Making It Happen

A Memoir of Peace Corps and Venezuela in the 1970s

Kendellen @ vi.
     org

Michael R
     Kendellen
202 - 545 - 0544
7513 14ʰ4 ST NW
Wash DC 20017

ISBN-10: 197-460-7473
ISBN-13: 978-197-460-6474

To Robert E. and Helen J. Kendellen

whites-only lodge. As late as 1961, they still had discriminatory policies that forbade blacks from staying there. The same year, the Chicago White Sox canceled their reservations when the hotel would not book rooms for the black players.

By the time I got there in 1974, the lobby looked old and worn out. In the 1980s, the historic McAllister Hotel fell into disrepair and became a target for developers. Now a fifty-seven-story skyscraper featuring luxury condos stands in the same location.

After I checked in, a bellboy hauled my luggage up to my room on the fourth floor. My roommate, Don, looking familiar, was already there. Then I placed him as the guy at the airport wearing a preppy sweater and carrying a tennis racquet. Don had been a producer for a local television station in Minnesota for eight years before getting the itch to travel and see the world outside his home state. So he quit a $10,000-a-year job, the equivalent of $52,000 in 2017, and joined the Peace Corps, figuring he could always re-start his career at age twenty-eight.

They had offered him a position in Asia as a Volunteer a year earlier, but the job fell through; so when an opportunity arose in Venezuela, he jumped at it. Don's favorite sports were football and hockey, which he assumed would help him to coach even though Venezuelans played neither of the two North American games. Upbeat and excited about being in the Peace Corps, he believed he could coach and serve as an advisor, exactly my attitude, though I was more subdued about the future than he was.

For the next two months, including the pre-training days in Miami, the trainers would inundate us with advice and guidance on what it took to be a Peace Corps Volunteer. We would learn the nuances of Venezuelan culture, become acquainted with the local heroes and deities, and gain insight into the country through the lens of ten years' worth of lessons learned. In our spare time, we read briefing papers, handbooks, and manuals to help us better understand Venezuela and our new organization.

In November 1961, Sargent Shriver, appointed by President Kennedy as the first Peace Corps director, met with Venezuelan President Betancourt, the first elected president of Venezuela, to talk about establishing a joint program. According to local media stories, the mission was a rousing success. *The Daily Journal*, an English newspaper, editorialized that the Peace Corps could help the country with its development goals. "Members of the Corps only go where they are wanted; they are serious, enthusiastic, and hardworking and they live like the people with whom they work. The whole approach to the idea is sound and sane." *La Republica*, the mouthpiece of the Democratic Action Party, also feigned enthusiasm. They believed the Peace Corps could "strengthen the ties of friendship and solidarity that unite" the two countries. Venezuela was looking forward to welcoming the first Volunteers.

The Peace Corps hired Roderic Buller, who came from the Rockefeller Foundation in Mexico, where he worked on the Mexican Agriculture Program (MAP) as the first country director. In July 1962, the first Volunteers arrived to work with the YMCA, 4-H clubs (known as 5-V clubs in Venezuela), and the University of the East. From 1962 to 1974, roughly 1,500 Volunteers served in community development, education, environment, agriculture, sports and recreation, and health projects.

At its peak in 1965–67, Peace Corps Venezuela averaged 400 Volunteers, which was way below the nearly one thousand volunteers that Colombia, Chile, Peru, and Brazil each had. More than half the Volunteers worked with the Ministry of Education to carry out a new physical education curriculum in primary and secondary schools and to train trainers at universities and vocational schools. Volunteers with the Ministry of Agriculture worked on improving crop and livestock production, as well as on resource conservation. Architects and city planners tried to improve local government. Volunteers also worked in hospital administration, sanitation, and with the Boy Scouts. The Smithsonian operated an environmental project through the Peace Corps.

We didn't hear what these projects entailed other than that many failed, and scores of Volunteers resigned from disappointment before the end of their two-year assignment. The Peace Corps acknowledged they should have had government approval before recruiting Volunteers; now knowing most projects would fail without it. Years later, the trainers stressed any other approach would be a "form of imperialism"—an unusual choice of words, probably not cleared in Washington—to describe the opposite of collaboration.

When I arrived in late January, 1974, 275 Volunteers worked in agriculture, crafts, forestry, municipal administration, physical education, teacher training, public health, rural development, sports and recreation, and YMCA programs. If the number of Volunteers in a country indicated success, then the Peace Corps in Venezuela, in 1974, could be considered one. If there were lessons learned from the past, I assumed they had applied them and that the Sports and Recreation program, if not other programs, was in good shape.

At the first meeting of the Sports and Recreation group in Miami, seventeen men and six women, all between 20 and 28 years old, filled the room on the second floor of the hotel. We had all graduated from public universities in the past year, except for the two who'd earned degrees from Trinity College and Stanford. Majors included Soviet, China, and international relations;

conservation; radio and television; physical education; secondary education; biology; sociology; theater; political science; psychology; communications; Latin American studies; administrative sciences; recreational therapy; marine biology; journalism; and American and English literature. A third of the group had been Physical Education majors in college and most of the rest were Liberal Arts majors with skill sets that put us into the category of generalists.

The group consisted of four teachers, two community organizers, one television producer, one YMCA supervisor, one photographer, one salesman, and a woman who had worked for two years on an apple orchard in California. Another woman spent fourteen months in a commune in Berkeley before joining the Peace Corps. There were two Vietnam Veterans: one a Marine and the other a pacifist who served in the Army Medical Corps. We came from sixteen states, with five from California alone. We were primarily white, Catholic, single, and college-educated except for one African-American and a 20-year-old college student who quit school to go to Venezuela. One of the two couples had been married less than a month. They confided both sets of parents were not pleased with their decision to join the Peace Corps.

Despite having been recruited for a sports and recreation program, jocks were not among us, just sports fans. One had played football and volleyball in college and two others baseball, and lacrosse. A surprising number detested spectator sports like football and baseball. The rest of us had participated in athletics for fun, in recreational or school leagues. No one had made all-state, all-conference, or had won a championship of any sort other than the former Stanford football player who had played in the 1972 Rose Bowl. No one admitted to playing soccer. Whatever the level of interest and athletic skill we might have brought to sports-crazy Venezuela, in two months we would be coaching, advising sports bodies, organizing tournaments, and, if lucky, playing on a baseball or basketball team, if the job description we received was accurate.

A psychologist led the first exercise in which we introduced each other. In the 1960s, according to Elizabeth Cobbs Hoffman writing in *All You Need is Love: The Peace Corps and the Spirit of the 1960s*, Peace Corps trainings were known for their unusual way of sorting out who would make a good Volunteer and who would not. Psychologists would ask questions such as "Have you ever talked to God?" and "Do you think your private parts are beautiful?" with the thought that whatever response they heard could be used to decide whether a trainee should be dismissed. In Miami, the psychologist leader posed no threat, as the Peace Corps had long ago done away with such inquiries and testing. Instead, the touchy-feely era was underway and bland questions were needed to start the ball rolling. With "Tell us about yourself," my Peace Corps life began.

Larry, the Volunteer I introduced, was a former juvenile delinquent and Vietnam veteran. At seventeen and facing a possible life of petty crime, he had joined the Marines and deployed to Vietnam, where he remained a second year as a civilian volunteer in a project that assisted Vietnamese street children. After he returned home, he earned a degree in Sociology. The psychologist asked me if he would enjoy Peace Corps work. Not having a clue after talking to Larry for ten minutes, I kept my reply simple and logical. "I would say because he liked the volunteer work he did in Vietnam, I think he should like working with Venezuelan kids."

Larry followed and introduced me as someone with seven siblings; a college graduate with a Liberal Arts degree who believed it was not whether you won or lost but how you played the game. I corrected him on the sports cliché and said winning was the goal, but you shouldn't let a loss linger, a belief developed after losing a close playoff game in a summer recreation league. Larry, repeating what I had told him, also said, "I paid my way through college by working part-time at a bank and I liked sports, particularly baseball."

Our physical well-being and how the Peace Corps office in Caracas functioned in case of an accident or illness occupied a large part of the orientation. Dolores, a middle-aged nurse from the Peace Corps Medical Department in Washington, DC, moderated the sessions. Until Miami, she had never briefed Volunteers before leaving the United States for their two-year stint. Instead, she would see them for the first time after they were sent home for health reasons. Washington had now given her the opportunity to share her wisdom and, hopefully, prevent such an early return from happening at all.

She started off by saying if we objected to medical treatments based on religious or philosophical beliefs, such as not wanting immunizations, then the Peace Corps was not for us. If so, we should pack our bags and take the next flight out. Wow. Up until this point, religion had not been mentioned in any context. Throughout the application process, the word "religion" never appeared in any form or briefing paper. Now in Miami, a Peace Corps officer said if our religious beliefs conflicted with certain medical practices, we should quit at once and go home.

If no one had been listening up to this point, she had our attention now. Slam-bang! Take it or leave it. Silence pervaded the room. No one stirred, or said a word. We sat and waited for the next bombshell.

After Dolores had allowed us a few minutes to review our religious beliefs in light of public health conditions in Venezuela and the policies of Peace Corps health care, she told us we would be better off following her advice than resisting it. She again went straight for the jugular and warned each of us would suffer from a "change of bowel habits," one of the most discomforting ailments known to the human race, otherwise known as diarrhea, in the months ahead. We could get it from the food or the water, which we should never drink. But even if we adhered to her advice, we should nevertheless expect to suffer from parasites and occasional diarrhea.

An even worse fate, Dolores warned, was to fall ill with unusual symptoms in a distant, isolated town without immediate access to a doctor. If we got sick and no doctor was available, we should call the Peace Corps medical office in Caracas, which had a 24-hour answering service. While it sounded comforting in Miami to know we had doctors and nurses on call, we would later learn phone connections in remote areas far from Caracas were often full of static or the connection would get lost in the middle of the call. However, as a fallback, we had the names of local health providers to contact, and for temporary comfort, our issued first aid kit.

The Peace Corps administered immunizations, hoping to keep us healthy. They also scheduled biannual gamma globulin shots to ward off hepatitis, and we received three rabies shots in the stomach before training ended. The Peace Corps manual warned we should beware of dogs, many of which spent their time roaming the streets. If we contracted rabies, we would probably die a slow death. As we lined up for our first rabies shot, Dolores jolted us out of our morning reflections on the hazards and challenges that lay ahead by shouting, "Anyone pregnant? Anyone pregnant? Raise your hand if you are." No one did.

Dolores also informed us that if we managed "to catch" a sexually transmitted disease (STD), the Peace

Corps would treat it, adding, "It's up to you to get [venereal disease] treated. It's your life." Her tone, betraying her real sentiment toward Volunteers who contracted STDs, was a variation of "you idiot." Dolores recommended we pick up condoms at the office in Caracas. Abortion was illegal in Venezuela, and the Peace Corps could not pay for one. They would, however, give contraceptives to the women Volunteers upon asking. In 1974, HIV/AIDS was unknown and thus not part of the orientation.

The Peace Corps Manual listed marijuana, cocaine, heroin, and LSD (lysergic acid diethylamide) as banned substances. The manual emphasized the criminal element of drugs over the dangers of use. Getting arrested for buying or selling drugs could impact the future of the Peace Corps in Venezuela, never mind the legal consequences for the Volunteer who got arrested for possessing drugs. Dolores finished her presentation with a question: "Are any of you a drug addict? If so, raise your hand now." No one raised their hand. With that, the health orientation was complete.

Cachivache, the 200-page Peace Corps manual for Venezuela, which roughly translates to "Useless Things To Know," was packed with information and advice on health conditions: some useful, most not, as the translation of the guide implied. For example, like diarrhea, we should consider dental problems inevitable, because we would consume carbonated sugar drinks, mostly Pepsi, Coca-Cola, and orange soda, more often at meals than water or milk. All potable water was contaminated, and before we drank it, we should boil it. If we were unlucky enough to get bitten by a snake, we should not panic and instead find a doctor and call Caracas, assuming we could find a working telephone.

The manual was not short of advice. We should not be alarmed by the number of lizards we would see.

We learned Volunteers who lived in *Los Llanos* (The Plains) in central Venezuela might sweat more than Volunteers who lived in the cooler higher elevations in the Andes Mountains. Because of the intense heat and tropical sun, we might become dizzy from too much of it. If so, we should take a nap. Men were more apt to lose weight than women because women knew more about cooking. Whatever hazards and dangers lurked and threatened us through water, insects, animals, and contagious diseases, the odds were greater we would die in a car accident. As a precaution against injury or death in an automobile, we should always sit in the back seat of a taxi, and if the driver fell asleep, we should get out of the car ASAP, which made sense unless the car was moving. Buckling seatbelts was unknown in the 1970s, where used American cars from the 1960s, the most popular vehicles in Venezuela, did not have them.

After two days in Miami, we flew to Caracas, arriving at midnight. While we waited in the Customs area for our luggage, a few in the group sang "The Battle Hymn of the Republic." The next day, the Peace Corps interviewed us to learn about any personal preferences and peccadilloes that might affect living with Venezuelan families. The Peace Corps placed ads in the local newspapers to solicit local families interested in hosting Volunteers. As an incentive, each family would receive $85 a month. In return, they provided meals and a bed, and were encouraged to include us in their social activities. Along with six hours of Spanish a day, living with a Venezuelan family was about all that would matter in training.

My single request was to live in a household without a dog. Having grown up with seven siblings and one bathroom, I didn't care about the size of the household with whom I would live; I kept my request simple.

My host family, led by Natalia, a 54-year-old, heavy-set fourth-grade teacher and part-time taxi driver, consisted of her; her husband; and Natalia's daughter, Mildred, who taught Spanish to American children and was married to Rufino, an accountant. They had a 10-month-old daughter. The couple had graduated from the University of Caracas and planned to move to the United States in a year. Rufino spoke a little English, which put uncertainty in his plans regarding whether he would adapt to the U.S.; he had heard Americans didn't like to teach English to Spanish-speaking people. Though not an expert on the subject, I still told him I was unaware of the issue. He also wanted me to confirm the rumor the government paid a monthly stipend to people, even if they didn't have a job. Instead of explaining welfare and unemployment benefits, which I knew little about, in basic Spanish, I pleaded ignorance and said that someone receiving an allowance for not working was news to me.

Natalia was always late, like most Venezuelans. During the Venezuelan presidential campaign the previous year, she went to a 1 p.m. rally but found the plaza empty. That was because it started at 10:30. On Sundays, masses didn't stick to the schedule. A Volunteer reported he accompanied his family to church for the 10 a.m. Mass. They arrived fifteen minutes early only to find the 9 a.m. Mass was just beginning.

Segundo, Natalia's second husband, worked construction and delivered flowers part-time. He talked little in the two months I lived in Los Teques. In fact, I only saw him around the house at breakfast and on special occasions like birthday parties. I remember him most from the night he came home drunk and fell off a chair, hitting his head on the kitchen counter while reaching for a glass. At breakfast the next day, Natalia nearly fell off her own chair from laughter when she recounted the story. Over the next two and a half years, I would frequently observe

Venezuelans laugh themselves silly watching a person trip or fall.

They lived in a three-bedroom house with electricity, a telephone, television, and hot water. Less than half of the families that Volunteers lived with had a telephone, and most did not have hot water. I never saw a house with a bathtub. The kitchen, with a table and chairs for three, a four-burner gas stove, a sink, and a refrigerator, was more than most host families had, so I was lucky. The bathroom consisted of a shower stall and a toilet with an attached seat. I deposited the used tissue in the wastebasket because the water pressure was too low and the pipes too small to flush it. The cleaning woman emptied it daily.

Despite my request for no pets, Natalia had three mangy dogs covered in scars, which barked when I came within fifty feet of them. The training staff ignored other preferences as well. One Volunteer wanted to live with a family that had kids in their mid-twenties with no pets; the same as back home in the U.S. They placed him in a household with six children from 5 to 21 years old, two dogs, and a pig.

Most Volunteers during training lived alone with their host families. I was one of the few who had a roommate, sharing a small room with Michael, a 30-year-old from Minnesota who lived on grains, vegetables, seaweed, and an occasional beer. Venezuelans had difficulty understanding his macrobiotic diet and wondered how he stayed alive. However, they did not try to change it and helped him buy seaweed by driving him to a store in Caracas.

Michael didn't last long. He grew disillusioned with what he was learning about his job and cited potential health problems in trying to sustain his diet in Venezuela, including feeling high after receiving a gamma globulin shot. He quit halfway through the training and went home.

Natalia's house in Los Teques where I lived during training.
(Photo: Mike Kendellen)

Before setting off for Spanish class each morning, I ate a breakfast of cornflakes or oatmeal, leftover black beans, and bread, though one morning, for a change, there was a box of Sugar Smacks on the table. While Natalia always bought regular milk for cereal, a few Volunteers reported their families put hot milk or chocolate milk on their cornflakes.

Lunch at the training site, the best meal of the day, was chicken, pork chops, ham, or beef, along with fruit and a vegetable except every Friday, when the cooks prepared fish, with the head intact and the eyes burnt to a crisp. It tasted better than it looked. Natalia's preferred dinner comprised meat, potatoes, noodles, and bread, sometimes leftover from breakfast or from the night before. By the third week, I craved a hamburger. In letters home, I complained about the starchy, greasy food and blamed it for the ten pounds I had gained in six weeks, along with drinking a minimum of two 12-ounce bottles of Pepsi every day and not getting much exercise. I was one of the few trainees whose bowels had not changed yet. Other Volunteers were not so lucky and were already on their second round of it; most blamed the food served by their host family.

Each morning I took a city bus to Camp Nora, a YMCA compound in the hills above Los Teques that the Peace Corps had rented for our training. Spanish class started at nine and went until noon. During the two-hour lunch, we played volleyball or bocce, a game played with wooden balls the size of a tennis ball with scoring rules similar to horseshoes: whoever got nearest to the pin or stake earned a point. Others studied, read, slept, or wrote letters. After lunch, we had two more hours of Spanish before returning to our host families or going to one of the bars in town.

Los Teques, a town of 20,000, twenty miles southwest of Caracas, is the capital of Miranda state. In February 1974, it was a small town several miles from the capital. Over the next thirty years, it grew into a suburb connected by the subway and the freeway while gaining notoriety as the location of the country's worst prison. In 2006, The Guardian reported widespread corruption and drugs and weapons there, including guns among the inmates. The murder rate was high, and riots occurred frequently. Some embassy representatives chose not to visit their jailed citizens because they considered it too dangerous. One prisoner was Paul Keany from Ireland, who the police arrested at the Caracas airport with drugs valued at a half a million dollars. In his memoir of his eight-year imprisonment, *The Cocaine Diaries: A Venezuelan Prison Nightmare*, he wrote of bribery, murders, drug dealing, and riots before he escaped and returned to Ireland. A prison raid in 2013 resulted in the police confiscating guns, two grenades, drugs, and more than 8,000 bullets. The police arrested one prison official when he swallowed the memory chip from his cell phone to hide evidence.

In non-prison news, in 2013, after the government had imported fifty million rolls of toilet paper in the midst of a nation-wide shortage, the police suspected the missing rolls were in Los Teques. A search found 2,450 bales of it, or approximately 100,000 rolls, along with 7,000 liters of fruit juice and 400 packages of diapers.

The first weeks of training focused on Spanish class and adapting to living with our host families. We didn't learn anything about our jobs as sports advisors except that the Sports and Recreation program had become the largest Peace Corps program when it had expanded five years earlier. At that time, then-President Dr. Rafael Caldera said, "There is no program in which the Peace Corps can participate and offer more to my country or bring our peoples closer together."

By 1974, when I arrived, Dr. Caldera's words had been long forgotten. I only read them while paging through the manual. We heard little about what advising IND would involve, though the trainers emphasized our accomplishments should be measured by how we contributed to the IND mission, which was to promote sports in schools and communities and develop sports programs for youth groups and farmers. From all the vagueness we were hearing about being a sports advisor from the training staff, I figured we would do whatever was required to put the national plan for young people and sports into action. It was up to each of us to know how to do it.

The more prominent challenges would be the lack of equipment, a shortage of playing fields, not enough basketball courts and swimming pools, and operating within the dysfunctional and disorganized IND bureaucracy. As the weeks passed, it became more apparent we might not do much more than coach in rural areas. In fact, I concluded, we would probably not do very much advising at all.

Part of the problem was the Peace Corps had recruited us before actual job openings materialized—not an unusual practice—so until the final week of the eight-week training, we did not know which town or city we would be posted to, except it appeared most of us would be sent to the eastern part of the country. A show of hands in Miami indicated that more than half the group preferred basketball. Swimming was the second choice. Three chose baseball, including me. When a list of probable locations and jobs was posted in the middle of training, the two that appealed to me were one in the Caracas slums and one coaching baseball for sixth graders. I was hoping to go to the Andean mountain region, but apparently the local IND didn't need Volunteer coaches.

Word spread that Wayne, the sports coordinator—known as a Super Volunteer because he never left his site and was always working—had proposed to the training director that he run a workshop to gauge our coaching qualifications and our advisory skills. He thought it important to know our abilities even though Washington did not consider it necessary when they evaluated our applications six months ago. Despite Wayne's well-conceived plan, the training director rejected it.

Wayne moved on to his next idea and scheduled sessions with different experts in IND. He scheduled me to work with 64-year-old Ernesto Aparicio, the former manager of the Venezuelan national team and the uncle of former Chicago White Sox shortstop, future Hall of Famer, and national hero Luis Aparicio. Instead of feeling honored to have Ernesto Aparicio as a trainer, I was apprehensive and couldn't concentrate in Spanish class the day of the training. However, to my relief, he never showed up, and the remainder of the workshops with

IND were canceled when the teachers went on strike, closing the schools and its facilities nationwide.

Sensing our relief at hearing the training sessions with IND had been canceled, Wayne berated us for our lack of motivation and general disinterest in them. He wondered why, as a substitute activity, we didn't organize volleyball and bocce tournaments among ourselves. "You will face many more unexpected canceled events and challenges over the next two years, and you should take this as an opportunity to practice your problem solving." No one understood what point he was trying to make. We didn't organize tournaments because the last thing we wanted to do was fill the two-hour lunch break with work. Most of us were struggling with Spanish and obsessing over where we would live for the next two years.

The endless possibilities we had as Peace Corps Volunteers was one of the themes of training. Success was up to each of us, but if I failed, it would be my fault. The staff warned us that progress might be slow and ultimate success, in whatever way we measured it, could take a while to achieve. We needed to be patient. The trainers repeatedly told us that whatever obstacles we would face, we could ease the awkwardness if we developed confidence dealing with the people around us. "The Venezuelans must believe in you, and only you can make it happen," the program officers told us in the same tone you might hear from a high school football coach.

While the idea sounded like common sense, there was a method to achieving it. If we wanted to make it happen and be successful, we needed first to gain the trust of the Venezuelans. There were no shortcuts to achieving trust. If we approached our work in a professional manner and were friendly and sincere, in time, we could attain *Confianza*, the Spanish word that combines good manners with its opposite, "don't be a jerk." The Peace Corps took a higher road and described the path to Confianza in quasi-religious terms:

Nobody knows him nor does he know anybody. He is unfamiliar with his new job in Venezuela and with the Venezuelan culture. To do his job effectively, and, in fact, in order to live two meaningfully years by forming relationships with Venezuelans, the Peace Corps Volunteer must regularly dedicate himself to the task of projecting a natural image with which Venezuelans can feel confident, of inspiring confidence in the Venezuelans with whom he works and, finally be developing his own self-confidence as a Volunteer in his program.

The road to *Confianza* included a blend of non-verbal communication, human relations, customs, superstitions, overcoming negative perceptions of foreigners, learning Spanish, including idioms, and knowing local ways of thinking and the range of political and social views in the country. While *Confianza* seemed like a reasonable theory, it appeared to be nothing more than a Peace Corps concept, since I never once heard a Venezuelan speak about it.

Engaging Venezuelans in conversation, meaningful or not, would go a long way in gaining Confianza. They liked to talk, in fact—so much I came to believe yapping was in their DNA. The conversations did not have to be substantive; it was the effort that mattered. Venezuelans spent an extraordinary amount of time talking about nothing of consequence, which raised the question of whether bullshitting and pointless conversation should be a part of the effort to attain *Confianza*. Could I bullshit? The Peace Corps cautioned us that going native, pretending to be Venezuelan was a phony way to behave and it would not be helpful in our jobs. Did bullshitting qualify as going native? Should we limit our bullshit? We were not offered an opinion.

No one considered cursing anything other than

bad behavior for Volunteers, even if Venezuelans swore. The Peace Corps advised us not to swear because Venezuelans might misunderstand and think we were making fun of them, or worse, think we considered them to be stupid. The advice on cursing struck me as an over-interpretation of human behavior and seemed too far-fetched. Was cursing so complicated? Would I be trusted less if I said "fuck," the one curse word of any significance in English, or if I called someone an asshole? Should I be worried if a Venezuelan swore at me? If I did, would it be more offensive to them or me? What if I cursed in silence and raised my middle finger?

The one gesture the trainers advised us not to do was making a circle with your thumb and forefinger while holding up the other three fingers. It did not mean "OK." In Venezuela, the sign said you were calling a person gay, and the consequences could be worse than giving the finger or saying, "Fuck you."

Rumors of Peace Corps links to the CIA plagued the program from the day President Kennedy tapped Sargent Shriver, his brother-in-law, to be the organization's first director and the Soviet Union announced that Shriver was a CIA agent.

One of Shriver's first tasks was to insist that the CIA could not use Volunteers to achieve their mission. Shriver fought with the CIA over this legitimate request and convinced them of the severe damage the Peace Corps would suffer if Volunteers and staff reported to intelligence agencies. In a memo to Allen Dulles, the director of the CIA, in April 1961 (which was released in 2015), the inspector general advised Dulles to keep away from the Peace Corps. "I believe you should stress to the Senior Staff the Agency will make no use of the Peace Corps and will take specific action to avoid in any way contaminating that group."

In a summary of a meeting on May 31, 1961, at CIA headquarters, the director insisted CIA policy regarding the Peace Corps include specific wording that it was in the mutual interest of the Peace Corps and the CIA "to stay apart." President Kennedy also directed the CIA not to use the Peace Corps for intelligence purposes.

The policy never became law. Instead, the CIA has agreed over the years not to use the Peace Corps for any reason, and former CIA employees are ineligible for employment with the Peace Corps. Even so, allegations of intelligence-gathering surfaced. Radio Moscow broadcast that Volunteers in Africa and Asia were "U.S. agents." China and Cuba described the Peace Corps as a "junior" CIA. A Havana newspaper accused the Peace Corps of poking "their noses into all places where meek rulers open the door for them." Cuba warned Venezuela to keep an eye on Volunteers. Whether they did or not is unknown; three decades later, Fidel Castro would admit to Connecticut Senator Christopher Dodd, a former Volunteer himself, the Cuban intelligence agencies never linked a Volunteer to the CIA. Still, when a new group of Volunteers arrived in Chile in 1965, a Santiago afternoon newspaper headline read "Forty-Seven Agents of the CIA Arrive at Airport Today."

When I arrived in Venezuela, the *Movimiento al Socialismo* (MAS), the Socialist Party, as a matter of party dogma, purported that the Peace Corps, most Americans, and American institutions and programs in Venezuela were working for the CIA. MAS, for their part, could not conceive of a world where an American abroad would not be gathering information.

Natalia's relatives believed I worked for U.S. intelligence because they saw no other reason for my being in Venezuela. Neyda, Natalia's 22-year-old niece, was a MAS supporter and a backer of Jose Vicente, the head of MAS and the Socialist Party candidate for president in the December 1973 election. We discussed politics and current events at the beach, over dinner, or when I stopped over at her house in Caracas during the eight-week training in Los Teques. Neyda studied law and had applied for a scholarship to a university in Rome. She did not believe in women's liberation, thinking freedom and independence were a state of mind and not a matter of rights. Besides, men needed liberating too, and she wondered why women did household chores and not men.

She was less open-minded about my real purpose in Venezuela, to coach baseball. She assumed I worked for the CIA because I scribbled notes as she told me the lyrics to songs by the Venezuelan composer, poet, and political activist Ali Primera and the Chilean singer-songwriter Victor Jara. In 2005, Venezuela declared Primera's music part of the national heritage and *Rolling Stone* magazine named Jara, whom the Chilean army killed during the coup in 1973, as one of the fifteen most important protest artists of all time. She grew suspicious from my questions and note-taking, but was ambivalent about it as well. "Give your notes to the CIA. I don't care," she told me. "Now, can you stop writing so we can go out for pizza?"

Neyda's twin sister, nicknamed Toto, who was always polite and cheerful when I saw her and who bore very little physical resemblance to her sister, thought I was a spy, too. It was nothing personal. Americans were spies, no evidence necessary. She told me she knew a Volunteer who had quit the Peace Corps because he no longer wanted to work for the CIA. I did not reply.

The Volunteer Handbook, full of advice on drugs, food, and sex, lacked suggestions on how to respond if a Venezuelan accused us of being a spy or if a person approached us and identified himself as a spy. The handbook stated we should avoid behavior that would even hint we came to Venezuela for any other reason than to coach sports, train teachers, or provide technical advice. We were on our own in figuring out how to respond if accused of an affiliation with the CIA. The embassy showed shocking disinterest in what Volunteers faced, as we learned when a diplomat at a reception for us shared his views on the work of the Agency: "If the CIA were half as successful as everyone thought they were we would be better off."

Venezuelans also queried me on a variety of cultural and political topics. People were curious how oil companies differed from the Peace Corps and how much money I earned and who paid me. The answer was simple, if long-winded and a bit officious. Oil companies were large international private corporations earning billions of dollars, while Peace Corps was a government program that promoted a better understanding of Americans and other countries by sending teachers and other professionals to assist countries in achieving national goals.

They also asked about the rumor that former President John F. Kennedy was living on the island of Scorpio with his widow, Jackie, and Aristotle Onassis, who she had married, a ludicrous story started by Truman Capote. I told them it wasn't true.

One rumor I did not dispute was whether I knew kung fu. One of the most popular television programs in Venezuela was *Kung Fu* starring David Carradine. Later, after I had moved to my site, one Venezuelan told me it was assumed I knew kung fu and other Chinese martial arts because I was an American. I never denied it, and I was lucky that no one ever asked for a demonstration. What would I have done if they had? The belief made me feel safe at night walking on streets with one street light or none at all; knowing people thought I could beat the shit out of them with a few kicks and chops to the throat.

Some of the trainers and Spanish teachers told us, "Venezuelans love Americans." At a bar in town after class, we laughed at the improbable love fest we had just heard the Venezuelan teachers describe to us. It made little sense considering our historical role in the Americas. Criticism of American oil companies profiting from Venezuela's resources, along with the coup in Chile a few months earlier, which many people assumed involved the CIA, cast skepticism on the "Love America" mantra. Much more interesting and pertinent was when a program officer, in his lecture on the views and perspectives of Venezuelans, said the *senoritas*, as he called young Venezuelan women, preferred to date American men. Really? Did the women prefer Americans to other foreigners, even us poor Peace Corps Volunteers? When a trainee questioned it, the program officer responded with, "It's the truth" (*Es la verdad*.)

The Peace Corps recommended that technical sports advisors should wear slacks and a shirt with a collar at the office and change into athletic clothes such as shorts and a t-shirt when coaching. Women who were swimming coaches should wear a one-piece suit when teaching and save their bikinis for the beach. In the 1970s, despite the tropical climate, cultural norms dictated that Venezuelan men wore shorts only at the beach or when taking part in athletics. Otherwise, wearing shorts in restaurants, in shopping malls, on any Plaza Bolívar, or when walking on the street was considered feminine behavior. If men wore them in such places, they could expect Venezuelans to taunt them with whistling and verbal jousting. Once, the police issued a warning to a Volunteer for the "unacceptable behavior" of wearing shorts while driving.

Despite the bias of law enforcement and immigration officials regarding long hair and beards, which they identified more with drugs than fashion, the

Peace Corps left it up to each one of us to decide on mustaches, beards, and the length of our hair. Since I grew a beard in my first year of college and had no intention of cutting it, I checked before leaving into whether beards were acceptable. No one said they were not.

Before leaving the U.S., I met a Volunteer who'd served in Venezuela in the 1960s. He told me, for reasons he couldn't remember, that wearing white tennis shoes was taboo. Venezuelans would laugh if they saw someone wearing such shoes, which, he said, I should probably not do as an advisor to a national institution. Notwithstanding that I believed what the former Volunteer said about this strange prejudice, I asked a program officer who had been in the country five years if it was true men should not wear white shoes. He looked at me like I was nuts. He shook his head with an expression of incredulity and responded that he had never heard of the practice, adding that men could wear sandals if they also wore socks with them.

Whatever clothing Venezuelans wore, they did their laundry by hand and hung it outside in the sun to dry, being generally unable to afford a washing machine and dryer, even if they had reliable electricity to operate them. The Peace Corps, which never seemed short of advice and cultural insights, told us our laundry would dry in fifteen minutes because of an abundance of sunshine and high temperatures. A few Volunteers who had been in the country a year or more agreed that clothes dried in less than thirty minutes. Based on their experience, they recommended that we sit and watch our laundry dry if we didn't want it stolen.

Like most countries, Venezuela has its heroes. The Holy Trinity of Simon Bolívar, a liberator; Luis Aparicio, a baseball player; and God, a deity, was as eclectic a group of national heroes as any in the world.

Simón José Antonio de la Santísima Trinidad Bolívar y Palacios Ponte y Blanco, shortened to Simon Bolívar, was born in Caracas, in 1783, the same year that George Washington resigned as commander-in-chief of the Continental Army and went home to Mt. Vernon. Bolívar's family was wealthy from land ownership and their sugar plantations in Spain, and from silver, gold, and copper mines whose labor force comprised Native American and African slaves. Both his parents died before he was ten. At fourteen, Bolívar enrolled in a military academy in Caracas, where he developed an interest in weapons and military strategy. At the age of sixteen, Bolívar went to Europe, where he studied the works of John Locke, Thomas Hobbes, Voltaire, Jean-Jacques Rousseau, and other eighteenth-century liberal thinkers.

In 1807, he returned to Venezuela; just a year later, he helped launch the Latin American independence movement. On July 5, 1811, Venezuela declared independence from Spain and Bolívar joined the army. Over the next twenty years, he led military campaigns that culminated in independence in Ecuador, Colombia, Peru, and Bolivia. Although Bolívar had other officers fighting battles for him, including Francisco Santander of Colombia, he is recognized as the liberator of Venezuela. In 1830, he died of tuberculosis in Santa Marta, Colombia.

Or did he?

In 2010, Doctor Paul Auwaerter, an infectious diseases expert at the Johns Hopkins School of Medicine in Baltimore, Maryland, discovered that Bolívar might have died in Colombia from a bacterial infection often associated with arsenic poisoning rather than tuberculosis. Hugo Chavez, the president of Venezuela at the time, recognized an opportunity to bolster his support and interpreted the new conclusions on Bolívar's death as meaning that Colombia, Venezuela's current nemesis, assassinated him, an end he assumed would appeal to the public. Chavez, who had renamed the country the Bolívarian Republic of Venezuela, "wept with emotion" when he ordered Bolívar's casket opened at 3 a.m. on national television. He also announced the exhumation of Bolívar's remains on Twitter to his 720,000 followers.

What impressive moments we have lived tonight! We have seen the remains of the Great Bolívar! Our father is in the earth, the water, and the air. You awake every hundred years when the people awaken. I confess we have cried, we have sworn allegiance.

Scientists took DNA samples from the bones and teeth of the skeleton to determine if, in fact, Bolívar had been poisoned. The scientists did find traces of arsenic, which doctors at the time used as treatment for some ailments, leaving open the possibility Bolívar died of failed medical practice, a common cause of death in the first half of the nineteenth century. After months of anticipation, the tests could not prove Bolívar was murdered.

Chávez would have none of it. On national television, he dismissed the science. In his view, Colombians killed him. "They murdered him and, even though I don't have proof, the circumstances in which he died point to it," he told the country. When the body was ready for re-burial, Chávez approved a new mausoleum at the cost of $27 million to re-bury the national hero in a mahogany coffin adorned with gold, pearls, and diamonds. One of the more outspoken critics, Bolívar's British biographer John Lynch, said, "It is an ugly monstrosity, a waste of money, and a monument to Chávez, not to Bolívar, who needs no further glory."

Modern science, though, could not kill The Liberator. He lives on through the currency, the bolivar, and in plazas bearing his name in every town, complete with a statue of him on his horse. Berlin, Cairo, London,

New York, Ottawa, San Francisco, Sofia, Tehran, Washington, DC, and in cities throughout Latin America have Bolívar statues. The country of Bolivia and a square in Cairo are named in his honor, as are Asteroid 712 Boliviana and towns in Texas, West Virginia, Missouri, and Ohio. India named a road in New Delhi after him. The U.S. Library of Congress houses more than 2,500 books and manuscripts on or related to Bolívar. *The Los Angeles Times* recognized *Bolívar* by Marie Arana as the best biography of 2013. I never once heard anyone crack a joke or show any lack of respect for him. Simón José Antonio de la Santísima Trinidad Bolívar y Palacios Ponte y Blanco is a revered hero in Venezuela.

The baseball player Luis Aparicio, born in Maracaibo, made his major league debut in 1956 as the shortstop for the Chicago White Sox. In his first year, Aparicio led the American League in stolen bases, assists, and putouts and was voted Rookie of the Year, the first Latin American player to win the award. Aparicio also played for the Boston Red Sox and Baltimore Orioles before retiring after the 1973 season. Lawrence Ritter and Donald Honig included him in their book, *The 100 Greatest Baseball Players of All Time*. In 1984, Aparicio was the first Venezuelan elected to baseball's Hall of Fame in Cooperstown, New York. Aparicio was later named the Athlete of the 20th Century in Venezuela. Aparicio is the son of Luis Aparicio Sr., who also played shortstop and owned a Winter League team with Aparicio's uncle, Ernesto Aparicio—the same uncle who failed to appear at a scheduled workshop the Peace Corps had planned.

The majority of Venezuelans were Christian, if not Catholic, making God a genuine hero. I never learned much about religion in Venezuela other than that significantly more women than men went to church and Mormons were in the country as missionaries.

Of the three immortals, Bolívar was the most

popular. He represented independence, which appealed to a larger crowd than baseball fans and Christians.

Midway through training, we encountered the Carnival festivities—the Latin American version of Mardi Gras, meaning "Fat Tuesday" in French—which concluded the day before the forty-day Lenten season began, followed by Easter. It was a welcome respite from the eight-week grind. I went to Punto Fijo on the southwestern coast of the Paraguaná Peninsula in western Venezuela where Natalia and her extended family owned a beach house. Even on the beach, there was no escaping discussion of my motivations for being in Venezuela. Holding a glass of whiskey, Mario, a cousin who worked for an oil company, said he didn't think I worked for the CIA, though he thought it possible. I denied it, of course, as if it mattered. He offered me another drink. It always bewildered me that no matter how convinced anyone was about me being a spook, everyone remained friendly and hospitable.

After Carnival, I met up with Larry, the ex-Marine I introduced in Miami, in Los Teques. We hitchhiked to Puerto Ordaz to spend three days with other Volunteers to get a feel for how Volunteers live and work. The long weekend was less fun than going to the beach with Natalia and her clan. The Volunteers we met admitted they weren't over-worked but didn't seem happy with their jobs. They were unanimous in declaring the National Institute of Sport (IND) a dysfunctional organization. One described it as a "hellhole."

"Just wait. You'll be like us in a year," was the general message. In return, we amused them with our eagerness to get our site assignments and with our naiveté on what we could accomplish as Volunteers. Still, the weekend was worth it.

On Sunday, we planned to hitchhike back to Los

Teques, a 450-mile trip that would take at least two days depending on our luck in getting rides. We stuck out our thumbs and stood on the side of the highway. After thirty minutes, a bus stopped. When we boarded, they asked us to pay the one bolívar fare. We refused and got off the bus and started walking with our thumbs out. After about a half a mile, the same bus we had declined ten minutes earlier stopped again. This time, they let us board without paying. Fifty miles later, the driver wanted a break. After a short rest, we re-boarded but not before the driver asked each passenger to pay once more.

Hitchhiking to Caracas on a Sunday morning.

Paying again seemed unfair, even if we hadn't paid the first time, so we got off the bus and continued on foot. We walked for an hour before a truckload of National Guard soldiers picked us up and drove a few miles before dropping us off. They apologized for not taking us further, explaining that if they did, they might get reprimanded for breaking the rules on picking up hitchhikers. We set off on foot once again. A few minutes later, a Cadillac pulled up and the Venezuelan driver offered a ride. He was listening to Beethoven at full blast. We passed the National Guard truck that had given us a lift earlier. The soldiers were standing on the roadside, out of gas. We waved as we sped by in the Cadillac. An hour later, the driver was close to his girlfriend's house and exited the highway, so we had to get out.

We walked for three hours. Cars passed us by, never slowing down; a few drivers and their passengers flipped us the bird, for no apparent reason other than being stupid enough to hitchhike on a Sunday afternoon. Along the way, we warded off wild dogs, a donkey, and a cow that charged us. After an hour, a police car stopped and the two officers introduced themselves as Hector and Miguel. They asked what we were doing in Venezuela. By now, I had learned enough Spanish to tell them I studied literature in college and now was teaching baseball. They both laughed, thinking I was joking. They dropped us off in Barcelona, a town founded in 1671, where we stayed the night.

The next day we resumed the trip, and after three more rides, arrived in Los Teques in the evening. The takeaway lesson was never to hitchhike on Sunday.

With five weeks of Spanish under our belts, training expanded to include lectures on the country's economy, history, geography, and culture. After one hundred hours of lessons, my Spanish was still not advanced enough to understand much detail. I felt more relaxed when, during the talk on the economy, they got to how Venezuela has reaped the benefits of higher oil prices since the international oil embargo four months earlier, and the Venezuelan economy was strong as a result. Other economic details were bewildering, if not altogether missed, with my limited Spanish.

One cultural orientation session where the teachers ran around half-naked and spread pudding on our faces in a candle-lit room stumped us. What the heck were they doing? Presumably, they were trying to prepare us for the unknown incidents and events we would soon be witnessing. With no one around to explain our observations, we would have to sort out the strangeness by ourselves. The exercise would have fallen into the category of useless cross-cultural bullshit if they had given us the chance to evaluate it.

After eight weeks of training, I had concluded there was no magic formula for developing the skills necessary to live in an unfamiliar setting; you were who you were, and that was it. In the Q&A sessions with the teachers, most questions were phrased as "What if" situations. What if, at a party, the host offered you one more *arepa* after already eating two? How do I refuse an offer of a third serving of cold spaghetti at dinner? How do I say I've enough without offending anyone? How do I disagree in a courteous way?

Years later, after working in six other countries and introducing myriad new employees to local customs, I grew tired of giving tips and insights on living in a different culture. Instead, I eliminated all theories, reduced the amount of information given, and condensed cross-cultural living to three options: "Don't Be Stupid," "Be Smart," or the longer version, "Don't Fuck It Up."

As the weeks passed and we got closer to being assigned a site, there was an increasing anxiety in the group over working in a remote town in a strange country where a national institution would depend on our recommendations to achieve their goals. In retrospect, it was classic Peace Corps: make it happen and never mind the details for now. More and more, as training came to a close, I thought of the day I would get on the bus and go to my site. I was counting the days until training was over. However, apprehension about the future was secondary to getting through the next two weeks.

Several days later, we learned of our assigned sites—that is, everyone except me. While everyone chatted during breaks and lunch about their assignments and their new jobs, I was left waiting and feeling awkward. Wayne said it would be a couple more days before they placed me, without saying what prompted the delay.

Three days later, he informed me I would be spending the next two years in San Carlos in central Venezuela, where I would coach baseball. *Where the hell is that?* I wondered. Not once during training did I hear "San Carlos" mentioned as a place. I didn't recall seeing it on the wall map I looked at every day. Natalia never heard of it. I felt better when a few of the teachers assured me the town was near Valencia, Venezuela's third largest city, though none of them had ever been there. One teacher from Maracaibo threw a wrench in the discussion when he said there was a village named San Carlos on Lake Maracaibo. Was I going to western Venezuela, near Colombia? Wayne assured me, however, that I was going to the San Carlos in the state of Cojedes and not the San Carlos near Maracaibo. Still, I wondered if it was a good idea to go to a place few Venezuelans knew much about and that seemed like the equivalent of Siberia.

I looked up San Carlos in the *South American Handbook*, the best-known tourist guide for Venezuela at the time. It was 170 miles southwest of Caracas and 60 miles from Valencia, in the *Los Llanos* region, an area of savannahs and wildlife, and was the capital of the state of Cojedes. Cattle and tobacco anchored the economy. The guidebook described San Carlos as "uninteresting," a polite way of saying, "it sucked." Spanish Capuchin missionaries founded it in 1678. By the early nineteenth century, the town had 39,000 people and seven churches.

During the fight for independence, Simon Bolívar retreated to *Los Llanos* to persuade the people Spain was their enemy rather than the landowners for whom they worked. Bolívar recruited them into his army, and they played a vital role in defeating Spanish troops in the Battle of Carabobo. By the middle of the eighteenth mid-century, war and malaria reduced the town to 3,000 and three churches. While San Carlos and Los Llanos had a rich culture and history, I would come to appreciate none of it.

Training ended on a Saturday night in typical Venezuelan fashion, with a farewell party known as a *despidida*. Our host families and Peace Corps staff in Caracas attended. At the party, a kid holding a beer and not looking a day older than seventeen accused me of being a spy.

"You work for the CIA," (pronounced "See Ya") he said as he sipped his beer.

"Me?" I asked, pointing my finger at my chest to make sure he was talking to me, "How do you know that?" I asked.

"Nixon is not good. Right?" he said in a tone that made me think he wasn't sure if he had offended me. Continuing, he asked in Spanish if the Peace Corps was part of the CIA.

Somewhat weary of the number of spy questions over the last two months, I replied, "If you are so sure I am a spy, why are you at the party with other alleged spies?"

"For the free beer," he said with a smile. I walked away.

The party ran into the morning hours. After midnight, the remaining crowd cheered two Volunteers who ran naked through the party. A hat was passed around, collecting enough to give each streaker $12.50 for their effort. Streaking—running naked in public—was the craze in America, occurring in a wide variety of venues. In Hawaii, the "Streaker of the House" interrupted a session of the state legislature. Fans streaked at baseball games, and a man ran naked across the stage during the Academy Awards. And there was money to be made from the mania. A company marketed a new running shoe they named the "Streaker Sneaker" and "The Streak" song by Ray Stevens rose to number one on the Billboard charts, as well as becoming a major international hit that sold over five million records. In fact, the Country Music Association nominated "The Streak" as the song of the year.

I received an average score on my Spanish test, which took the form of a conversation with Rosita, the language training director. It might have been a generous grade, although it didn't matter, since the Peace Corps did not pass or fail trainees based on language skills.

I welcomed the end of training. Natalia cried at the bus station when I left and wished me luck, saying I would always be her son, and her home was my home. My host, who laughed often and talked nonstop, said that when I left after two years of service, she would go to the United States at the same time and sell her 1965 Pontiac to cover expenses.

At the time, the end of March 1974, Bob Woodward and Carl Bernstein reported that a government employee they code-named "Deep Throat" had been a key in uncovering the crimes committed by the Nixon administration, an incident known as Watergate. *The Sting* and *The Exorcist* were America's favorite movies and *Jaws* a bestseller. As the bus pulled away from the station, I wondered what lay ahead in San Carlos.

Three

Play Ball!

I arrived in steamy San Carlos a little before midnight. No local officials or media met me at the bus station. Even Fred Schram from Ashland, Wisconsin, the other Volunteer in San Carlos, downplayed my arrival and waited for me at the Pensión Esperanza, a rooming house near Plaza Bolívar, where a room cost $1.25 a night. I arrived drenched in sweat after walking twenty minutes from the highway with a backpack that weighed close to thirty pounds.

It was late, so after we introduced ourselves and talked about what we would do the next day, beginning with breakfast at nine, he showed me my room, which would be my home for the duration of my time in San Carlos due to the lack of affordable and safe houses for rent. A bare low-wattage bulb, surrounded by cobwebs, hung above the bed in the tiny room. A wardrobe stood against the wall, and opposite the bed was a wooden table covered with a sheet of plastic with a floral design. Abdelatif Omar Abdelkarim, an immigrant from the Middle East and the owner of the largest furniture store in San Carlos, had published the calendar hanging on a nail on the wall. There was no sink with running water. The room was stifling and the temperature was about eighty degrees. I might have to buy a fan.

Vertical iron bars covered the only window. Dogs barked nearby. The ten tenants shared two bathrooms and two showers, which were in the rear of the building near the refrigerator containing recycled Pepsi bottles filled with cold water. Each tenant had a glass with their name on it. Cobwebs covered the corners of the ceiling in the lobby where a fan, tropical plants, three leather chairs, and a black-and-white television kept it pleasant. Every weekday night, the owner's wife and their daughter watched *Dona Barbara*, the popular *telenovela* (soap opera).

F. Depons, a representative of the French government to Caracas from 1801 to 1804, described San Carlos in his book, *Travels in Parts of South America During the Years 1801, 1802, 1803, and 1804*, as a hot, well-designed, attractive, and growing city with a population of 9,500. Spanish Capuchin missionaries founded it in 1678, soon followed by Spaniards from the Canary Islands who populated the city. Wealth was measured by the number of oxen, horses, and mules one owned.

In 1974 when I arrived, the population of 20,000 was half of what it was one hundred years earlier, although it appeared even less than that. Most buildings were one or two stories, and either painted white or left uncompleted with bare brick. The few cars on narrow streets were American from the 1950s and 1960s. Native-born Venezuelans held the government jobs, and Middle Eastern and Italian families owned the clothing and hardware stores. Chinese owned the one grocery store in town.

On my third day, Fred, who coached basketball, introduced me as the new baseball trainer at the scheduled 8 p.m. meeting of the Cojedes Baseball Association. We arrived a half-hour late, and the meeting had not started yet. When I met Juan Carlos Rojas, the director, who had majored in Spanish literature, Fred mentioned that I too majored in literature in college, making an effort at forming a bond between us that would open the door to achieving *Confianza*. However thoughtful, the gesture failed. Rojas showed no interest in admitting we had the same major in college or anything in common—which, of course, we didn't.

The meeting of players and coaches began with Eduardo, a middle-aged man, walking on stage while gesturing to his son. He pretended to unbuckle his belt and throw his arm up as if he planned to hit him. The crowd howled. Señor Rojas then came on stage and took over. He announced the schedule of games and practices for the week. A discussion followed about a coach's complaint that the umpires at his team's games were lousy. Señor Rojas had no comment. With nothing else to discuss, the meeting ended. Before leaving the stage, Eduardo peered into the crowd and, playing tough, pointed at me, the one guy there in the crowd with a beard and looking out of place, and said, "Who's he?"

Hotel Esperanza in San Carlos where I rented a room.
(Photo by Mike Kendellen)

Señor Rojas introduced me to the baseball ruling class in San Carlos, and everyone applauded, making me feel welcome and making the coaches happy because there was now another person to share the workload. Later, I concluded they were just being polite. I would learn over the next year that my introduction, accompanied by applause, was as good as it gets for working in the Peace Corps Sports and Recreation program. Many of the Volunteers in my training group arrived at their sites and found a general disinterest in and even surprise about their mere presence. One IND director asked a Volunteer, "Why are you here?" At least no one asked me that.

Venezuela's local sports historian, Javier Gonzales, has written that you can't understand the cultural history of Venezuela unless you understand baseball. Ivan Medina, the author of *Registro del Beisbol Venezolano*, Venezuela's baseball statistical bible, said, "Baseball is in our blood." The Peace Corps understood Venezuela prized the game when they put Luis Aparicio on the same pedestal with Simon Bolívar and God. The local newspapers illustrate the national fanaticism in the way they cover the sport. Each day, the sports sections have game summaries and box scores, along with a separate article reporting how the Venezuelan players performed the previous day.

Baseball was the national pastime in Venezuela long before the Peace Corps arrived. Historian Gonzales attributed its origins in

Play Ball!

Venezuela to British miners in the 1860s and 1870s, who introduced rounders to the country. That game, played in Ireland, involved a bat, a ball, and four bases like baseball. In the 1890s, after Cuba had established the La Cubana cigarette factory in Caracas where the employees played on the weekends, baseball replaced rounders as the country's favorite game. The sport reached a crescendo when two thousand people attended a game Emilio Cramer, the cigarette entrepreneur, organized with the El Caracas Base Ball Club. Seeing an opportunity, Cramer soon formed a league with four teams.

When the U.S. Marines were patrolling the Caribbean in 1902 in the aftermath of the Spanish-American War, they went ashore and played games with local teams, which set off a new surge in popularity. A few years later, the oil industry brought more Americans and established more playing fields. By 1915, there were more than one hundred teams in the country. In Maracaibo, American businessman William Phelps, best known for his study and expertise on birds in Venezuela, imported baseball equipment from the United States to sell in his department store, American Bazaar. He then hired coaches to teach local children the game, through the "Sports Social Club," primarily to sell his merchandise. He also built the first baseball field in Maracaibo.

Over the next two decades, Venezuela hosted tournaments with teams from Puerto Rico, the Dominican Republic, and Cuba. The country's victory over Cuba in the 1941 Caribbean World Series cemented baseball as the undisputed national pastime. In 2000, local sports writers voted it the greatest Venezuelan sporting event of the twentieth century. After World War II, Venezuela became a winter haven for American players. Satchel Paige and Josh Gibson from the American Negro League played there, as did Jackie Robinson and Roy Campanella before they played for the Brooklyn Dodgers. Today, Venezuela has a league that plays from October to February, using both home-grown talent and players from U.S. professional leagues.

IND asked me to coach in Tinaco and La Aguadita, two small towns about an hour by bus from San Carlos. IND explained that my job was to conduct practices while someone else, usually the father or brother of a player, would manage the teams on the weekends in San Carlos. Being new to the job and Venezuela, I didn't question the arrangement. I went to Tinaco on Tuesday and Thursday afternoons and to La Aguadita on Wednesday and Friday, also in the afternoon. In the mornings, the kids attended school. Every other Monday evening was for meetings of the Baseball Association, but more often than not, Señor Rojas canceled them when the coaches said there was nothing to talk about. On Saturday, I watched the teams I coached play.

I never understood why Venezuela, with all their baseball talent, needed Peace Corps Volunteers as coaches, but I was also curious how I ended up in San Carlos. According to Fred, Caracas had asked him if IND could use a baseball coach. Although dubious when IND told him they would welcome one, he liked the idea of having another Volunteer in town and having someone to eat meals with and finish the night with a beer, so he told Caracas there was an opening in town.

During training, the Peace Corps had delayed telling me I had been assigned there because IND was slow putting their request in writing. In response, they sent me, the one person in the training group who couldn't use his right arm, fielded left-handed, threw left-handed, and batted left-handed, a rare and underappreciated combination of skills to the central plains of Venezuela. It didn't appear to bother IND. No one ever explained the supposed need for baseball coaches, but based on being sent to tiny towns with cow pastures as playing fields, they mostly needed able and willing coaches to fill more vacancies in remote places. Venezuelans weren't volunteering to go. They knew only teams from the cities win championships.

Tinaco, founded in 1754, where cattle-raising anchored the economy, was sixteen kilometers northeast of San Carlos. Twice a week after lunch, I stood on the highway, holding the first baseman's glove I had brought from home, two baseballs, and two bats from IND, waiting for a bus. When it came into sight, I held the equipment between my legs so I could flag it down. If I weren't waving as if I were lost or in dire need of help, it would not stop for me. As the bus came to a stop, I heard "Tinaco. Tinaco. Tinaco," rolling off the conductor's tongue, while he gripped a bar with one hand and held a book of tickets and a paper puncher in the other. The bus, emitting thick black fumes from the exhaust pipe, stopped for a few seconds, allowing me to jump on board. The driver revved the engine as I put my foot on the first step of the bus. I always looked for the nearest empty seat to avoid falling in the aisle when it started to move again.

The Cordillera de la Costa mountain range presented a scenic background to a field where cows and pigs roamed the outfield. Before practice, I would tell the kids to shoo the animals away with a few swats of a stick to their backside. A few times, I arrived to find a pile of pig shit between first and second base. I ordered the kids to clean that up, too.

The sandy and uneven field that passed for a baseball diamond produced many hits when a batted ball in the infield bounded off a bump or rock and careened out of reach, turning an out into a single or a double. A Major League scout once said the poor field conditions in Venezuela made the players better fielders, but I had my doubts.

La Aguadita, a town of a few hundred people, a few bodegas (corner grocery stores), two bars, and a school was a forty-five-minute bus ride from San Carlos and a few kilometers from Tinaco. Small rocks dotted the outfield where cattle grazed. Like Tinaco, part of the pre-practice ritual was removing a calf or two from the field. First, the kids would throw rocks at it. If that didn't work, they would grab its tail and throw it to the ground, the same as their fathers did at the *Coleo* at holiday festivals. Holes and rivets from the festivals left the field in even worse condition than the one in Tinaco. I made bases from whatever materials littered the area. A piece of aluminum from a discarded can of motor oil was first base. Cloth sacks filled with dirt served as second and third bases, and a piece of cardboard was home plate. The field did not have a backstop behind home plate, ensuring that an errant throw or wild pitch or foul ball would land in the bushes, requiring a time-consuming search that halted practice.

Baseball field in Tinaco
(Photo by Mike Kendellen)

I coached two teams of 10- to 12-year-olds and two teams of 13-

to 15-year-olds. Five, six, or seven players regularly came to practice, which was not enough for a simulated game, a problem that appeared to bother only me. A complete team of nine players never attended one practice together. Like the managers, players were more interested in the games than in the practices. I would teach fielding through hitting ground balls, pitch batting practice, and hitting fly balls to the outfield. If enough players showed up to fill six positions, we would play a few innings. After a couple of hours, practice was over.

Before I gathered the equipment and walked out to the highway to wait for a bus back to San Carlos, the players would ask questions. Why did I wear the same t-shirt and pants to practice? They wondered if I owned other attire. Some probed further by inquiring if the pensión where I lived had a bathroom and if it had a mirror. I didn't know what motivated them to ask those questions. Was it really that odd that I always wore the same pair of pants? Was my beard that unkempt? The questions, even if juvenile, were a welcome break from being accused of spying, or being asked my opinion on Watergate and Richard Nixon, or why I liked Hank Aaron even though he was black. I would get back to my room around 6 p.m., just before dark. I wrote letters home saying work was going well.

Despite a mere two hours of practice on poor fields each week, all four teams made the playoffs, making it difficult to prove a correlation between my coaching and the teams' success. When the junior teams played each other, I quietly rooted for Tinaco and hoped La Aguadita would lose because of their lousy attendance at practice. However, I could not will them to victory; La Aguadita won 8-1.

During training in Los Teques, Wayne—the Super Volunteer— said we might have opportunities to play on a local team in our sites, but nothing ever developed. Instead, I umpired and watched games on weekends. It started one Saturday when the umpire failed to show up. A member of the Baseball Association saw me in the seating area and asked if I would work the game. I agreed, even though I didn't have the tiny gadget I used to count balls and strikes with me. Without it, I would have to keep track in my head, a challenge I relished, though a risky one since coaches and players kept track of the count, too. I didn't need a coach to tell me in my umpiring debut in Venezuela that I had called a batter out on two strikes instead of three or walked one on three balls instead of four.

Play Ball!

Before joining the Peace Corps, my experience as an umpire was in the Cub Scouts and 8- to 11-year-old girls' underhand softball leagues. I lasted one season in the girls' league. When a coach accused me of taking bribes from the opposing coach after I called one of her players out in a close play at home plate, I knew fifth-grade girls' softball was not for me. Being accused of bribery in girls' softball was too much to take. I never called another girls' game.

For three years, I umpired two Cub Scout games a week in April and May. I have two lingering memories of the experience. One involves leaving a student rally protesting the invasion and bombing of Cambodia and the deaths of students at Kent State and Jackson State Universities in May 1970 to work a game. Student demonstrations were multiplying across the country, leading to the closing of more than 450 universities. More than forty years later, I recall the episode as a case of misplaced priorities.

While I was skipping out of an anti-war demonstration, more than 100,000 people gathered in Washington, DC for a similar march. At 4 a.m. during a weekend of protests, President Nixon went to the Lincoln Memorial to meet student protestors, hoping to understand their motivations better. He told them, "I hope [your] hatred of the war, which I could well understand, would not turn into a bitter hatred of our whole system, our country, and everything it stood for. I said that I know probably most of you think I'm an SOB. But I want you to know I understand how you feel." According to students from Syracuse University, he also tried to engage in a discussion on football.

Also in Washington at the time was the Committee of Returned Volunteers, the first Peace Corps alumni group. They were unhappy with U.S. foreign policy, particularly on Vietnam, and accused the agency of championing the "imperial-like" policy. In protest, sixteen members of the New York chapter occupied the fourth-floor offices of the East Asia and Pacific Region at the Peace Corps office, a few blocks from the White House. The protestors flew the Vietcong flag from the window. They also posted banners in solidarity with Bobby Seale, the Black Panthers, Ho Chi Minh, and Che Guevara. The takeover ended thirty-six hours later without the authorities intervening, principally because the director, Joseph Blatchford, whom President Nixon had appointed a year earlier, refused to call the police, despite demands from congressmen and the White House, who were incensed over the

Vietcong flag—and because the group thought they made their point and there was no reason to continue the occupation. The next issue of *The Volunteer*, the Peace Corps' in-house magazine, published several scathing letters from both present and former Volunteers denouncing the staff, bureaucrats, and paper-pushers, as one letter writer called them, for not supporting the protest.

My other memory of Cub Scout baseball—I was never a Scout myself—was a game when an 8-year-old came to bat with the bases loaded and two outs in the ninth inning, a situation every player dreams about. The coach, following his A-Walk-Is-as-Good-as-a-Hit strategic approach to youth baseball, ordered him not to swing at any pitch, with the hope he would walk and tie the game. The coach told the kid to do nothing, putting the outcome of the at-bat in the umpire's hands—which in this case was me, as I had to call a ball or a strike for each pitch.

It was stupid. I did not like this approach to youth baseball. When players are under 12 years old, the coaches should encourage the kids to swing at the ball, not stand there hoping the umpire makes the correct call. Still, whether I disagreed with the strategy or not, the 8-year-old, four-foot-tall kid looked terrified, standing in the batter's box and listening to his coach instructing him to look at every pitch and leave the bat on his shoulder. The coach, standing less than twenty-five feet away, was screaming, "Don't swing, don't swing!"

I felt sorry for the kid. He had no choice but to follow his coach's orders. This put the outcome of the game in my hands. I would determine the result, which could affect the kid for the rest of his life.

I called them as I saw them, to use a cliché for expressing neutrality in umpires. The count reached three balls and two strikes. A parent standing behind me shouted, "Hey, ump, you need glasses?" Whose side was he on? Did he want me to call a ball or a strike? I ignored him.

With three balls and two strikes, the next pitch could end the game. The coach continued to scream, "Don't swing, don't swing!" The kid trembled as he stood in the batter's box three feet in front of me with a bat on his shoulders. Parents from both teams yelled encouragement to their kids out in the field, despite knowing the batter was not going to swing and, thus, that there would be no play in the field.

Cub Scouts are not known to rebel and resist. There was no way the kid would swing at the pitch. I wanted to strangle the coach. I stood behind home plate, ready for the next pitch. It was slow and over the plate. The kid followed orders, doing nothing. I did my duty and called it as I saw it. "Strike three. You're out," I yelled. The tyke burst into tears. The game was over.

Parents from both sides shouted at me: "Hey, ump, you're blind." I walked away.

Less than five years later, I was walking out of the stands in a foreign country wearing jeans and a t-shirt to umpire a game. I stood behind the pitcher, alone, without protective gear or even a hat or sunglasses against the tropical sun, ready to call balls and strikes and keep the count in my head. Did I join the Peace Corps to do this? The job description didn't mention umpiring.

Coaches in Cojedes had a more aggressive approach to hitting than the Cub Scouts of America did. They ordered batters to swing. "Hit the ball. Hit the ball," they yelled before each pitch. One coach gave even more explicit orders: he called a time-out to yell at a batter to hit a triple. A triple! Nobody tries to hit a triple, the rarest of the four possible hits in baseball. Still, it was music to my ears, and so much better than hearing "Don't swing, don't swing." Venezuelans know how to play ball!

If I made a few bad calls, I did not expect the coaches to argue with me. They knew my Spanish was not adequate to carry on a heated discussion and, anyway, umpires never changed their calls. The coaches asked me to umpire because they presumed I was neutral and fair. My first game did not have any controversial plays, and I didn't lose track of the ball and strike count. No one accused me of favoring one team over the other, and no one offered me a bribe. Overall, it was a good day. They asked me to umpire more games.

The quality of play for 14- to 16-year-olds was below average, which increased the likelihood something weird would occur. Players dropped easy fly balls and kicked every other ground ball. I often witnessed such plays at my practices. The batters swung and missed at so many bad pitches I considered moving closer to catch a whiff from their swinging strikes to cool me off in the ninety-degree weather. Few players hustled, reflecting the pace of slow-moving Venezuelan society. Outfielders jogged after a ball or to snag a sinking line drive. When the ball fell for a hit, the player expressed surprise at the outcome of his effort. "*Cuno*, I missed it!" Others misjudged balls and ran in from their position to catch instead of backing up, only to have the ball sail over their head, at which point the outfielder would sprint after the ball, too late to matter. By the time he caught up with the ball, the batter was passing third base and trotting home to score.

I worried a play out of the ordinary would happen, requiring me to rule on it. For instance, I might have to make a call when two players found themselves on the same base, or when the ball hit a runner, or when the catcher dropped the ball on a close play at home. I didn't want to see any of those oddball plays occur.

Inevitably, though, bizarre plays did happen. In one game, the manager called in the left fielder to pitch in relief of the starter. Two innings later, when he faltered as a pitcher, the coach moved him to right field and the right fielder became the pitcher. The opposing manager objected. He said the left-fielder-cum-pitcher should have left the game like all pitchers do when the manager replaces them. An argument ensued between the two coaches. They asked me to decide. The players and fans assumed the rules allowed the pitcher to move to right field and stay in the game, and I did, too. "Play ball!" I yelled as the former pitcher walked out to right field. I ordered the other players to their positions. No one argued. I umpired several more games, and they all proceeded without incident or argument.

Baseball players in Cojedes were often actors, similar to basketball players flopping and hoping for a foul, or soccer players feigning near death after being tripped by an opposing player. When hit by a pitch, marked as an HBP on the scorecard, the 14-year-old batter would go into various contortions and grimace as if he had been hit over the head with a hammer. After a few minutes of rubbing the sore spot on his arm, the usual place where batters got hit, over and over, he would walk to first base and stay in the game. In one game, the batter was hit on his hand, tearing a fingernail. He left the game, and from the bench declared he couldn't play for two weeks. A fan sitting behind home plate called him a wimp.

Before and after games, coaches would pester me about game strategy. For instance, a coach once asked me what he should do if runners were on first and third with one out and the batter had two strikes on him. Fans debate this situation all the time. I gave the obvious answer: "He should swing at the pitch if it was over the plate."

They were also curious about my ideas on physical conditioning. "What are some exercises to stay in shape?" Again, I kept it simple and suggested they could start by running, something I thought most Venezuelans should consider, as many seemed in poor physical condition. A Baseball Association official, eager to gain insight into my coaching techniques, though never curious enough to go to Tinaco and La Aguadita to watch me coach, asked if I favored disciplining the players. Was I hard on them during practice? "Discipline is important," he said without irony.

I wasn't sure what he meant and shrugged off the question of being tough by responding in one word, "*Alguna*" ("Some"). I didn't think yelling at players made them better or motivated them. Even though the meaning of discipline remains vague and too often meant shouting at players when they made mistakes, two former Venezuelan Major League players cite it as a major factor in saving their careers. Melvin Mora, from Agua Negra, Yaracuy, northwest of Valencia, struggled at first, before playing thirteen years with the Baltimore Orioles and three other teams; he said in a speech thanking all his former coaches and the scout who recommended him, "Discipline is the key to the game. Listen to the coaches; work hard and be disciplined."

Another player, Richard Hidalgo, from Caracas, who played most of his nine years for the Houston Astros, said, "Discipline is the most important thing. We had to work hard to get where we are now (in the Major Leagues)."

While it sounded good, the meaning was not clear. Yasiel Puig may have clarified it. Puig fled Cuba in a boat in 2012 and signed a seven-year, $42 million contract with the Los Angeles Dodgers. After two outstanding years, his production slumped, and he finished the 2016 season on the bench. Some of his teammates thought Puig lacked maturity. When he reported to spring training in 2017, healthy and fit and looking forward to having a good year, a sportswriter asked him what caused the change in his demeanor and outlook. "Discipline," was his reply. Could he explain? Was it his workouts? His nutrition? His swing? Or was it his general behavior? Puig said it was all those things.

In the 1980s, Major League scouts thought players from Venezuela were not hungry or ambitious. They were lazy, too, the scouts said. Few played in the United States. Instead, teams looked to the Dominican Republic and Mexico for players. Venezuela broke out of its funk in the 1990s, when Major League Baseball added four teams and needed more players to fill rosters and the Houston Astros established a baseball academy in Valencia, resulting in more Venezuelans signing contracts to play in the United States.

Since 1939, more than 350 Venezuelans have played in the Major Leagues. Among them are shortstops Chico Carrasquel, who made his Major League debut with the Chicago White Sox; national hero Luis Aparicio; David Conception, Hall of Fame shortstop for the Cincinnati Reds; and Ozzie Guillen, who played fifteen years with the White Sox. In 2017, some of the more prominent Venezuelans were Avisail Garcia (Chicago White Sox), Miguel Cabrera (Detroit), Jose Altuve (Houston), Ender Inciarte (Atlanta), Salvador Perez (Kanas City) and Felix Hernandez (Seattle).

Three players from San Carlos have made it to the Major Leagues. Luis Rodriguez, the most successful of them, played for five teams, including the San Diego Padres, where the local media called him "The Franchise." Oakland released pitcher Iván Miguel Granados after two seasons in the minor leagues. After the major leagues, he went to Spain, where he played on their Olympic baseball team as the worst pitcher on a bad team. Pitcher Yfrain Linares, a kindergartener in San Carlos when I was living there, played for the Milwaukee Brewers and in Mexico and Italy before finishing his career, according to Baseball Reference, in rural Massachusetts playing for the Berkshire Bears. In the 2016 season, no one from San Carlos was playing professionally in the United States.

However, in Venezuela's political and economic meltdown, Venezuelan players have become U.S. citizens or made the United States their base over fears about safety and social situations at home. There are fewer academies, fewer scouts visiting the country and baseball has taken a backseat in an uncertain future.

While umpiring, I learned of the quirkiness in Venezuelan names. Before a game, the managers of the teams exchanged starting lineups, a ritual that never amounted to anything. I skimmed the two lineup cards to make sure they each had a player at all nine positions, and each team fielded the nine players listed on the manager's lineup.

At one game, one particular name on the lineup card caught my eye: Hitler-Stalin Gomez was playing third base for one team. Since it wasn't my job to check for cheaters, I didn't question the coaches or ask the player for his cedula (ID card) to see if that was his real name. Yet I wondered.

After the game, I asked Reyes Franco Herrera about it. Reyes, a 27-year-old native of San Carlos, coached at the Park Recreation Center, though I didn't know what sports because I never saw him at work. Fred had introduced me to him, and after Fred left, he was my friend in the area. Reyes confirmed that Hitler-Stalin was a legitimate name, offering no explanation on why parents would name their child Hitler or Stalin, much less both.

Years later, I discovered Venezuela was known for unique names. In 2007, sixty registered voters had the name Hitler. Other voters included one Batman, eight Hochiminhs, a Dwight Eisenhower Rojas Barboza, Hengelberth, Maolenin, Krishnamerk, Githanjaly, Yornaichel, Nixon, and Yurbiladyberth. Ílich Ramírez Sánchez, the Venezuelan-born terrorist also known as Carlos the Jackal, was named in honor of Vladimir Ilich Ulyanov, better known as Lenin. His two brothers were Vladimir and Lenin.

The naming situation was such that the National Assembly debated a bill that would limit the number of names parents could consider for their children to one hundred, primarily to "preserve the equilibrium and integral development of the child." Defenders of the bill believed it would protect kids from bullying; assuming difficult-to-pronounce names like Yurbiladyberth would make life a living hell while growing up. Others hoped the bill would eliminate any doubt about the child's gender. For instance, was Yornaichel male or female? Newspaper editorials described the measure as "malicious." The bill never passed.

All four teams I coached made the playoffs, which turned out to be two weeks' worth of error-prone games. Over the course of the 62 games played in the tournament, the players committed an unbelievable 326 errors—more than five per game. The Major League average is less than one.

In the bottom of the ninth in one game, my team from La Aguadita was behind 6-3. With a walk and two hits, they loaded the bases with one out. The next batter hit a fly ball to centerfield and the runner on third tagged up and headed for home. The throw got past the catcher and the batter scored, making it 6-4. Meanwhile, the runner on second had also tagged up on the play, and when the ball went past the catcher, he ran for home. The catcher retrieved the ball and threw it to the pitcher covering home, who tagged the runner. The umpire called him out; being the third out of the inning, that ended the game. It was a close call. I thought the runner was safe. The coach for La Aguadita rushed to home plate, screaming at the umpire that he was stupid and a cheat, but refrained from punching the umpire. The manager and the umpire continued to argue as they left the stadium and, once on the street, threw punches at each other. No one tried to break it up.

During the next game, the umpire who made the call at home plate and survived the post-game fight spotted me in the bleachers and came over to chat, looking for empathy. A university student in Caracas, he didn't care if the manager called him a cheat; it meant nothing to him. He believed he had integrity and was just a sports fan who wanted to help out in the community. He was more disappointed than angry and said he wasn't going to let an unsportsmanlike, dumb manager change his outlook.

In another game, a fan ran out of the stands and slapped the umpire on the side of the head after making a controversial call, before the coaches hauled him away. Fans also threw stones at umpires. I was lucky; no one argued any of my calls.

The tournament, an action-packed and bizarre series of games, ended the baseball season. Now what?

Four

What Do I Do Now?

The San Carlos baseball league season ran from April to September. With the season over, I needed something to do. Fred had left to become the regional volunteer coordinator for western Venezuela, leaving me as the sole Volunteer in the state. His departure created an opening for a basketball coach, a post I hesitated to inform IND I could fill until Peace Corps decided if they planned to replace Fred. Meanwhile, in a letter to a friend, I mentioned selling lottery tickets, painting, or taking fares on a bus as job possibilities.

Teaching chess was an option, too. I learned to play at 12 from a neighbor who considered himself an expert. It took a year before I beat him. After the world championship in 1972 between Boris Spassky and Bobby Fischer, the world, including Venezuela and San Carlos, experienced a chess renaissance. Although it had been two years since the epic match in Iceland had captured the world's focus, taxi drivers played on the hoods of their cars while waiting for passengers, teenagers sat on sidewalks and older folks occupied benches in Plaza Bolívar until the police arrived and chased them away. I started a game by letter with a friend, and Reyes and I played a few days a week in the lobby of the pensión where the overhead fan kept us cool. Hoping to enhance my skills, I bought a chess set in Caracas along with an instruction manual for $10 titled *How to Improve Your Chess*.

Players formed local chess clubs and associations. Some enthusiasts in Tinaquillo, another town in the state noted for cattle raising, asked the director of IND to guide them through the paperwork to form an association, a necessary step for players to be eligible for national tournaments. The group elected Jose Hernández its first president. *Historia Del Ajedrez En Cojedes (The History of Chess in Cojedes)* cites players from the state who have won medals in regional, national, and international tournaments since 1974.

In San Carlos, Reyes formed a club. He nominated me for president of the six-member association, thinking having an American as the head of the group might give it some prestige. I thought otherwise. The last thing the San Carlos Chess Club needed was a Peace Corps Volunteer as its president, but I didn't want to embarrass Reyes, so I agreed to run for the position. We voted by secret ballot. I was relieved when Reyes announced the results and I had lost 4-2—and I was not one of the two people who voted for me.

The Chess Association of the State of Cojedes has enjoyed some success since those initial days. In 2014, their Facebook page reported that Venezuela sent a team of five players to the Chess Olympics in Norway, including José Luis Castro Torres from San Carlos. Venezuela finished 47th in the tournament, out of 172 countries.

Each month, Caracas sent a packet of memos and newsletters which served as my source of information about the Peace Corps in Venezuela. The memos concerned policies on accommodations and vehicle use, doctors we could contact, the dates of future regional Spanish courses and the next Foreign Service exam, and staff travel plans. I especially looked forward to reading *The Peacemaker*, later renamed *El Clarin*, a newsletter that kept us informed on the latest departures and arrivals of Volunteers. For entertainment, there was the occasional recipe (how to make granola), attempts at humor ("Since we have taken so much flak from so many Volunteers about our yacht being incompatible with the Peace Corps way of living, we have decided not to extend again. So there!"), opinions (unhappiness about scheduling a language course over the July Fourth holiday), complaints (staff needs more backbone), and travel suggestions (see more of Venezuela and less of Colombia). One Volunteer, who taught swimming in the YMCA program, griped over the number of Volunteers arriving with technical skills. He thought the Volunteers in rural development and public works and the environmentalists brought attitudes of superiority, and then, through no fault of theirs, Caracas assigned them to government offices where qualified Venezuelans already held these jobs. What kind of sense did that make? The argument wasn't much different than questioning Peace Corps' recruitment of baseball coaches.

Visits from Peace Corps staff were infrequent and consisted of lunch at a restaurant on the outskirts of town known for its broiled chicken. The Caracas staff, a mixture of Venezuelans and Americans, consisted of a director, a deputy, program officers, the training team, and the administrators and a nurse. Walt Thomas, an African American, was the program officer responsible for the Sports and YMCA programs in western Venezuela, which included San Carlos. When I first met him, he introduced himself as a man of few words. Unfortunately for Walt, his more energetic and outgoing colleague in eastern Venezuela visited Volunteers primarily to bullshit with them. Walt was less sociable, and appeared distant in comparison.

It didn't help that Tony, his counterpart in eastern Venezuela, fit perfectly into the Venezuelan culture: he was an extrovert, had the gift of gab (a highly coveted skill), and acted as a fixer with IND, solving a variety of problems for Volunteers. Maybe people like Tony were a better fit for Peace Corps staff, but Walt suffered in comparison. He had grown up as a poor African American during both segregation and the Civil Rights Movement. He wasn't about to buy groceries, pick up passports and run other errands for Volunteers, or pretend to be friends with them. It wasn't his style.

Many Volunteers interpreted Walt's more low-key approach as a sign of incompetence. It didn't help that he found only two jobs in western Venezuela for Volunteers in my training group, whereas Tony, his more exuberant colleague, placed twenty east of Caracas, making Walt look bad, if not lazy or incompetent. Few people gave Walt the benefit of the doubt, even though western Venezuela had fewer sports facilities and a smaller population, making IND less interested in Peace Corps no matter how many coaches were available.

In the eastern part of the country, Tony stacked the deck by convincing the Caracas office and IND that placing Volunteers close to each other would promote inter-city competitions and intra-state tournaments, which seemed to be the lifeblood of sports in Venezuela. The result was eight Volunteers in the state of Sucre, four in Managas, three in Bolívar, three on Margarita Island, and one in Amacuro. The lopsided arrangements contributed to the belief that Tony worked harder than Walt, who was thought to not work at all because he could only find two positions in Barquisimeto, where he lived.

But Walt's problems started before I arrived in Venezuela. A few months earlier, Caracas terminated two Volunteers for smoking marijuana based on snitching from one of their own. Caracas thought Walt should have been the one reporting the offense, not Volunteers. Walt disagreed. He didn't see his job as being a monitor, babysitter, or lackey who brought food from the supermarket that wasn't available at a rural Venezuelan bodega or retrieved passports from the Colombian Embassy so that Volunteers could take a vacation.

Since everyone was well aware of the drug policy and the consequences of not following it, Walt saw no reason to remind people of the policies each time he heard a rumor of marijuana use or witnessed it at a party. As he saw it, Peace Corps promoted recruitment as a rigorous process in which 75 percent of the applications were rejected. Walt reasoned if that was true and all the Volunteers in Venezuela had survived that process, then he shouldn't need to go around repeating drug policies to smart and talented people.

But Walt had responsibilities as a staff member. Caracas wanted him to be more of a policeman during a time when rumors were rife of marijuana use, possibly threatening the Peace Corps' future in the country, and Volunteers were spending too much time away from their sites on unauthorized vacations. Walt, though, did not believe those tasks were part of his job.

There were ugly undertones as well. On top of the criticism of Walt's work, some Volunteers did not like that he rented a house with air conditioning, hired a maid, and drove a Cadillac, even though as a professional staff member, he could afford the rent and cleaning service. Besides, Peace Corps policy allowed staff to ship a personal vehicle to their posting. What role race played, if any, was not clear. But one Volunteer who liked to brand himself as a white guy who grew up in "Nigger Town" perceived Walt as a big black guy who refused to bow to the power structure—but should have sucked it up and adjusted his lifestyle to keep his job. Other Volunteer complaints were trivial, like the few who didn't like Walt's preference for Motown music. Still, Walt may not have helped his case; he preferred talking about race relations in the U.S. rather than listening to Volunteers talk about the difficulties they were having with their Venezuelan bosses and colleagues. On one occasion when he visited two Volunteers, he insisted they sit around and think of derogatory names white people called black people.

My contact with him was no different from my contact with most other staff: minimal. While I was in San Carlos, he visited me twice in six months. During one visit to San Carlos with the director and deputy director, the discussion during lunch turned to revising jobs and tasks at the Caracas level so staff could better serve the Volunteers. Walt criticized the plan, which drew a response from the deputy director: "Walt, I'm only trying to make your job easier," exposing the rift which had been rumored between them.

On his other visit, he took me to lunch at the best restaurant in San Carlos, known for their roasted chicken. At the time, I was working twelve hours a week and needed a few more baseballs, but I had no plans to ask him to intervene with IND about giving me more work, being doubtful that any visiting Peace Corps staff could improve my situation. Whatever issues I had with IND, I was not going to ask staff from Caracas to intervene. I don't recall what we talked about over lunch, but it wasn't race. After the pleasant meal, he returned to Barquisimeto. I never saw him again.

A few weeks later, the packets of memos and newsletters Caracas sent each month arrived. On the cover page of The Peacemaker, the travel schedule showed that Walt would be in Caracas the whole month, while on page three, it said Wayne, the Super Volunteer, was now the interim Sports and YMCA program director. If Wayne was the director, why would Walt still be in Caracas?

It turned out he wasn't; he had left Venezuela for Washington, DC to appeal his dismissal. The saga continued when I received a letter from him asking me to write to a Mr. Lawrence Speiser, a leading civil liberties lawyer in Washington, DC, who specialized in workplace discrimination, and confirm he had visited the Los Teques training site and the swearing-in ceremony and that we had conversations during those times. In the same envelope was a letter from the Equal Employment Opportunity Commission (EEOC) asking me to comment on the Peace Corps working environment and how it may have affected Walt, who was claiming the Caracas office discriminated and conspired against him.

Even though I was new and didn't know that much, I told the

EEOC that a lack of trust between Volunteers and staff permeated Peace Corps, and that Walt, from what I heard, did not meet the expectations of how a Peace Corps staff member should live and conduct himself. I didn't know if race factored into his clashes with staff, but I told the EEOC that he was most upset that the Caracas office expected him to act like an undercover agent, reporting on volunteers who violated rules. If Volunteers broke rules, they often pertained to owning a motorcycle (forbidden); taking a vacation without authorization (not advised); and smoking marijuana (against the law).

The next thing I heard, Walt was back in Caracas at his old job, though one Volunteer who had been in Caracas reported he had no real work to do. ACTION, the federal umbrella agency that included Peace Corps, sent an investigator to Caracas to look into the discrimination complaint and soon after, Walt was no longer with the Peace Corps. There was never an announcement that he had left Venezuela.

Back in San Carlos, life continued; I was watching my everyday expenditures. Since high school, I had been tracking my expenses and continued recording them in Venezuela, no matter how small, in a notebook in San Carlos. At the end of each month, I tallied the figures and concluded, "That's interesting. No action required." I didn't think my expenses were outlandish. With three restaurants, two movie theaters, a few bars, an ice cream parlor, bodegas every few blocks, a furniture shop, and a hardware store, I had little opportunity to spend much money. I put beer, movies, newspapers, magazines, and stamps for the snail mail I sent weekly into the categories of rent, food, transportation, and travel. I paid 180 bolivars ($45) for my room, which was 30 bolivars ($7.50) more than the monthly allowance for housing Peace Corps sent me and I still saved about $25 a month. My bank balance kept increasing.

Long before I arrived, Volunteers had been complaining that the extra $75 living allowance provided for Volunteers in Caracas over the lowest allowance—in 2017, the equivalent of $500 more—was unfair. Volunteers were not paid a salary or a stipend, but rather were given a living allowance and money for rent. Management, agreeing the issue needed further study, established the Cost of Living Allowance Commission, a group of staff and Volunteers tasked with analyzing our compensation using information from the Central Bank of Venezuela, the sole credible source of economic data in the country.

What Do I Do Now?

	MEALS	SNACKS	RENT	WORK	BEER	MOVIES	STAMPS	HEALTH	NEWSPAPER	TRAVEL
Apr 74	115.50	16.00	147.00	10.50	27.75	8.00	9.10	28.40	0.00	45.00
May	270.00	50.75	150.00	29.50	75.00	40.00	22.00	8.10	3.75	0.00
June	240.00	40.35	150.00	23.75	63.25	82.00	12.00	8.35	8.00	6.00
July	185.00	18.35	180.00	18.75	29.50	25.00	16.00	1.25	25.00	111.60
Aug	241.25	31.60	180.00	26.00	23.25	41.00	2.70	11.50	25.25	0.00
Sept	185.00	36.10	180.00	0.00	16.25	35.00	18.50	0.00	31.50	89.75
Oct	185.25	23.70	180.00	0.00	44.25	40.00	2.40	4.95	18.25	139.45
Nov	277.25	19.25	180.00	0.00	84.50	30.00	6.75	5.50	54.25	178.25
Dec	162.50	10.25	180.00	0.00	30.25	12.00	4.40	1.00	11.25	95.50
Jan 75	88.50	2.50	180.00	0.00	7.50	9.00	19.50	1.50	2.00	290.00
Feb	222.30	7.20	—	—transport	28.50	4.00	22.00	1.50	12.25	128.65

The spreadsheet in bolivars tracking monthly expenses I kept in a notebook. Four bolivars = $1. In June 1974, I spent 240 bolivars or $60 on breakfast, lunch and dinner.

The Commission, after months of work, recommended that no one's living allowance should be decreased by more than ten percent. San Carlos, one of thirty locations that received the lowest allowance, was listed as a site where Volunteers should receive fifteen bolivars ($4) less. My new allowance would be 165 bolivars. I checked my expenses and concluded I could live with the decrease. Although it was a ten percent cut, that meant a mere four dollars. I could still save a little for vacation.

More interesting, the review group also suggested reducing the rent allowance by 25 percent if two or more Volunteers shared accommodations. The practice that all Volunteers received the same housing allowance regardless of whether they lived alone or with others rankled enough Volunteers that the Committee recommended a lower rent allowance for Volunteers who shared a house or apartment with more than two other people. I didn't know how many people this would affect, but I didn't like the policy. The rent allowance should have nothing to do with how many people are sharing an apartment or house.

The settling-in allowance was a separate matter. At the end of training, each new Volunteer received 1,200 bolivars to acquire household items such as furniture and a refrigerator. I had spent only a tiny portion of my settling-in allowance because I lived in a hotel. I put the unspent money in the bank. The Commission recommended the amount be increased, as Venezuela was getting more expensive.

Washington, however, rejected the suggestion because Congress was reducing the Peace Corps' budget, making it a bad time to increase Volunteer costs. I did not respond to the memo. The recommendations appeared to be solving old, simmering problems and the amount of money involved was too small to care about.

In fact, never once did I hear Volunteers talk about the memo. Budgets were not our domain and the gap between the Caracas allowances and the rest of the country had been reduced. I also assumed that because so many Volunteers were nearing the end of their service and rumors were circulating that the Peace Corps would close in Venezuela, policies and finance had lost their relevance.

I stayed informed on national and international developments, including Watergate, through the local papers, *TIME*, letters, and the magazines and hometown newspapers my father sent me a few times a month—the same thing his mother did for him when he was in the Army during World War II. I was watching my teams from Tinaco and La Aguadita battle in the playoffs when President Richard Nixon resigned. The Venezuelan newspapers used the opportunity to review his career, paying particular attention on his visit to Caracas in May 1958 when he was vice president, an incident Nixon included in his 1962 book *Six Crises*.

In 1958, relations between the U.S. and Venezuela were at their nadir. The Venezuelan government wanted Washington to focus less on the Cold War and the threat of Communism and more on protecting American investments—especially oil, the lifeline of the Venezuelan economy. The military had ousted President Marcos Pérez Jiménez in a coup, and he had fled to Miami along with the chief of the Secret Police, Pedro Estrada. Most people assumed the U.S. government had supported Jiménez, which led to further resentment. In this environment, Nixon came to Venezuela. The visit is remembered for a mob attacking his motorcade with a volley of rocks as a protest of U.S. policy in Latin America. The embassy, fearing the worst, canceled the ceremonial trip to Simon Bolívar's tomb. In response to possible further attacks, President Eisenhower dispatched troops to the Caribbean in case Nixon needed to be rescued. But a rescue proved unnecessary when he cut short his visit and flew back to Andrews Air Force Base outside Washington, where Eisenhower and 10,000 enthusiasts welcomed him home as a hero.

What Do I Do Now?

Sixteen years later, he quit the White House in disgrace. Letters from home had been warning me that Congress either would impeach him or he would resign, so when I heard the news, I expressed my reaction in one word: finally! Venezuelans had a difficult time comprehending Watergate and grasping the specific reasons for Nixon's demise. A few cynical local pundits thought Watergate illustrated the inherent corruption of capitalism, while newspaper editorials considered the reporting on the crisis a victory for democracy, a position they did not take two years later in the midst of their own national political trauma. Polls showed Venezuelans were wary of Nixon leaving office and the effect it might have on world peace.

Nelson Rockefeller had a much longer history with Venezuela and a more constructive impact on the country than Nixon. Though the Rockefellers were the majority owners of the Creole Petroleum Corporation, a subsidiary of Standard Oil of New Jersey and the largest oil company in the nation, Rockefeller was more interested in linking American know-how in capitalism with economic development in Latin America. To further his interest, in 1947, he created the International Basic Economy Corporation (IBEC) on the premise that profitable enterprise could best fulfill basic needs for food, clothing, and shelter in the developing world.

In Venezuela, Rockefeller wanted to build a sustainable local food industry that would reduce imports. His vision was to establish industrial farms to supply the supermarkets with produce grown on Venezuelan-owned farms, an approach to development Rockefeller believed would neutralize the leftist propaganda heard throughout the region which held that more government involvement in all aspects of society would be fairer and less exploitative. "It's hard to be a Communist with a full belly," Rockefeller quipped when questioned about his plan of replacing the unprofitable corner bodega with businesses that offered more choices, with most provided by local farmers, that would theoretically result in a stable middle class. If people could afford to buy enough food for their family, they would be less likely to follow revolutionary movements. It was an ambitious vision.

But Venezuelans were skeptical. A Caracas newspaper opined that Rockefeller's plan to make the country self-sufficient in food was just another demonstration of British-American imperialism and a disguised attempt to buy all the farmland and profit from it.

While the politicos debated the merits and demerits of the scheme, Rockefeller had serious practical obstacles to surmount. For one, few people lived in rural areas and even fewer owned land. Because the country's lack of roads and bridges made transportation very expensive, few companies could afford to move agricultural produce around the country. Rockefeller also needed the government to show interest and some enthusiasm for his ideas if his plan was to succeed.

Development, though, was a hard sell. The government lacked the expertise and motivation to grasp what Rockefeller envisioned; Venezuela, with its oil, could buy everything they needed. Whatever benefits Rockefeller enterprises promised, local food producers believed his main aim was to drive them out of business so he create a monopoly on agriculture. One radio station in Maracaibo, the center of the oil industry, where there was little farming, declared that Rockefeller wanted to turn the country into nothing more than a large plantation of economic slaves. How could development move forward in such an environment?

Despite Venezuelans' tendency to buy what they needed from international markets rather than develop local enterprises, Rockefeller moved ahead with his vision. He brought in consultants from Cargill, the largest agricultural company in the United States, to assess the state of farming in the country. The "experts" from Iowa concluded that agriculture in Venezuela was "incredibly backward, biblical some of them said, and reliant on ancient technologies: fire, stick, and hoe" while missing the details of the uphill struggle farming represented. They recommended farmers spray their fields with DDT and other pesticides to increase yield like the farmers in the U.S. did. However, the American specialists reached their conclusions and made suggestions without speaking to Venezuelans. If they had, they might have found out that armyworms frequently destroyed crops, and were difficult to kill. Plus, spraying with DDT took up so much time there was no time left to fertilize. And even if spraying and fertilizing were workable ideas, the region's tropical rains, also foreign to Iowa, drowned whatever plants survived the pesticide onslaught.

IBEC, frustrated with unending problems, fired Cargill and replaced the firm with Charles F. Seabrook, the so-called "Henry Ford of Agriculture" who, along with Clarence Birdseye, had built America's frozen-food business. Without much effort, they recognized that industrial farming that relied on machinery and pesticides would not work in the tropical soils and climate of Venezuela. When the new consultants reassessed the problem, in fact, they concluded that free-enterprise private sector agriculture in the United States was more myth than fact. With little government visibility in rural areas, most experts and politicians had no reason to think the success of American agriculture was anything more than a result of good old American know-how combined with a hands-off non-interference approach from Washington. IBEC analysis, however, concluded the opposite: American agriculture thrived because of government-funded research and technology and by providing land and subsidies.

In Venezuela, no such expertise, mandate, or interest existed. Worse, oil revenue, the source of funding for agriculture, competed with other government priorities. Rockefeller had assumed the oil companies would want to buy produce from Venezuelan companies and gain cheaper food for their employees. But he was wrong. The oil companies, flush with money, didn't care if local farms produced fruit, vegetables, and meat at a lower cost, nor did they care if thousands of people working in the oil fields and living in camps ate imported or home-grown food. Food was food; where it came from did not concern the oil giants. And as long as a sufficient amount of oil revenue flowed to Caracas, the scheme of promoting local food production lacked a financial incentive to make it happen.

IBEC listened to the criticism and shifted its focus to establishing retail supermarkets. Analysis from other countries had shown that locating stores in prosperous areas, preferably populated with a lot of North Americans, would be the quickest way to make a profit. So it was not surprising when in 1949, IBEC opened its first supermarket, called CADA (*Compania Anonima Distribudora de Alimentos /Anonymous Food Distributor Company*), on Bella Vista Avenue in Maracaibo, an affluent area of the second largest city in the country, with a thriving North American community, most of whom worked in the oil industry. By 1956, there were eight supermarkets, which increased to twenty-one by 1966.

Although CADA and its affiliated American-like restaurants offered one sector of society more food options, most Venezuelans did not like the supermarkets. They viewed them as symbols of imperialism and foreign intervention, a common theme in international politics at the time. Angry mobs burned, robbed, and attacked them in the 1960s as a protest against U.S. support for an unpopular government. In November 1966, the leftist Armed Forces for National Liberation (*Fuerzas Armadas de Liberacion de Nacional*) fire-bombed CADA stores as a protest against the lack of inclusiveness in Venezuela. Demonstrators equipped with machine guns and stones also attacked several of the store's twenty-four locations to protest President Lyndon Johnson sending the U.S. Marines to the Dominican Republic to curb a civil war and prevent a Communist takeover.

Despite the challenges, IBEC expanded its retail business and built shopping malls. Examples included the *Centro Ciudad Comercial Tamanaco* in Caracas, a complex of shops, restaurants, and banks, along with a smaller one complex in Maracaibo that included a supermarket, retail, and Big Boy restaurants under a single roof. By the time I arrived in the mid-1970s, IBEC was selling the facilities to local investors because they were losing money and, as with the oil companies, rising nationalism raised concerns about the future of foreign-owned companies.

Venezuela never did develop an agriculture sector despite promises to do so. In response to the food shortages in 2014, in fact, President Maduro formed a council of farmers, fishers, and rural food producers to address rapidly plummeting nutrition, food scarcity, and production. He also created a Ministry of Food. Maduro promised the council would "revolutionize" decision-making regarding agriculture and food production. Three years later, in 2017, a study found the average Venezuelan had lost nineteen pounds because they didn't have enough to eat.

Whatever the history and politics surrounding the Rockefeller-owned supermarkets and restaurants, Peace Corps Volunteers frequented them. The nearest CADA store to San Carlos was about sixty miles away in Valencia. It turned into a morale booster where I could enjoy air conditioning, a beer, a burger, and a banana split. I overlooked any connection it might have to colonialism, imperialism, or exploitation. I would sit and sip my beer, forget the politics of IND, read *TIME* magazine, and watch the Venezuelan upper class and American expatriates shop.

In San Carlos, I could also reap the benefits of Rockefeller-owned enterprises through the *Tio Rico* (Rich Uncle) vendors, who peddled popsicles, pineapple bars, and creamsicles. When I sat in Plaza Bolívar eating an ice cream on a stick, called a "paddle-pop," I wondered why a billionaire like Nelson Rockefeller had invested in a product that sold for a mere five cents.

When Gerald Ford chose Rockefeller as his vice president after Nixon resigned, he remained invested in oil, cattle, and retail in the country and could have been cast as an "American imperialist." One Congressmen joked, "Rockefeller will have to put the United States in a blind trust and then sell Venezuela," if he wanted to be vice president. Venezuelans, however, approved of his choice. Whatever may have happened in the past with farming, pesticides, and supermarkets, they presumed his connections would bode well for the country and were confident their interests would be well-represented with Rockefeller in the White House.

While in Venezuela, I wrote, on average, two letters a week, which I sent snail mail from the San Carlos post office. They took seven to ten days to reach the U.S. The Peace Corps, always forthcoming with advice, suggested we stress our positive experiences when writing to our families so they wouldn't worry. Food and people we met were better topics than the latest bout of diarrhea or the arrest on Saturday night for public drunkenness.

My first letters from Los Teques were full of negative impressions. In one, I expressed shock at the availability of electricity: "They aren't as primitive as I expected." Caracas, noisy and polluted, with ubiquitous American cars, had the worst drivers I had ever seen. It was a miracle I didn't see more accidents. In the midst of the chaos in Caracas, I noticed many people were missing an arm or a leg. At first, I attributed the excessive number of amputees to physicians making rash decisions rather than thinking through what an amputation could mean to the person's psyche. But I was way off the mark. I would learn doctors severed limbs because hospitals lacked the equipment to treat certain illnesses, leaving amputation as the most realistic choice to save a life. Forty years later, in 2014, in the midst of Venezuela's latest economic crisis, the number of amputations rose because the hospitals didn't have the proper equipment and medications to address infection or illness.

I also wrote home about the slow mail service, the tropical climate, and the quality of *The Daily Journal*, a journalistic disgrace, though I read it as often as possible. Garbage and plastic bags littered the streets, and radio stations played The Beatles, the Rolling Stones, and James Brown—cultural imperialism at its finest—which disappointed me. I wanted to hear local music, whatever that was. One letter summarized my observations after five months in San Carlos:

I thought I'd tell you the grass was green here; the sun is hot and baseballs are round. The banks are notoriously inefficient, and bananas are scarce, contrary to popular belief. Rockefeller is considered an imperialist running-dog-lackey. Nixon is hated, and people have accused me of being a spy several times. The food is horrendous. There's more sugar in the Venezuelan diet than in Castro's backyard. I live in a condemned building and sleep with cockroaches. Politicians are corrupt and buses are cheap. There are more dogs and pigs than apples, and Venezuelans just love Americans.

The food was greasy and people drank too much Pepsi; as a result, Volunteers gained weight and suffered from bad teeth. I also wondered how the three flickering street lights in San Carlos, when they worked at all, reduced crime.

Despite all the complaints, I liked being in Venezuela, the travel, meeting people, seeing the world from another perspective, the adventure, were appealing.

The middle-aged mail carrier delivered my letters and parcels, filled with books, newspapers, and magazines, right to the pensión. I received around a letter a day from friends, my parents, and each of my seven siblings, though they usually arrived in clumps of three and four at a time. My father typed one-page letters, while my mother wrote several pages in long hand. The mailman was a fan of American culture, following it through music, television, and movies, particularly ones with car chases. From it, he had concluded that gangster life in America would be right for him. He hoped one day to go to the United States. I never discouraged him from pursuing his dream.

My mother wanted to know things no one else asked about. First, though, as a way of boosting my morale, she said the kids in San Carlos needed someone like me to coach them. In the next paragraph, she wondered whether the people were happy. She enquired about infant mortality rates, a topic of interest to her after having lost a child a few days after birth. She was curious about teenagers in the area, and what kids did when they grew up, topics that would concern a mother who raised eight children. I didn't know how frequently babies died, but I knew tuberculosis, hepatitis, birth defects, and malnutrition were common public health issues. Heart disease was one of the leading causes of death in the state of Cojedes, followed by traffic accidents. I wrote that the Cojedes residents had the dubious distinction of drinking more beer per capita than those in any other state in the country, something that might interest people in Wisconsin, where I grew up. In other correspondence, each of my siblings told me about my sister Mary's wedding, including that everyone at the church said a prayer for my well-being in Venezuela.

After five months in the Venezuelan heartland, I was still healthy despite the grease-filled meals at the Hotel Roma, where the French wife of the owner gave me a discount and allowed me to keep a running tab as a regular customer. I paid bi-weekly or whenever the bill reached fifty bolivars, about $12. At around nine each morning, after finishing twenty-five deep knee bends, I would walk over to the restaurant and have two greasy over-easy fried eggs; bread, often stale; and a soft drink or glass of water, after I was assured they had boiled the water. On some days, I would skip lunch and go to the corner *bodega* off Plaza Bolívar to buy a hot dog (*perro caliente*) with onions, mustard, and ketchup, which was a pleasant change. I would return at seven-thirty for a dinner of beef, rice, black beans, and fried bananas. On a few nights, spaghetti would be the main meal, along with a cold Pepsi. When Fred was living in San Carlos, we ate together, but after he left at the end of my second month, I sat alone and read a newspaper or magazine while waiting.

So far, my issued medical kit remained unused. It included cold tablets; mouthwash; antihistamines; cough syrup; eye drops for conjunctivitis; Phisohex, an antibacterial detergent; antidiarrheal tablets; nasal spray; milk of magnesia for stomachaches; disinfectant; vitamins; Band-Aids; adhesive tape; Q-tips; gauze; and a thermometer. In comparison, today's medical kits include dental floss, condoms, calamine lotion, lip balm, scissors, eye drops, insect repellent, oral rehydration salts, and antacid and iodine tablets. If I became ill with anything more serious than the flu or if I was in an accident, Plan A was to go to the closest local doctor. If that didn't work, Plan B was to call the Peace Corps office in Caracas. Luckily, I never needed either plan.

One night, I returned late to the pensión to find the door locked with a sign on it: "CLOSED." What had happened? How could it close if I was renting a room? I knocked, and after a few minutes, the owner opened the door in his pajamas. He said that as part of a national crackdown on unsanitary conditions in public places, hotels, and restaurants, a health official had issued him a warning. If he did not upgrade the bathrooms and shower area within two weeks to meet the national sanitation codes, the Ministry of Health would close the pensión.

For some reason, I was not worried. In the following days, the owner requested more time when he learned that stores in San Carlos did not have the floor tile he needed to renovate the bathrooms. So until the materials arrived, an army of cockroaches would continue to occupy the shower, requiring me to exterminate five or six each time I showered by smashing them with a broom. When the repairs got under way, the shower was turned off; for two weeks, I bathed by pouring pails of water over my head.

The pensión was not the only business swept up in the national movement for sanitation. The San Carlos Municipal Council ordered a city-wide cleanup, recruited volunteers to sweep the streets, and kicked the food vendors off Plaza Bolívar, though they were back in a few weeks.

The hot and humid weather and the ordinary days inspired me to write a poem:

STAGNATION

Day after day, week after week,

Month after month, year after year

The sun shines.

Sun on Monday, Tuesday, Wednesday, Thursday, Friday, sometimes Saturday

And always on Sunday.

No change in the forecast, for tomorrow or next week or next month or next year.

There is a ninety percent chance of sun tomorrow.

What Do I Do Now?

*Babies are born, liquor consumed, games
played, schools attended, profits made,
marriages announced, divorces fixed, people
buried and governments rule under the sun.*

But Sonny isn't made to think.

Weather dominates conversation.

"Oh, how's the weather?" Hot, sunny.

What if it rains?

*Shine, shine, my boy, for that is your job.
No hail. No wind. Little thunder, little
lightning, little excitement, and no change
but should your duties make other lives so
stagnant?*

I passed the time reading newspapers, books, writing, and going to movies. San Carlos had one movie theater and a ticket cost three bolivars, or about seventy-five cents. Most of the movies were subtitled in English, though they were ones I would never dream of seeing in the U.S. Two of them were *The Cross and the Switchblade* with Pat Boone and *Black Caesar* with Fred Williamson as the Godfather of Harlem. One of the worst was the Italian movie, *The Night Evelyn Came out of the Grave*, about a man whose obsession with his dead wife caused him to prey upon other women; one had been declared insane and performed a striptease in a coffin. One reviewer called it suitable for Euro-trash fans.

Some nights I would go for a nightcap at the Los Ranchos bar, whose owner was going through a divorce after his two sons caught their mother in bed with a local policeman. The owner had run for state assembly in the recent elections, but received just two votes, neither of which was his wife's. After the election, he spent the remaining campaign money on a party at Los Ranchos.

At the bar one Saturday afternoon, an IND board member sitting to my left told me I was a spy and asked why I wasn't working more; so much for small talk. A patron occupying the bar stool on my right overheard the charge and chimed in with, "Half of San Carlos thinks you're a spy." I was unaware of these suspicions and let it go. If I responded, it would be the usual boilerplate denial ("I am not a spy"), and besides, they would not have believed me.

The IND official returned to reading the day's racing sheet. He wanted to know the latest odds on the week's horse races at the La Rinconada hippodrome in Caracas. Each town in the country had an off-track betting office. In San Carlos, it was at the Los Ranchos bar. After asking a few more forgettable questions about my connection to the CIA and showing no interest in what I might have to say about my (nonexistent) endeavors in espionage, the IND official walked over to the police officer sitting at a nearby table to place a few bets in the Cinco y Seis (5 and 6) racing lottery.

The object of Cinco y Seis was to pick the horses of the day's feature race in order: first through sixth. If you selected five of the six runners, you won a small percentage of the pool. In 2013, according to the Paris-based International Federation of Horseracing Authorities, the horse-racing industry in Venezuela handled more than $120 million in legal bets a year. However, tight government regulations spawned an illegal betting industry inside the state-sanctioned gambling halls known as "offices" where so-called "bankers" took bets in person and by phone. With so much money being wagered, violence pervaded the sport in the form of kidnappings, threats to jockeys, and poisoning horses. Yet Cinco y Seis flourished.

Fans today can place bets through a mobile app, a sign of progress. At the Los Ranchos in 1974, when life was less complicated, bets required completing a racing form with a pencil and paying in cash.

With the baseball season over and in need of something to do, I decided I would try to replace Fred as a basketball coach. It would be a challenge, since I had a hard time explaining how to cross the street in Spanish. I was impressed watching him teach a zone defense in Spanish. Still, in my mind, I could coach basketball. I was qualified based on attending hundreds of practices as the team manager in high school and one year of coaching in a Catholic Youth Organization league. I just had to make it happen.

The IND agreed in principle for me to replace Fred—there were no other candidates—but they remained noncommittal on buying equipment and filling the potholes scattered around the fenced-in, padlocked outdoor court. While coaching basketball was a possibility, I also realized it would not happen soon.

A more promising prospect was the request from the San Carlos

What Do I Do Now?

Baseball Association to coach at the local orphanage. Reyes, the friend who also coached and worked for IND, and had suggested I run for the president of the chess association, and I met the director see what he had in mind. He wanted me to start practice the following Friday morning at eight, at which time he would give me the key to the equipment room containing balls, bats, gloves, and helmets. That was easy. Our meeting with the president of IND in Cojedes was not for another two hours. So we walked to the post office to check for mail and then played chess for an hour. The sole point of meeting with IND was to find more work for me than the one day at the orphanage.

When we arrived at the IND office, the secretary showed us to the director's office, where he was talking to a roomful of people. We walked in and interrupted the meeting. Reyes introduced me. After shaking hands, the director told us to wait in the hallway. Half an hour later, he called us back. The director did not introduce us to the track coach and a third person in the room. Reyes grabbed two chairs, and we pulled them up to the front to make sure we had everyone's attention. Reyes then presented my plan. I would coach basketball after IND installed a basket, replaced a backboard, and filled the potholes on the only court in San Carlos. Without commenting, the director asked if I would coach on Tuesdays and Thursdays in the Las Vegas barrio, three kilometers from San Carlos, where a basketball court was already in playable condition opposite the motocross race track where, in three years, the Venezuelan motorcycle Grand Prix would take place.

That was when I realized the third person was the sports coordinator from Las Vegas. I could not refuse the request. Whatever problems Las Vegas had, I seemed to have solved the need for a basketball coach. I left the meeting feeling better. Now, I would at least work six hours a week.

I arrived at the orphanage as scheduled on Friday. The director informed me the equipment had not yet arrived. I was disappointed, though not surprised. Plans in San Carlos seldom played out as intended. The next day, Reyes told me there was a misunderstanding and the real problem was that the key to the equipment room was missing. The good news was the director expected to find it before the next scheduled practice. A few days later, Reyes learned that the president of the municipal council, in Caracas for a conference, found the key in his hotel room. When he returned with it, I could begin work.

The next night, I attended the weekly Baseball Association meeting. A discussion on whether beer should be banned at all sporting events in the state of Cojedes monopolized the session. The Association had heard of an incident that occurred a few weeks earlier in Cleveland, Ohio when fans rioted after consuming endless barrels of cheap beer. After fans complained that the beer sold at the stadium did not contain the amount of alcohol advertised, Cleveland management, already concerned with declining attendance, announced there would be a night when beer with an alcohol content of 3.7 percent would be for sale in twelve-ounce cups for ten cents, compared to the regular price of sixty-five cents. The game drew 25,000 people, more than double the average. As the game progressed, fans became drunker and rowdier. At the bottom of the ninth inning, hordes of fans, some carrying bats, knives, and chains, charged the field. When a folding chair hit an umpire on the head, his colleagues concluded that Cleveland, the home team, could not maintain order and declared the game a forfeit. The local newspapers reported the episode in depth.

Members of the Baseball Association believed if they didn't curb drinking at games in San Carlos, the town could experience a Cleveland-like incident during a game "We cannot have drunken fans run on the field in Cojedes. It would be an embarrassment to us," said one.

I wasn't aware that drinking at games was a problem. If a fight broke out, machismo appeared to be the reason for it, not alcohol, such as the times I witnessed spectators and coaches attack umpires. Problems related to drinking at games seemed like a red herring. Yes, fans liked to yell at the umpires, players, and coaches like typical baseball fans, but they usually behaved themselves. It strained the imagination to think spectators at an amateur game in San Carlos would riot—maybe at Venezuelan professional games in the big cities, but not in rural Venezuela.

Still, at the start of the meeting, support for the proposed beer ban appeared widespread. Then, halfway through the debate, a member raised a question: "Who will enforce it?" The room fell silent for a few seconds before everyone talked at once. I was ready to give my opinion, but no one asked. When the votes were counted after a secret ballot, the proposal lost. It was obvious the lack of willingness to enforce a ban was the reason. No one wanted to tell their friends they couldn't drink beer while watching a baseball game. It was like telling someone they couldn't eat popcorn in a movie theater. With no other business to discuss, the meeting adjourned. For me, the discussion on prohibiting beer at sporting events was disheartening—honestly, it was the last straw. I left more convinced than ever that I should not stay in San Carlos.

Early terminations and unhappy Volunteers were not uncommon. A letter published in *The Peacemaker* from a couple who resigned illustrated an ongoing problem with Peace Corps:

Dear PCV and Staff,

We are early terminations. Not because we don't like Venezuela or because we don't like Peace Corps ideals or because we failed to make a commitment to our two years here. We terminated because Peace Corps could not provide us jobs, which isn't anything new; it happens a lot, a lot more than it should. We realize coordinating programs is not an easy job. But to our mind, that doesn't excuse Peace Corps from repeatedly failing Volunteers over and over again.

My husband is a forest economist. When we applied to the Peace Corps, we received a job description which stated that because forest economists in Venezuela were incompetent and didn't know the field well enough, they were bringing in an expert from the U.S. The problem was, Peace Corps also sent the job description to the Venezuelan counterparts, who have PhDs. They were so insulted they refused to let my husband work there.

Since January, we have been in one hassle after another trying to get something to do. Now, four months later, we have had it. What should have been one of the most fantastic experiences of a lifetime has been a bitter, frustrating experience. Some people get good jobs, good support, and have a good experience. Can't staff try to improve the quality of programs so that a satisfying Peace Corps experience can be available to all Volunteers?

Goodbye and Good Luck.

I understood their sentiments. In a state where the literacy rate was 60 percent, unemployment was high, and most people had health complications, sports seemed an odd focus for the Peace Corps. Even though Venezuela gave tens millions of dollars of its petrodollars to other Latin American countries, it could not afford textbooks for children in school. In a letter to a friend, I wrote, "Over half the people in San Carlos can't read or write, and I'm teaching kids how to hit a goddamn baseball?"

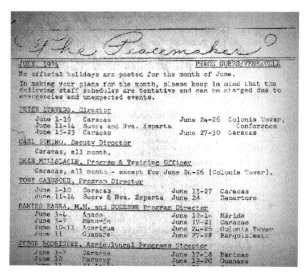

The front page of the Peacemaker always included the travel schedules for the month of the Peace Corps staff.

I didn't want to be asked any more about my baseball "career" in the United States ("What team did you play for?"). Maybe I was naïve, but I never assumed they were joking. I was bored and annoyed with Venezuelans curious to know if I was a racist by asking whether I liked Hank Aaron, who had broken Babe Ruth's home run record a few months earlier, despite his being African American. I wanted to be more than a walking encyclopedia of American sports trivia.

Venezuelan baseball would survive without me. It needed engineers, mathematicians, scientists, and honest politicians, not the superstar wannabes and lazy outfielders I watched and coached in San Carlos. But I liked the challenges living abroad presented; I just wanted a more fulfilling job. I had no idea what else I could do, but I needed a change. I wanted to make a larger contribution to national development than teaching a kid to hit a ball, run the bases, or checkmate his opponent in less than ten moves in a chess match.

If Caracas couldn't find a different line of work for me, I would leave. To use a baseball metaphor, I concluded the count on Peace Corps

What Do I Do Now?

in San Carlos was no balls and two strikes. One more strike and I would be out.

By now, I had been in San Carlos for six months. I was not enjoying coaching. In the big picture, whether the other guy or the other kid could throw or hit the ball did not concern me much. Besides, I didn't want to be known as a baseball coach. Whatever altruistic reasons I had for joining the Peace Corps, the sports culture in Cojedes had extinguished them. As a sports advisor and baseball coach, I didn't see myself contributing to Venezuela's development.

I questioned the usefulness of what I was doing while nursing a beer at the Los Ranchos bar. Maybe I should quit and go home. If not, I might disappear into oblivion. It was 2 a.m., the jukebox was turned off, and I was alone. Before walking back to the pensión, I played two games of pool while imagining my fate. My mind wandered while listening to Demis Roussos, a popular Greek singer. I began thinking about my future. Decades, if not centuries later, someone, probably a tourist, would write about a skeleton he saw in a glass case of a species known as PeaceCorpsman in the Cojedes Natural History Museum. A plaque would describe how a hiker in the year 2121 had discovered the bones while walking across a former baseball diamond. The volunteer docent would speculate he came to the area by land rather than by sea. Characteristics included eyes unlike any others in the region. Anthropologists thought the hair protruding from the side of his head could be from a beard. His clothes suggested he came from a lower class of people, though the absence of jewelry made it impossible to be sure of his precise group. The fragments of cotton indicated he held a low-paying job such as a baseball coach, which the shreds of cheap underwear found with him also showed. It was not known if he spoke Spanish. The word Hola, tattooed on his elbow, raised anthropological theories. The remains might have been of a day laborer or a shopkeeper Or Hola could be a secret code for an alien civilization. He looked to be from the twentieth century, and tests showed he had 1.8 percent Neanderthal DNA. To this day, his origin remains unexplained.

While the PeaceCorpsman was not yet extinct, the latest memo from Caracas suggested he might be on life support. Caracas had canceled training for the next Sports and Recreation and YMCA groups without saying whether budget reductions or the quality of the programs caused the cancellations. Based on the recent weekend language classes I attended in Barquisimeto, it appeared that other Volunteers from my group were having varying levels of success or failure, depending on whether you looked at the glass half full or half empty. Volunteers reported such activities as developing a basketball program for an elementary school and building an athletic field; running physical education classes during the day and spending nights coaching wrestling and gymnastics.

A less noteworthy accomplishment was the Volunteer who organized a baseball tournament and then went on vacation. One spent four months waiting to inaugurate a new gymnasium so that he could coach basketball, and when it opened, IND gave him mid-day hours, the worst possible time in Venezuela to work. A Volunteer raised eyebrows when he conducted press conferences criticizing the local sports authority for its lack of organization and misplaced priorities. Four Volunteers from my group had resigned, including one who left because he believed IND had disrespected him. Despite the departures, Peace Corps remained dynamic, with 188 Volunteers still in the country in August 1974.

After weeks of pondering my future, I woke up one morning, sat up in bed, looked around at the fading paint on the walls and the cobwebs in the corners, and said to myself, "Fuck it, I'm not doing this anymore." I decided to quit and go home. I was fed up with IND and the fiasco at the orphanage over the missing equipment and the so-called lost key and being asked to coach basketball on a court full of holes whose primary use was to train army recruits. What was I doing coaching eight- to ten-year-olds, umpiring games, and joining a chess club?

I sent the Peace Corps a letter saying I had resigned, without giving a date when I planned to leave or mentioning a transfer and a new job as possibilities. I then wrote to family and friends telling them I would be home by Christmas. Calling Caracas was not a good option. The telephone at the pensión was out of order most of the time, and when it worked, the connection was so erratic and scratchy, I figured the line would go dead in mid-call. I didn't want that to happen when discussing an issue as serious as quitting. Besides, the cost of calling Caracas exceeded what I was willing to pay. In any case, I had made up my mind; there was nothing to discuss.

Ten days later, I still hadn't heard from anyone. In the meantime, I weighed the pros and cons of staying; maybe I would change my mind.

What Do I Do Now?

Part of my predicament was, despite a poor state of affairs at work, I liked the adventure of being in Venezuela, and there was some value in learning a new language. I had no ideological qualms with Peace Corps, nor did I blame them for my situation. I simply wasn't making it happen.

The American economy also gave me pause when it came to calling it quits. According to the hometown newspapers my father sent me, the unemployment rate in the U.S. had reached almost 7 percent, an increase of 1.5 percent since I left. With figures like that, continuing in the Sports and Recreation program, even in San Carlos, seemed a better choice than going home in the middle of a recession. Employment prospects in such an environment would be terrible.

I didn't know if Peace Corps accepted resignations without an interview, if they would call me to talk about my situation, or if they would try to get me to stay. Oblivious to the process, I went camping with Bill, another Volunteer, and his girlfriend in an abandoned sugar mill in Guatopo National Park for the weekend and enjoyed a hamburger and a beer at the Big Boy restaurant in the Rockefeller-owned CADA in Valencia on the way back.

When I returned to San Carlos, I sent a telegram to the Peace Corps telling them I would prefer to change jobs and location rather than resign and go home. The three days of travel had changed my mind. I proposed teaching English as an option, not knowing how Caracas would react to the idea.

A few days later, I received a reply saying they had assumed all was well and were surprised that I'd quit, while adding they were happy I had decided to stay. They suggested I come to Caracas to discuss it further. I left the next day.

At the Peace Corps office, I made a pitch to teach English, based on how the teachers in San Carlos spoke the language. I recorded several tapes for two teachers who wanted their students to hear an American speak English. Based on the difficult time the teachers had explaining what they wanted, I concluded the schools could use some native English speakers. The program officer, Neil Volkmann, did not jump on the idea. He said he would let me know after he talked it over with the director.

I returned to San Carlos and waited. Two days later, a letter arrived saying they would not try to place me as an English teacher because it would take a job away from a Venezuelan. While I accepted the rationale, I also thought, *But would it?* Didn't schools have vacancies just like IND had hundreds of openings for coaches? Would I really replace a Venezuelan English teacher? The letter added there were other job possibilities, without mentioning what they were or their location, which government ministry, or what field. However, it was enough information to conclude that if I changed jobs, I would also change sites.

I did not inform IND or the Baseball Association of my thinking. The last I heard, the orphanage still maintained that they couldn't find the key to the equipment room and the president of the municipal council returned from Caracas without the key or any idea of where it might be. Then I heard that the president of the council had found the key, meaning I might work yet. But the following day, the director of the orphanage told me he didn't have the key while assuring he would solve the problem soon. He wanted me to coach. All I could do was wait.

A few days later, the truth was revealed. The director admitted the orphanage owned no sporting equipment and the coaching job for me never existed. The whole story about the lost key was a fabrication. I was baffled. The director did not try to explain why he made it up and I didn't waste any time using the incident to get insights into the culture. Even if the orphanage had the equipment, I would have been unable to conduct practice because the soccer coach, after an argument with the park officials over the use of the field, moved his practices to the baseball field. Add the fact that the gate to the basketball court remained padlocked, leaving no place for practice, and I was out of options.

Even though the Peace Corps was looking for another job and site for me, I was still officially working in San Carlos. I would have discussed the messy situation with IND and the Baseball Association, but they were busy preparing for the fourteen and under National Junior Baseball Tournament the first week in December. I was excited about the tournament. No matter what the sport, it was a big deal to have national competition in your town. Remaining optimistic, I even hoped IND would ask me to be one of the coaches on the Cojedes team, but they never did. Why would they?

Volunteers talked about corruption, both real and imagined, but I never observed it firsthand until the baseball tournament. The team from Cojedes won their first two games with a few players I didn't know. I thought I had seen every player in the state and wondered who these

82

older ones were. After they won their second game, I overheard the coaches joking about the number of "old-timers" on the team. The next day, the tournament officials ruled six over-aged players on the Cojedes team were ineligible and disqualified the whole team. A few days later, the officials suspended a player for four years, a lifetime for a teenager, for throwing a ball at the umpire after he disagreed with a call.

All this happened before I received a telegram from Peace Corps telling me I should go to Maracaibo for an interview at the *Asociacion Zuliana de Padres y Amigos de Ninos Excepcionales* (Zulia Association of Parents and Friends of Exceptional Children), known as AZUPANE (pronounced A-ZOO-PA-NAY). Although I had never heard of the project, the possibility of working and living in Venezuela's second-largest city intrigued me.

At this point, Neil Volkmann, a member of the Chippewa and Cree tribes, was the Peace Corps program officer covering western Venezuela, replacing Walt after he had been terminated. He picked me up in San Carlos and we drove to Maracaibo, stopping in Valera, a small town in the foothills of the Andes, for the night. We stayed with two Volunteers. We chatted for an hour before going out for dinner. Someone suggested a movie, so on the way back we checked to see what was playing. No one was in the mood for a Bruce Lee film, making it a short night. At the Volunteer's house, I slept on the floor under a few blankets and Jim, one of the Volunteers who lived there, took his usual spot in a hammock, wrapping himself in an American flag. The next day, we left before dawn

We arrived at AZUPANE by mid-morning, where two Volunteers, Brian and Jeff, worked. Father Jose Gregorio Finol, the director and a Jesuit priest who was always referred to as "Padre," was on his way back from a conference in Europe. Dr. Angela de Ferreira, the deputy director, gave us a tour of the center; afterward, I met with the AZUPANE psychologist, the only other senior staff member available. By way of making small talk, I said that I liked to read. Perking his interest, he asked whether I liked science fiction. Though not a big fan of the genre, I had read *Fahrenheit 451, The Martian Chronicles*, and *Childhood's End*, which I had found in the Peace Corps library in Caracas. We then discussed our favorite authors, Ray Bradbury and Arthur C. Clarke, for a few minutes. The awkward discussion ended because the psychologist's strong accent was hard to understand. We sat in silence until Jeff said that I would be around for three days, and we could talk more about books later.

The next day, I accompanied the kids to the YMCA swimming pool. It was my first exposure to people with disabilities, mental or physical, despite having had polio at three and being unable to use my right arm. Until the visit to Maracaibo, I had never known anyone with a disability other than a cousin who was blind; I certainly didn't think of myself as disabled.

I met the Padre on my third and last day in Maracaibo. In the short interview, he asked about my job in San Carlos and what I would like to do at AZUPANE. Jeff had advised saying that I would like to work in the Recreation area, so that's what I said. AZUPANE planned to launch a camping program in the next few months, and the Padre suggested I run it. If so, it would mean that I'd stay at the beach for three days each week, which sounded appealing. If I wanted to change jobs and leave San Carlos, I couldn't be too choosy. I was open to most anything.

When I returned to San Carlos, the baseball tournament was over. A few days later, I received a letter from Caracas approving a transfer to Maracaibo in February. I accepted the offer without further questions. Knowing the details of my job at this stage was unnecessary; they could be worked out later. With that news, I left for a three-week vacation to Colombia and Panama.

Five

Colombia

Two days before Christmas, I hitchhiked to Merida, a city five thousand feet above sea level in the Andes Mountains, taking three rides to get there. A half-dozen Volunteers were in town for the holidays, all congregating at a local Volunteer's roof-top apartment. Getting there required climbing a ladder to the top floor and leaping six feet over a courtyard to get inside. After I had performed those acrobatics, I discovered the apartment did not have a toilet, though it did have a beautiful view of the Andes Mountains. Without a toilet, the Volunteer's *modus operandi* was "Piss over the side and crap in the restaurants." It seemed inconvenient to have to go to a restaurant whenever he needed to take a dump, but then again, the landlord gave him a break on his rent.

The guy's library contained books on Vietnam, a biography of Janis Joplin, and a book of poems by D.H. Lawrence. In the corner were two *Playboy* magazines and National Lampoon's *The Job of Sex: A Workingman's Guide to Productive Lovemaking,* a parody of the 1972 bestseller *The Joy of Sex.* Some of his music cassettes included John Lennon, Elton John, and the Grateful Dead. It looked palatial compared to my room in San Carlos.

On Christmas Eve, we grilled hamburgers, ate fresh salad, drank beer and wine, and finished the meal with a crème de menthe. Afterward, some of us went to the Cathedral Basilica of the Immaculate Conception for Midnight Mass to have a cultural experience where the women outnumbered the men by a large margin. People drifted in and out throughout the Mass as if it were a sporting event. Unlike the one I attended in San Carlos with Reyes a few days earlier, no one was smoking. Otherwise, they fixed on the priest, who said the Mass in Latin. Ushers passed small baskets for the collection, but few people dropped in money. We left before communion and walked to Plaza Bolívar, where a small crowd was dancing to "Jingle Bells" while others roller skated or lit sparklers, two Christmas traditions in Venezuela. At midnight, the bells tolled.

Christmas Day was quiet. It didn't feel like Christmas despite the seasonal decorations, Midnight Mass, and familiar carols. The warm weather and lack of snow kept the holiday blues from sneaking in. Stores were closed, forcing us to go five miles beyond the city limits to find a restaurant for dinner. For my first Christmas away from home, I had kung pao chicken and rice. The next morning, I took a bus to Colombia.

Over the next two weeks, my first international trip consisted of bus rides, cheap hotels, border checks, new foods, tourist sites, bargaining at stores, and meeting other travelers. I would stop or pass through eleven cities and towns and detour to Panama. My first adventure in Colombia occurred in Pamplona while buying ice cream. Before I chose a flavor and placed my order, I asked the price.

"Six pesos (twenty-five cents) for a cup," said the vendor.

"I'll take a vanilla cup."

"That'll be ten pesos," he said, handing me a cup of vanilla ice cream.

"How much?" I asked, faking shock at the higher price.

"Ten pesos," he repeated.

I handed him six pesos, said *gracias,* and walked away with the ice cream. I wasn't paying ten pesos after we had agreed on six. The vendor chased after me and demanded ten pesos. I refused to pay.

"You said six. I gave you six." He wanted ten. I calmly repeated six. My limited Spanish kept the argument simple. This dialogue went on for a few minutes. "A deal is a deal," I said. During the exchange, a crowd gathered and appeared to back my argument that ten pesos was too much. Maybe the vendor had a reputation for ripping off customers.

The ice cream seller gave up and crossed the street to complain to the police.

I went off looking for Flipper, the business that made the ice cream. I informed the owner that his vendor was overcharging me. He was not sympathetic, explaining that vanilla ice cream cost more than other flavors, and I should pay the ten pesos. Absolute nonsense. I walked away without paying. No one tried to intervene, not even the policeman who stood on the corner, smoking cigarettes and looking bored.

Getting out of Pamplona was more complicated than walking away from an ice cream vendor. Bus tickets to Bucaramanga, the next stop on the way to Bogota, were sold out. The second transportation option in the Andes was a truck. At the far end of the station, I found a parking lot with twenty-five cattle trucks. I hurried up as people were climbing onto the trucks. I jumped on one whose passengers included two nuns, a young woman, an elderly couple, and four Colombian men. The women sat in the cabin, and the rest of us stood in the open but empty cargo bed.

The next morning I bought a bus ticket from Bucaramanga to Bogota. After two hours, we pulled up in front of a white stuccoed house for a meal of rice, beans, and a piece of beef. Over the next three hours, the bus took a series of curves at an altitude of more than five thousand feet, causing some of the men to vomit over the side. As dusk approached, the police stopped the bus in the middle of nowhere to inspect our baggage for possible smuggling. Peace Corps Volunteers who had taken the same route said the road checks were routine and rarely resulted in the police confiscating contraband or making any arrests.

I seized the opportunity to get off to fetch a sweater from my backpack in the baggage compartment underneath the bus, as it was getting cold. As soon as I stepped off the bus, an official sitting a few feet away waved to me that I should come over to the inspection table.

"What's this?" he asked, grabbing my Instamatic camera off my belt.

"Es una camera" ("It's a camera"), I told him.

"Where are your papers?" the inspector wanted to know.

I handed him my passport. "Come here," he ordered as he directed me off to the side where he paged through it, finding my visas for Colombia and Venezuela and then skipped to my international health card, known as the Yellow Card, which intrigued him. Maybe the doctor's impenetrable penmanship regarding the rabies shots and inoculations Peace Corps administered amused him.

Next, he asked for my backpack. I retrieved it from the baggage compartment. When he opened it, he found the dirty laundry I had placed on top to ward off thieves and nosy officials, like him. A speck of color caught his eye. He dug beneath the underwear and pulled out the paperback version of *The Pump House Gang* by Tom Wolfe, a book of articles on surfers, bikers, the Beautiful People, Hugh Hefner, New York and London, wrapped in a bright pink cover. He stared at the small photograph of three men and three women on the cover in various sorts of dress, including a woman in a bikini. On the first page were excerpts from reviews. One from the *Saturday Review* read, "NORMAN MAILER ON THE STEPS OF THE PENTAGON..." The inspector put his forefinger on "PENTAGON" and looked me in the eye with a slight twinkle: "Yes, now I know who you are." After he had concluded Wolfe's book was not a spy manual, he put it down and browsed through the postcards I had bought.

Throughout the search, I remained silent. The inspector didn't ask any questions, not even "Where are you going?" By now, the inspection was holding up the bus. All the passengers were on board and waiting for me, and the engine was running. The inspector got the hint: "You can go." I shoved my dirty laundry, the book, and my postcards back into the backpack. The inspector who observed the ordeal thanked me, *Gracias*. For what, I wondered as I climbed back on the bus.

I spent the New Year in Bogota. The next day, I took a bus to San Agustin, a town of dirt roads, surrounded by coffee fields, in southwest Colombia. It is best known for its archeological park, declared a World Heritage site in 1995, which contains hundreds of religious monuments and sculptures representing the pre-Columbian culture that flourished from the first to the eighth century. Tourists could rent a horse for less than five dollars for the round trip to the park.

But first, I needed a place to stay. At the bus station, hotel employees, including some managers, met the buses and negotiated room rates while passengers retrieved their luggage. I accepted an offer

88

to stay at a hotel for seventy-five cents a night; for an extra sixty cents I could have dinner. Other guests included an accountant and his wife, who calculated they had enough cash for ninety-three more days before they returned home to Florida. A carpenter from Boston was on his fifth consecutive South American winter holiday. Two guys from Oklahoma, including a graduate of the London School of Economics, had already been in Colombia three months and were on their way to Ecuador and the rest of South America. A couple from California was always arguing over their travel plans. A man from Canada with a tennis racket hoped to find employment at a Caribbean island resort where he could use their courts at no cost to improve his tennis game. Bob, a 40-year-old American English teacher living in Venezuela, wanted to buy a car. He introduced himself with, "Hi, I'm Bob. I've been eating pussy for twenty-five years." However, women were not his primary interest. Instead, he wanted to own the hottest car in San Cristobal, where he lived. He said Colombia was saturated with used cars at reasonable prices, and it was just a matter of time before he would come across one. I had no reason to question him. However, it was unclear how he would find a "hot car" to buy in an area where horses and Jeeps served as the chief modes of transportation.

The next day, four Colombians and I rented a Jeep for a tour of the archeological sites. In the evening, I caught a night bus to Popayan, arriving at 4 a.m. I walked to a hotel a few blocks away and woke up the young guard sleeping in the lobby. He checked me into a room and then went back to sleep.

Hours later, I was scratching my legs from bed bugs. I ignored them, thinking the itch would go away like a mosquito bite. I got dressed and toured the city, enjoying its tranquility until it was time to catch the bus to Medellin, an eleven-hour, 270-mile journey. It was an unusual bus ride in that the passengers laughed and talked among themselves. With reading lamps and light headbands still years away from being must-have travel gear, it was too dark to read. Some of the riders in the back of the bus wanted music and shouted, "*Musica, musica, musica,*" to the driver. In Venezuela, passengers never had to ask for music, as the drivers always listened to the radio or cassettes. In Colombia, though, music was an option.

A few days earlier, en route from San Augustin to Popayan, I had asked the driver to put on some cassettes, but he said music was for parties and dancing and refused. On the way to Medellin, however, the driver complied with the passengers' request. With the music came the drinking. Riders pulled bottles of rum from their bags. One woman drank so much that in response to the curving mountain roads, she vomited out the window in the middle of the night. Another woman walked to the front while her mother slept and sat down on the console, lighting cigarettes for the driver to keep him awake. The booze eventually put everyone to sleep. We arrived in Medellin without incident.

The Medellin Cartel, the notorious network of drugs, corruption, and murder led by Pablo Escobar, was in its formative years and had not yet established itself as a global criminal enterprise when I passed through Medellin on my way to Panama in January 1975, though the city was already known as a den of thieves. The police and tourist offices advised bus riders not to wear watches or jewelry when putting their arm out of the window for fear someone would walk by and grab it.

In the mid-1970s, marijuana was a billion-dollar business in Colombia. Drug kingpins Carlos Lehder and Fabio Ochoa shipped tons of it to the East Coast of the United States from the Guajira Peninsula and the Sierra Nevada de Santa Marta on the Caribbean coast. The government dismissed warnings from the U.S. Embassy on the growing problem, which they described as a problem of usage rather than one of supply. Then-president of Colombia Alfonso Lopez Michelson took the opposite view. He believed U.S. consumption fed the demand in the global market. Whatever danger the drug trade created, the presence of 250 Peace Corps Volunteers sent the message the country was safe.

Over the years, Colombians, historians, journalists, and novelists have perpetuated the urban legend that Peace Corps Volunteers introduced coca leaves and taught farmers to process it into cocaine, despite the lack of evidence to prove this theory, to say nothing of the absurdity of the claim, given that coca leaves have been used in the Andes for centuries.

The fiction can be traced to the 1970s. Jaime Gaviria, a former schoolmate of Pablo Escobar, has said Escobar believed Peace Corps Volunteers "began to invade this country, sent by the government up there, saying they had come in search of peace, but they ended up in search of cocaine." Since then, the preposterous idea has penetrated Colombian popular culture through cinema and literature. In 2004, the plot line of the movie *El Rey,* which the critics loved for its authenticity, had Peace Corps Volunteers introducing farmers to cocaine. That year, Colombia entered it as the country's choice for the Academy Award for best foreign-language film, but the Academy did not nominate it as a finalist. The director and screenwriter, Antonio Dorado, said he had anecdotal and documentary proof that Volunteers played a role, even if a small one, in the beginnings of the drug trade. He told the *Miami Herald,* "I'm not selling this as the real story. It's the people who say this is the real story." The film is available from streaming services if you want to check it for yourself.

Meanwhile, the novel *The Sound of Things* by Colombian Juan Gabriel Vasquez, published in 2014, repeated the myth. In his book, he describes how Peace Corps Volunteers trained farmers in the Cauca Valley to cultivate marijuana and process coca leaf into a paste and transport it by airplane to the United States. And that's how the drug industry in Colombia was born. Despite being a work of fiction, the author's depiction of Peace Corps rattled some Volunteers who served in Colombia, leading them to denounce it in an online forum.

In an article for the Social Science Research Center, Lina Britto, a Colombian journalist, reported she found former Volunteers had stayed in the Sierra Nevada de Santa Marta after completing their two years of service. While there, they engaged in modest drug sales that grew into a larger trade run by Colombians, but she unearthed no proof that Volunteers were involved in anything more than getting high. Anecdotal evidence, however, led her to conclude that Americans, hippies, and mercenaries had a role in establishing trade routes the drug cartels later expanded. Several memoirs by Vietnam veterans describe how they went from war to transporting drugs from Colombia to the U.S. in the 1970s.

Accusing Peace Corps Volunteers and others working in American foreign aid programs in Latin America of intelligence activities was nothing new, but accusing them of being criminals was something else. However, polls show that more than a quarter of Americans are convinced that not only did a UFO crash near Roswell, New Mexico, in 1947, but that aliens were on board. Three percent believe Paul McCartney died in a car accident in 1966, and a further 15 percent are "undecided," about his being alive despite his frequent television appearances, on the premise that the person on television could be an imposter. Long live Paul! In 2016, more than 41 percent of Republicans said Barack Obama was not born in the United States. One in seven thinks the U.S. government staged the September 11 attacks on New York, Washington, DC, and rural Pennsylvania. People believe what they want. With such a large number of people holding these beliefs, it is not so shocking that Colombians might think Peace Corps Volunteers in the 1970s were responsible for starting or expanding the drug trade, even though it's as ridiculous as thinking the Holocaust didn't happen and vaccines cause autism.

In January 1975, before the drug cartels became a rampant threat, I spent two days sightseeing in Medellin, including visiting the Zoo, renowned for its exotic birds, and then flew to Panama, where I encountered immigration officers critical of my appearance and lack of dollars. In the 1970s, crossing international borders could be an adventure for world travelers, known as WTs, as well as a tedious affair—at least if you had long hair, a beard, or both, and especially if you were dressed in what the police interpreted as a hippie look. If you wore a tie-dye t-shirt, had shoulder-length hair, or were a woman not wearing a bra, it often meant delays at a border. Border police and immigration officials in many developing countries often assumed travelers with certain clothing, facial hair, and hair lengths were troublemakers looking to buy drugs or foment local political and social unrest. In Singapore, border officials would send travelers to a barber before issuing a visa and denied entry to anyone with a beard.

At Tocumen International Airport in Panama, immigration was less interested in my grooming habits than the amount of money I had with me.

At the airport, I declared $30 and 1,600 bolivars. The immigration official, not impressed, said I needed more than thirty dollars, the official currency of Panama, for my three-day stay. I said the bolivars were worth $400 and would exchange them as needed. He ignored what I said, pointed me to a room, and told me to wait there.

Forty-five minutes later, a different immigration official entered the room and asked me the same question: "How much money do you have?" I repeated the amounts, and again he repeated that thirty American dollars was not enough for three days. I did not want to argue with him, but I had budgeted for three days based on what Volunteers who had been to Panama told me about exchange rates and the range of prices for hotels and food. So again, I said 1,600 bolivars was more than enough. The official said banks in Panama didn't change bolivars, and anyway, told me for the third time that I would need more than $400 for three days.

I wasn't buying it. Why would banks not accept a currency from a country whose economy was based on oil? Besides, I knew people who had changed bolivars at banks in Panama City. Again I insisted I had ample funds for my stay. Without responding, he turned around and left the room. I sat down. A half an hour later, he returned and said I could enter Panama. After stamping my passport, he gave me a little advice. "Before you go back to Colombia, you better shave your beard."

I toured the Canal Zone, still an American enclave with manicured lawns, bowling alleys, golf courses, and post offices with U.S. postal rates, while splurging on hamburgers, French Fries, apple pie, ice cream, pizza, and Chinese food, and buying books and magazines and mailing film home for development. I spent $65 in Panama and left with more than a thousand bolivars.

I flew out of Panama, unshaven, ignoring the advice of the immigration officer. Before leaving, I read that the Pittsburgh Steelers and the Minnesota Vikings were playing in the Super Bowl. But I would miss the game, as it was not yet a worldwide televised event. After a few days of sight-seeing in Cartagena, I made my way by bus to San Carlos.

When I arrived back at the pensión, a tenant surprised me when he said he had watched the Super Bowl on television.

"Who won?" I asked.

"The team wearing white," he said with enthusiasm. It would be two weeks before I learned that was the Pittsburgh Steelers.

I didn't stay in San Carlos long. I packed my bags to attend a mid-service review conference of the Sports and Recreation III program in Caracas. It had been a while since I'd heard much about the Peace Corps' future. Maybe there would be some news.

Six

The Peace Corps Cuts Back

It had been almost a year since we finished training and scattered across the country to fifteen sites in seven states, where IND welcomed us with various levels of enthusiasm. Of the twenty-three Volunteers who had gathered in Miami, six had already left, including one who returned home to get married and another who left for medical reasons. Of the remaining seventeen, seven changed locations and the other ten remained involved in their original project. It was a mixed record of success.

A year earlier, the previous group of Sports and Recreation Volunteers complained their projects lacked visible results, and that interest and motivation in them were waning. They pointed out that the job description the Peace Corps offered had no basis in reality and IND provided little support, including equipment and playing fields. Most believed an able Venezuelan could do their job, and the bottom line was that the Venezuelan sports world didn't need Peace Corps Volunteers.

Twelve months later, not much had changed. One Volunteer in my Sports and Recreation group arrived at his site to find out he didn't have a job. Not giving up, and believing in the spirit of the "you can make it happen" philosophy, he played pickup basketball with IND staff as a way to develop a relationship with them and build *Confianza*. However, the approach failed, and within a month, the Volunteer transferred to a new site.

The Peace Corps Cuts Back

The initial reception from local IND directors was disappointing. We assumed Caracas had notified them that we'd be coming to work in their town, but much to our surprise and frustration, that was not the case for everyone. Instead, the IND offices appeared clueless and asked a lot of questions, beginning with, "Who are you? Why are you here? What do you want to do?" Then they'd move on to: "Why basketball? You say you represent the Peace Corps? Could you repeat that? Are you a Volunteer? Let me check with my supervisor in Caracas. Where are you staying? I will contact you." We had expected better.

My introduction in San Carlos with the half-drunk official shouting, "Who is he?" at the Baseball Association meeting was more welcoming than most. IND and the Association might have been indifferent about my arrival, but nevertheless, they found work for me, unlike what happened to some Volunteers in other locations. The combination of a shortage of baseballs, bats, gloves, basketballs, and playing areas often resulted in Volunteers not working until they fixed the problems. My trouble at the orphanage over a phantom lost key to the equipment room was unusual. At other sites, the IND or sports director told the Volunteer up front they had no equipment. They didn't lie about it.

One Volunteer, sent to a city of 180,000 to coach baseball, moved to a new site after only a week, realizing that having a single trainer for the entire town was not a good situation. A few months later, he transferred to Chile, where Japanese miners had introduced the game in 1918. In 1990, baseball played a role in international terrorism when the Palestinian Liberation Organization chose a game in Santiago between a university team and the Chilean-American Chamber of Commerce as the scene to protest an upcoming visit by President George H. W. Bush. The bomb, placed in an aluminum bat, killed a Canadian and injured one American when a pitch thrown at over seventy miles an hour hit the bat, causing it to explode.

During the review conference, the majority of remaining Volunteers in the Sports and Recreation III program, my group, recommended they not be replaced when they completed their two-year service. This became a moot point just a few hours later when Peace Corps Caracas learned that IND did not include Volunteers in its 1975 budget, although their overall budget had increased from 55 million bolivars to 80 million. The news about the IND budget confirmed everyone's suspicions that IND wasn't interested in getting more coaches and trainers from Peace Corps while fueling the speculation that the future of Peace Corps in Venezuela was more in doubt than ever.

Congress wanted the Peace Corps to reduce spending in response to the recession caused by higher oil prices. While the Peace Corps budget for fiscal year 1975 (FY1975) was $80 million, which was $8 million less than requested. Before eliminating projects, Washington proposed that host governments make up the budget shortfall by increasing their contributions, which differed from country to country.

Latin American countries contributed less than any other region, though Nicaragua, Costa Rica and Paraguay provided more budget assistance than Venezuela, as did Chad, Upper Volta, Benin, and the Central African Republic—some of the poorest nations in the world. In 1975, Venezuela gave just $23,800, or 2 percent, to the $1.33 million budget.

The country's lack of commitment was not new. Five years earlier, a budget crunch resulted when the local government offices with which Volunteers worked did not send Caracas the funds they promised, resulting in a shortfall of $200,000. Caracas admitted they were not vigilant in following up with the agencies to ask for the money Venezuela had committed to pay.

However, not everyone would be asked to contribute more. Washington set $100 as the per capita income level to determine which countries Peace Corps should approach. Venezuela stood out as the wealthiest country, with a per capita income of $1,240, far exceeding the $950 in Malta and $810 in Jamaica, the second- and third- ranked Peace Corps countries, respectively. In comparison, in Upper Volta, it was $70 and in Afghanistan, Ethiopia, Nepal, and Burkina Faso, it was $80.

According to Peace Corps staff, Venezuela, a founding member of OPEC, was asked to give $500,000, close to half the 1975 budget. Staff in Caracas were not optimistic about receiving a favorable response, even though it appeared the country could afford it based on projected oil revenue. I calculated that with a barrel of oil selling for $11 in late 1974 and production at 2.8 million barrels per day, Venezuela was earning $31 million a day. With the oil wells operating 24/7, the requested contribution to Peace Corps was the equivalent of 45,000 barrels, or about forty minutes worth of drilling a year, which made the proposed contribution seem more than fair and affordable.

Still, the embassy admitted the odds did not favor the government increasing its funding to the level Peace Corps wanted, or at all. Before Washington made a final decision, however, they asked each country office if they thought requesting more money from the host government was an appropriate strategy. Would it work? Was a smaller program better than no program at all? If Peace Corps closed, how would it affect U.S. interests in the country?

The twenty-one countries that responded to Washington opposed the "give more or we're leaving" strong-arm approach. Such a threat would harm long-term relations with the host country, they argued. Most would rather take a 10 percent budget cut and downsize rather than threaten the host government with closing Peace Corps operations. Embassies around the world described various scenarios and dynamics that could result from the hardball tactics Washington proposed to get more money. Some feared the host government might view the request as an unacceptable ultimatum, while others considered it counterproductive to use such tactics to pinch paltry sums from host countries to offset budget cuts in the richest country in the world.

Most countries looked at the big picture and argued the Peace Corps was an important part of the overall aid program in host countries. Peace Corps directors and ambassadors saw nothing positive coming from reducing or eliminating a program that addressed basic human needs and fostered goodwill and friendly relations. The embassy in Colombia wrote that the Peace Corps worked with those who did not have an influence on the government or access to the media. It also helped the poor, facilitated development, and played a useful role in guiding and complementing national efforts. Ecuador thought playing the role of the bully regarding host government support was alien to the Peace Corps' philosophy. The embassy in Bogota summed it up best:

> To attempt to make the Peace Corps a cost-effective operation by demanding financial inputs from the host country misses the point of why the Peace Corps should be a sign of our commitment to raise the standard of living of the poor. To ask a poor country to contribute substantially to a rich country in exchange for a volunteer program that benefits our country as well as

the host country strikes me (the ambassador) as anomalous.

The ambassador in Zaire (now the Democratic Republic of the Congo) lamented the lost opportunity for young Americans to learn about other countries and cultures if Peace Corps phased out. He expressed the grand idea that fewer Volunteers would mean less influence on future leaders who would have been students in classes taught by the Volunteers. One ambassador criticized Washington for being unable to recruit the technical experts the host country wanted, adding it would be incongruous to ask them to fund Volunteers they might not be able to recruit or retain. The embassy in Kingston argued that the Jamaican government might see a request for an increase in financial assistance to the Peace Corps as retaliation for its new tax on mining and exporting bauxite to the U.S., which could cause more taxation and regulation of American products. A few directors and ambassadors pointed out that the United States, a wealthy country, would look silly quibbling over the small amounts of money involved, less than $125,000.

Venezuela was one of the least articulate countries in explaining Peace Corps' relationship with the government:

> The national government would most probably respond negatively to any request for financial support to the Peace Corps program which would necessitate the legislative approval of new funds specifically for such support. If, however, Peace Corps requested a change in its programming structure, which would restrict all future requests for which funds are already approved and available, the decision made by the government would be kept at the level of programming and thus be made by the national planning agency rather than a decision about new funds which would be made by the Venezuelan Congress.

The Peace Corps in Venezuela believed asking the government for more money was an act of futility, not because it would insult them but because Venezuela had already set its priorities for 1975, and funding for the Peace Corps was not among them. Threatening Venezuela with the loss of sports advisors, coaches, cartographers, and environmental experts was not going to rattle them in the midst of taking over the oil industry.

At first, the embassy said a smaller program would not provide much value. A few months later when Peter Stevens, the new director, and Harry Shlaudeman, the new ambassador, arrived, they changed course. They said a reduced program was better than none at all. Even a small program would show American interest in the people through the Volunteers' "selfless" participation in local communities, a trait other Americans apparently did not have. If the Peace Corps left or reduced operations to a minimal level, it would result in the loss of the most visible positive image the United States presented to the Venezuelans. Without Peace Corps Volunteers, oilmen, the military, embassy personnel, and tourists would be the face of the U.S., a situation Peter Stevens considered untenable:

> I would regret to see the Peace Corps close down in Venezuela because it has been psychologically a welcome adjunct to our diplomacy in this country. The widespread Peace Corps Volunteers are almost an assertion of faith in the future of Venezuela. In many cases, the only Americans the lesser privileged classes of this country have contact with are either U.S. industrialists, oil camp executives, or Peace Corps Volunteers with whom they relate on a much more friendly basis. In consequence, the departure of the Peace Corps would not serve our interests, but its value is difficult to project regarding dollars and cents.

After the one-day conference, kept brief because of a tight budget, I took a bus to Maracaibo, where I started my new job. I didn't know it at the time, but I would never see most of the Volunteers with whom I trained again.

On the long ride, I reflected on the last twelve months. Without question, I had learned a lot by living and working in a strange land and learning a foreign language. Even if my work as a sports advisor and trainer was unfulfilling, I traveled, met new people, and saw new places. As I looked out the window at the mountains and green landscape, I expected my ideas and interim conclusions about Venezuela and Peace Corps, and maybe about life in general, to develop further over the next year.

Seven

A New Job

I arrived at the Las Pulgas transport terminal in Maracaibo in the late afternoon and took a taxi to the La Lago section of the city where Jeff and Brian, two Volunteers who had transferred from the IND Sports and Recreation program eight months earlier, shared a small house. I stayed with them until I found my own place to live. But I wasted no time starting my new job and went to work the next day at AZUPANE (pronounced A-ZOO-PA-NAY).

In 1968, a group of parents with developmentally disabled children founded the *Asociacion Zuliana de The Padres y Amigos de Ninos Excepcionales*/Zulia Association of Parents and Friends of Exceptional Children (AZUPANE) to ensure their kids reached their individual potential. Its motto, *"Queremos Realizarnos,"* roughly meant, "Everyone has the right to be the best they can be without limitations." One hundred children, adolescents, and young adults came to the center Monday through Friday. A typical profile was a child between 10-12 years old who had a physical and intellectual impairment and might also have mobility and speech issues.

The center was located in the former Creole Oil Camp near the Hospital Coromoto in the La Lago section, a posh neighborhood known for its single-family homes, manicured lawns, and white-washed walls. It comprised four buildings: the office, a residence for the Padre, and two work areas. A wall, embedded with broken glass, surrounded the lush grounds of fruit trees and tropical floral. For added safety, an armed guard patrolled at night.

AZUPANE: Center of Human Development I want to realize myself
(Photo by Mike Kendellen)

On my first day, Padre Gregorio Jose Finol, a 47-year-old native of Maracaibo who had been the director of AZUPANE since 1973, introduced me at the weekly staff meeting. He told everyone I would be there for one year and, always the optimist, as I would find out, he said it would be more likely for three. This was not complete hyperbole. The Padre wanted a long-term association with the Peace Corps. Beyond the cheap labor Volunteers provided, the Padre believed Peace Corps Volunteers, being Americans, could bring new ideas and innovative ways of doing things. His approach was not much different from the third goal of Peace Corps, "Helping promote a better understanding of other peoples on the part of Americans." In other words, we would learn about them, and they would learn about us. Compared to IND and other government offices, the Padre was a breath of fresh air.

During my visit and interview back in December, the Padre said he would like me to direct the camping program, which was in the planning stages at the time. When I arrived six weeks later, a permanent program at the two-bedroom, one-bathroom beachfront house on Lake Maracaibo, owned by an AZUPANE board member, had yet to begin. Staff scheduled beach excursions on an ad hoc basis. My first outing was for three days with fourteen kids between five and ten years old and five other team members. Even though they all had a physical disability and needed assistance to eat, dress, and move about on their own, the kids did what anyone else would do at the beach: hike, swim, play ball, and hang out.

We ate well during the three-day outings. Somebody had the idea that instead of the usual fare of spaghetti, rice, *arepas,* and watermelon, we should have eggs every meal. So the people in charge of the food bought ten dozen, enough to eat scrambled and hard-boiled eggs twice a day. After dinner, we sat around a campfire, and each of the kids sang or performed. Eleven-year-old Paco impersonated a matador and a baseball player, which drew applause. He received the most laughs for his dead-on and hilarious impression of the Padre, which did not amuse him as he watched from the back.

Padre Jose Gregorio Finol, a native of Maracaibo.
(Photo by Mike Kendellen)

For sleeping, we strung hammocks in two rooms from hooks built into the walls, an arrangement found in most homes in Venezuela. The excursion ended on Sunday after breakfast with the Padre saying Mass on the beach as we stood around in shorts and sandals. Afterward, we got on the bus and returned to Maracaibo. The three days were a satisfying beginning to my new assignment.

The three Volunteers at AZUPANE perplexed the staff. Curious about our motivations and emotional states, they asked us a lot of questions. How could we leave our families and live so far away from them? One woman in her early twenties even wanted to know if I loved my mother, thinking I couldn't possibly do so if I left her to come to Venezuela. Another woman, who followed a meatless diet, practiced yoga, and changed religions every other month hoping to one day find the right path to happiness, wondered if I would feel any emotion when I left AZUPANE or if I would just run off and go to the next country the Peace Corps sent me. Leaving San Carlos was an unemotional event for me but I didn't know what to say about Maracaibo, having been there only two weeks. She was both curious and concerned. She believed Americans were cold-blooded business people who worshipped money, though she admitted her stereotype of Americans didn't match with Brian, Jeff, and me working abroad as low-paying Volunteers. When she asked for an explanation, I hesitated. Not having thought much about it, and realizing that even if I had, my Spanish was not at a level to express it, I kept it simple: "*No sé*," Spanish for, "I don't know."

When the AZUPANE staff heard that most Volunteers returned home after completing two years of service, they changed the direction of their inquiry and wondered why we would do that rather than transfer to another country. Some things you can't explain. It was even more baffling to them that Jeff and Brian did not have a refrigerator in their house to store cold water and make ice. They found it incomprehensible the U.S. government would provide so little money they could not afford to buy one in a tropical country like Venezuela. In truth, they chose not to purchase a refrigerator because the electricity in their neighborhood was unreliable.

I shared a room with Brian while living with them for a few weeks, which made me feel more like a guest than the third tenant. It was evident right away that the arrangement was inconvenient for them. Jeff drove me around on his motorcycle on Saturdays to look at accommodations after checking out ads in the morning paper. After my experience in San Carlos of living in a rooming house and upon seeing the high rents in Maracaibo, I decided renting a room with a family was the best option.

After a three-week search, I found one: a household of a mother, her three children, and a dog near Avenida Bella Vista. The rent of three hundred bolivars a month, one-third of my combined living and rent allowance, was an exorbitant price to pay, but I considered the arrangement temporary. When Jeff and Brian finished their two years of service in a few months, I planned to move into their house. My freshly painted room included a bed, two chairs, a closet, and a desk. The owner's house cleaner dusted and vacuumed my room every day as part of the rent, and I paid her to do the laundry every Monday. I shared a bathroom with another tenant and could not use the kitchen except to keep a pitcher of cold water, so I ate my lunch and dinner at restaurants while skipping breakfast. The owner said she would only worry about me if I got sick; otherwise, I was on my own.

I didn't see the family very much, nor the man who rented the other room until we both arrived home from work one evening at the same time. We engaged in small talk on the front porch before moving on to politics, a topic Venezuelans loved. He was the first Venezuelan to tell me that President Carlos Andres Pérez was a demagogue. Worse, he believed the president's plan to use oil revenue to reduce poverty and diversify the economy would either lead Venezuela to a great social revolution or take it down the road to political and economic disaster. Twelve months in office was not long enough, I told him, to be so sure about the direction the country was going. Pérez was popular, I pointed out: "Look, the Communist Party even met him at the airport on his return from the OPEC conference in Algeria. He must be doing something right." At the gathering, OPEC repeated that each country had the sovereign right to own its resources, a point Venezuela liked to repeat in its negotiations with foreign companies on nationalizing the oil industry. This principle should have boosted his popularity. The renter—I didn't know his name—was unimpressed with my viewpoint and changed the subject.

"Is AZUPANE connected to the CIA?" he asked.

Ugh, not this spy crap again. No one had mentioned the CIA since the IND official told me in a bar in San Carlos that I worked for the agency. Denial was never an adequate response. Any spook worth his or her mettle denies each accusation. So I denied any connection to intelligence gathering. For clarification, I added that neither I nor AZUPANE was attached to any spy agency. I have no doubt he thought I was lying.

I had assumed leaving San Carlos would be the end of my ties to IND, but I was wrong. My final chapter with them occurred when the coaches went on a nationwide hunger strike in a call for an increase in compensation and to protest the lack of equipment. If coaches in the U.S. tried this ploy to get athletic directors and team owners to address their demands for better working conditions and higher salaries, sports fans would have been screaming, "Let them die!" One casualty of the strike involved our ability to go to the IND pool. When the work stoppage petered out a few weeks later, AZUPANE did not resume its relationship with them, as they were considered too unreliable. Soon after, though, the Jewish Club also informed us we could no longer use their pool because the custodians had grown tired of picking up the mess from leaving half-eaten snacks on the changing room floor.

Although I cannot use my right arm due to the after-effects of polio, AZUPANE was my real introduction to the world of disability, a world I knew little about other than the developmentally disabled were then called "mentally retarded." History has not been kind to people with developmental disabilities. The Greeks and Romans believed babies were born with an intellectual disability because they had angered the gods. The Spartans let the deformed ones die. Over the course of centuries in Europe, they imprisoned people with psychiatric impairments.

In the 1800s, persons with disabilities served as entertainment in circuses and exhibitions, the consensus being they were "abnormal" and not intelligent enough to do anything else. Disabled persons often spent their whole lives in institutions and asylums. As urbanization spread in the latter half of the 1800s, academics, government and elected officials, and activists blamed the "feebleminded," a label also given to prostitutes, illegitimate children, and epileptics as well as the mentally deficient, for the rising operating costs for schools, prisons, and hospitals.

In 1869, Sir Francis Galton, a cousin of Charles Darwin, published *Hereditary Genius*, a groundbreaking work that concluded that intellectual competence, the primary determinant in life, was inherited rather than the consequence of poverty, education, and nutrition. Eugenics, the social movement, adopted Galton's ideas, which looked at the disabled as a long-term problem society could best solve by having fewer of them.

Proponents of eugenics, including such renowned figures as Charles Darwin, H.G. Wells, Alexander Graham Bell, John D. Rockefeller, Theodore Roosevelt, and Margaret Sanger believed nature determined personality and intellect, not socioeconomic factors. They identified euthanasia and sterilization as the preferred methods to get rid of, or at least reduce, what they called the "inferior" population.

Finding a means to achieving this aim was problematic. A 1911 Carnegie Institute report recommended gas chambers as the most efficient way to shrink the number of weak and disabled. The academicians behind euthanasia, however, dismissed the hideous idea because they did not think the American public would support such a program. Instead, they advocated for sterilization to ensure reproduction did not occur. If adopted, the argument went, the birth rate among the feebleminded would decline, and eventually, intellectually disabled persons would be gone, which would be better for all.

In 1907, Indiana enacted a sterilization law for "imbeciles," and in 1924, backers of the Virginia Sterilization Act declared that reproduction among the "feebleminded" was a threat to society. When the Virginia State Colony for Epileptics and Feebleminded petitioned its board to sterilize Carrie Buck, the family appealed, arguing the state had based its case on faulty science and incorrect information. State officials had used results from the Benet-Simon Intelligence Test, the same flawed test administered to more than a million recruits during World War I. Of these, 47 percent were declared feebleminded, yet were nevertheless sent to Europe to defend freedom. The test categorized Carrie as a "middle-grade moron," a higher level than "imbecile," despite being an above-average student in school. Carrie also bore a daughter, which the institution blamed on her alleged promiscuity rather than being raped by a family member. The court, using Carrie Buck, her daughter, and her mother as an example of what can result from defective genes, ruled the Bucks were a threat to the community.

The case went all the way to the U.S. Supreme Court in 1927, where an 8-1 decision in *Buck v. Bell* ruled a state could permit compulsory sterilization if the purpose was to prevent "feebleminded and socially inadequate" people from having children. Justice Oliver Wendell Holmes wrote, "Three generations of imbeciles is enough."

The court decision ranks with *Dred Scott* (African Americans were not citizens, and the federal government could not regulate slavery), *Plessy v. Ferguson* (upheld the constitutionality of segregation under the separate but equal doctrine), and *Korematsu* (allowed the federal government to put American citizens of Japanese descent into detention camps during World War II) as being among the Supreme Court's worst decisions. *Buck v. Bell* led to the sterilization of almost 70,000 Americans, with California and a host of Southern states leading the way. The decision also inspired Hitler to praise America for having an enlightened racial policy. In 1933, Nazi Germany adopted a Eugenic Sterilization Law and sterilized more than 300,000 men and women. Denmark, Norway, Sweden, and Switzerland also passed eugenics sterilization laws.

The Kallikak Family: A Study in the Heredity of Feeble-Mindedness by Henry H. Goddard, a best-selling book in 1912, further claimed a variety of mental characteristics were genetic and that society should limit reproduction by people possessing these traits. More recently, analysis of the Kallikak family has speculated that a combination of poverty, poor diet, and undiagnosed fetal alcohol syndrome had caused their mental disabilities.

As late as 1942, medical professionals advocated children thought to be "idiots" also be sterilized to ensure their genes would not be passed on to another generation. The term "idiots" remains in use today. The Kentucky, Mississippi, New Mexico, and Ohio constitutions prohibit "idiots," meaning severely intellectually disabled persons, from voting, though it appears from recent election results that some of these states were not enforcing the law.

At AZUPANE in 1975, "mental retardation" was the term used to describe children and adults with low IQs and developmental disabilities. Though it might seem insensitive today, it was an improvement over other common terms. The Padre was adamant about careful use of terminology. He banned nicknames and words like *loco* (crazy) and *enfermo* (sick), which implied the kids had caught a temporary illness and could be cured, or other words that inferred a diagnosis that was false and insulting. He also wanted us to describe the kids as "exceptional," the meaning of "E" in AZUPANE.

Samuel Kirk, a pioneer in the fields of special education and learning disabilities, defined "exceptional:"

> The exceptional child is defined as a child who deviates from the average or normal child in mental, physical, or social characteristics, to such an extent he requires a modification of school practices or special educational services to develop his maximum capacity.

By 1952, forty-six of the forty-eight states had enacted legislation on the rights and services for the intellectually disabled. By then, the civil rights movement was well along the way to overturning discriminatory laws against African Americans. Disability advocates saw the federal courts ruling that discrimination based on race was unconstitutional, and sought the same for people with disabilities. By the end of the decade, Congress and most states had passed laws allowing access to public transportation and government buildings, due process, voting, and education for the disabled.

Further advancing the disability rights movement, President John F. Kennedy, whose sister, Rosemary, lived in an institution in Illinois after undergoing a lobotomy that left her permanently incapacitated, established the President's Panel on Mental Retardation (now the President's Committee on Intellectual Disabilities). Kennedy also signed the Community Mental Health Centers Act of 1963, the last bill he signed before being assassinated.

However, in 1964, Congress failed to provide sufficient funding. They allocated nothing for professional staff and only enough to build half of the proposed centers. As a result, states closed expensive state hospitals and whatever community-based care there was ended. Patients then moved to adult homes or moved in with their families. Others became homeless. In response, President Jimmy Carter signed the Mental Health Systems Act in 1980 to support community programs. A year later, the Reagan administration repealed the law, saying mandates were bad policy, and cut federal mental health spending by one-third.

The right to mental health treatment was also fought in the courts. In 1971, a federal court in Alabama held that persons with mental illness or developmental disabilities in state institutions had a constitutional right to treatment. U.S. District Court Judge Myron Thompson summed up the implications of *Wyatt v. Stickney*:

> There can be no legal or moral justification for the State of Alabama's failing to afford adequate treatment for persons committed to its care from a medical standpoint. Furthermore, to deprive any citizen of his or her liberty upon the altruistic theory the confinement is for humane therapeutic reasons and then fails to provide adequate treatment violates the very fundamentals of due process. The enormity of what this case has accomplished cannot be overstated. The principles of humane treatment of people with mental illness and mental retardation

embodied in this litigation have become part of the fabric of law in this country and, indeed, international law.

The court case set minimum standards for treatment, although the Wyatt Standards were not finalized until 2003. They are now part of state mental health codes and federal regulations. The Wyatt case not only created mental health law, but it also led to the deinstitutionalization of patients with mental illness. However, with limited funds available, states were unable to hire more professional staff, and instead of providing better care, the institutions released the patients and closed down. Many believe *Wyatt v. Stickney* and deinstitutionalization led to widespread homelessness among the mentally ill in the U.S.

Activists lobbied in the 1980s to put the various laws on disability under one broad civil rights statute that would protect the rights of people with disabilities. In 1990, thanks to their efforts, President George H. W. Bush signed the Americans with Disabilities Act (ADA), which addressed equal treatment and access to employment while prohibiting discrimination in public services, transportation, and communications. The U.S. courts are still sorting out the law, notably regarding reasonable accommodation in the workplace. Meanwhile, the ADA became the model for disability legislation and law around the world.

As in other emerging countries, funding to assist people with disabilities in Venezuela is a work in progress, though even in the 1970s it had come a long way since 1912, when legislation referred to the developmentally disabled as "abnormal." Special education gained momentum in 1960 when teachers who specialized in working with hearing-impaired children began to emerge. Throughout the following decade, inclusive schools opened, though mostly private ones, because the Ministry of Education said it could not afford to fund them. In 1963, a group of parents established the nonprofit Venezuelan Association of Parents and Friends of Exceptional Children (*la Asociación Venezolana de Padres y Amigos de Niños Excepcionales*, AVEPANE). Its mission was to train and integrate the developmentally disabled into the community. In 1968, another group, led by Doctor Roberto Lara and his wife, Elsa, founded AZUPANE in Maracaibo. It was the only institution of its kind in the city.

By 1971, the Ministry of Education reported children with special needs attended forty-nine schools, of which twenty-three were for the developmentally disabled. Of those, eighteen were private, meaning the students came from wealthy families, leaving the less well-to-do families with no options but to keep their disabled child at home. All schools suffered from a shortage of trained teachers, as no university in the country offered classes or a program in special education. Recognizing the problem, Venezuela sent teachers to Uruguay for training.

The Padre was studying in the U.S. when the disability movement was gaining traction. He became a champion of the view that denounced institutionalization, one of the issues espoused by the movement. He wanted AZUPANE to be a model for a humanistic approach to working with persons with mental disabilities. Its mission was to improve the lives of the intellectually disabled on the principle that as individuals who had the potential for personal growth, they should be treated with dignity.

AZUPANE enrolled children who could not on their own perform major life activities such as seeing, hearing, eating, walking, and speaking. After an assessment by a psychologist, the kids were divided into one of three groups: Dependents, Trainables, or Educables, and then assigned to the most appropriate of the seven activity sections. Infants less than three years of age were put into the Sensory Stimulation section. The Motor Coordination area for children between four and six stressed mobility. Social Conduct and Expression focused on personal hygiene habits and self-fulfillment through painting, drawing, theater, and music. Recreation emphasized physical activity through exercises, games, and swimming. In Academics, a small group of teenagers learned reading and mathematics. Arts and Crafts trained the oldest kids in gardening, mechanics, handicrafts, and housework.

Staff and volunteers from Venezuela, Colombia, Ecuador, Chile, and Costa Rica consisted of men and women in their twenties, of whom none had graduated from college, though a few were attending night classes at the University of Zulia. Other staff were over forty, married, and had children.

I started in the Recreation section. The coordinator, Dario, was a former IND swimming coach. We spent nine hours a week at the YMCA, IND, the Jewish Club, or the Creole Oil Club, better known as the

American Club, swimming pools. The outings were the highlights of the week and the core of the Recreation program. Exercises, basketball, and playing on swings and slides filled the rest of the time. At the pool, I swam too, an endeavor which consisted of holding my breath from one end of the Olympic-sized pool to the other, unable to coordinate my breathing while moving. I still called it swimming.

At the pool in Maracaibo with an instructor
(Photo by Mike Kendellen)

AZUPANE had its detractors. The Padre had introduced a novel approach to working with the developmentally disabled. The radical experiment had few true believers, even among the staff. At a symposium on special education at the Zulia state school for the disabled, former employees accused AZUPANE of corruption, exploitation, and being nothing more than a school for rich kids. Most amusing were the allegations that the weekend beach outings were nothing more than hours of debauchery, an accusation Venezuelan politicians liked to use to put down their adversaries. Years later, President Hugo Chavez accused his so-called enemies of the same behavior when he said Venezuelan oil executives spent too much time drinking whiskey and engrossed in orgies. While I laughed at the accusations at the conference, I also realized AZUPANE and the Padre might have rivals.

Working with children and adolescents at AZUPANE presented many challenges. I knew little about each child's medical condition and background. Looking back, I am astounded how infrequently we talked about each child, if for no other reason than to understand them better. Most of them were disabled at birth and their ailments frequently had no cure. My technical vocabulary came to include epilepsy, cerebral palsy, spina bifida, and the now out-of-date "mongoloidism" (Downs Syndrome), which some of them suffered from, but I didn't know much about the conditions.

A few students may have been autistic, but I never heard the term used. At the time, autism was linked more to research on schizophrenia than associated with disabilities. It seems like far more than just forty years ago when you realize that studies in the 1970s concluded that lysergic acid diethylamide (LSD) and electric shock treatments could change behavior in children with autism.

The Padre advocated for a more humanistic approach to working with people with mental disabilities. It was all too common to treat persons with mental disabilities as if they were stupid. The Padre preached that they deserved better and had emotions and feelings like the rest of us. He wanted AZUPANE to develop people with disabilities into whole human beings. We all admired him for his sincerity and the staff did not consider his ideas crazy; they just didn't always understand them.

The Padre had three degrees from American universities, including a PhD from the University of Pittsburgh. In contrast, there were no college graduates among the staff, though a few staff were enrolled in night classes. None had been trained in Special Education, either. Even if degree holders applied for a job, the Padre could not afford to employ them because the school's funding was so uncertain. AZUPANE received no money from either the state or federal government. All of its revenue came from private sources.

To address the need to improve the staff's knowledge of mental disabilities, the Padre instituted a professional development program in coordination with York University in Toronto, Canada, that consisted of four months of classes in sociology and psychology, the philosophy of education, and methodology. The Padre believed Venezuelans were an alienated people who suffered from group-think and accepted everything they heard, including whatever he said. Between the awe, respect, and fear they felt for him, staffers seldom challenged his ideas or statements, a practice he detested. He wished the staff would think more for themselves. Just once I wanted to hear someone say to him, "I disagree with you for the following reasons…," because that would show progress, but it would never happen.

The Padre also offered classes to stimulate the staff, encouraging them to think on their own and be creative. A natural teacher, the Padre liked to sit cross-legged in the middle of a circle when conducting a class. He lectured, handed out papers, and gave reading assignments. His favorite authors and thinkers were three controversial mavericks in liberal and counterculture circles, each representing a different era in the twentieth century, who wrote about Christianity and its relationship to secular life.

Pierre Teilhard de Chardin, a Jesuit priest, philosopher, paleontologist, and adventurer, was involved in the discovery of Peking Man and in bridging science and religion. Some have called him the religious Indiana Jones.

Ivan Illich, a former Benedictine priest, born in Vienna into a family with Jewish, Croatian, and Catholic roots, became a critic of institutional education.

Khalil Gibran, a Lebanese poet and popular in the 1960s with New Age movements, is best known for *The Prophet*, a book of twenty-six poetic essays on love, family, beauty, pain, and death; it still sells well today. Only poems by Shakespeare and Lao-Tzu have sold more copies. He died in 1931 at age 48 of cirrhosis of the liver and tuberculosis.

Teilhard, who died in 1955, was one of the cutting-edge thinkers of the twentieth century, ranking among the top three or four most significant influences in modern Christian theology. He wrote about a new bridge between religion and science and between Christianity and the life and politics of humans. His theory of cosmic evolution put man in the center of the universe, and he thought evolving human consciousness would lead to social change.

But the Vatican disagreed. It accused him of being too ambiguous and contradicting Catholic doctrine. They censored his radical writings, of which few were published while he was alive. Rome even issued a statement asking religious and educational leaders around the world to protect the minds of the world's youth against the dangers of Teilhard's works and his followers.

Yet Teilhard and his ideas have not disappeared. Behind the 2014 newspaper headline, "U.S. nuns haunted by dead Jesuit: the ghost of Pierre Teilhard de Chardin," was the story of Rome complaining that too many nuns believed in "conscious evolution," one of Teilhard's main concepts.

Ivan Illich was the only one of the Padre's three favorite authors still living when he introduced their works to the AZUPANE staff. Throughout the late 1960s and early 1970s, Illich ran the Centro Intercultural de Documentación (CIDOC) at Cuernavaca, Mexico, a training site for all kinds of volunteers bound for Latin America. Illich criticized programs like the Peace Corps, which he thought did more harm than good because volunteers represented the values of their native countries. To him, Catholic missionaries were not much different. He dismissed foreign volunteers who worked in under-developed countries as nothing more than "vacationing salesmen for the middle-class American way of life." To my mind, regardless of what Peace Corps Volunteers were after in the 1970s, the ones I knew weren't selling American values. If anything, they might have been running away from them.

In a 1968 address to the Conference on Interamerican Student Projects, a Catholic youth service program, Illich analyzed the concept of volunteering abroad:

> Next to money and guns, the third largest North American export is the U.S. idealist, who turns up in every theater of the world: the teacher, the volunteer, the missionary, the community organizer, the economic developer, and the vacationing do-gooders. Ideally, these people define their role as service. Actually, they frequently wind up exacerbating the damage done by money and weapons, or "seducing" the "underdeveloped" to the benefits of the world of affluence and achievement.

Illich might be best known for *Deschooling Society,* published in 1970, in which he argued that rather than educating them, schools made people complacent and dumb. He maintained that homeschooling or learning in casual situations was preferable to relying on formal educational settings. He also condemned aid agencies, non-governmental organizations (NGOs), and others for creating self-

114

perpetuating international bureaucratic organizations that came with sustainable development.

Illich remained popular, even trendy, throughout the 1970s. His books were bestsellers; believers packed auditoriums to hear his lectures, and the *New York Review of Books* and the *Saturday Review* published his essays. Today there is an online publication, *The International Journal of Illich Studies*, dedicated to his ideas and writings. When he died in 2002, *The Guardian* called him one of the world's great thinkers.

The Padre never talked about politics, foreign aid, or the value of the Peace Corps, nor did he go into depth on what his three favorite authors represented in the world outside of AZUPANE and Venezuela. What intrigued the Padre was how they thought outside the box on the linkages between Christianity, the secular person, and education. AZUPANE's motto *"Queremos Realizarnos"* ("We want to realize ourselves") mirrored these themes. He wanted the AZUPANE staff to think, be innovative, and become better people for it.

No matter how much the Padre wanted to enlighten the staff, like everything else at AZUPANE, budget was an issue; he could not offer the classes for free. Moreover, he believed he had no choice but to make the staff pay because Venezuelans considered anything that was free to be of low quality, or at least that's what the Padre said. The fee was one thousand two bolivars, about a month's salary. He did not charge me. Besides the contents of the course, he also pitched the class as a way of earning credits toward a university degree. He talked York University into granting three credits for taking the courses, the opposite approach of the Ministry of Education in Venezuela, which refused to recognize the program.

It's uncertain what was learned over the weeks of lunchtime sessions. I never once heard the staff utter a word outside of the classes, much less discuss the authors or any of the assigned readings. Personally, I did not expect this kind of education as part of being a Peace Corps Volunteer.

After a few months, I had a better idea what each of the kids was capable of doing and knew a little about their family situations. The parents of Segundo abandoned him at the hospital after he was born because of his severe disability, not wanting to care for him the rest of his life. Now three, he seemed like a happy kid and smiled a lot when you spoke to him. But then, without explanation, he stopped coming to the center. The social worker, an American nun, went to see him at the hospital. According to the medical staff, he had relapsed since going to AZUPANE and would be better off in the hospital.

When I first heard this, I wondered how a person with such limited physical and mental faculties could regress. The doctor said Segundo threw his milk at dinner and cooperated less with the nurses after returning every afternoon—behaviors, they insisted, Segundo did not exhibit before he started at AZUPANE. The Padre was livid when he heard that explanation. He made it clear to the doctor that Segundo was not regressing, but rather expressing himself as a human being, making choices, and, by definition, developing as a person. The next day, Segundo returned to AZUPANE.

Eighteen-year-old Martin spent a lot of time in a cage his father built for him in the backyard of their home. At AZUPANE, he sat in a lotus position without making a sound while others in his group played; without warning, he would get up and walk away. Unable to stand up straight after spending so much time sitting in the cage, he walked stooped over like a bear. His middle-aged father affectionately called him "my little animal." His parents' primary interaction with him was when they brought him meals.

When he arrived at AZUPANE, he could only utter, "Que? Que?" ("What? What?"). Over time, he learned a few words, though he never spoke in complete sentences. Once in a while, he responded in a soft and tender voice. When staff tried talking to him, he would answer in a loud, deep voice which, after a few minutes, would turn into a barrage of obscenities aimed at no one in particular. Sometimes he imitated the staff. The impediments he faced due to having so little human interaction as a child were incomprehensible. It was sad.

Louisa was a sixteen-year-old girl who seemed mute because she rarely said a word. At home, she stayed in her room, alone, limiting interaction with her siblings and parents, or any other person. Her parents did not come to AZUPANE for social visits like most of the other parents. When someone would talk to her in a provocative or aggressive tone, she would rattle off a barrage of unintelligible words in what appeared to be an angry response to the hostile sounds directed at her. Like many of the kids, she never put together a string of words to form a complete sentence.

Gustavo could not speak and had trouble walking after twelve years of sitting on the floor in his room at home. But he would move his head and hands when listening to music, even the strumming of a toy guitar that I played once while working with him. According to the social workers and staff who visited his home, his parents kept him out of sight from shame and because they didn't know what to do with him. At AZUPANE, he would, with help, take a few steps every day, and each Friday, he would have shown enough progress to see that it would take just a little exercise to improve, only to lose all the gains over the weekend from sitting alone in his room. Each Monday he would return to AZUPANE and start over. It was hard to assess and quantify Gustavo's development when the primary concern was the relationship between him and his family. Being mentally disabled was a lonely existence.

Although there were moments of surrealism, such as when we would play basketball with the music of Mozart blaring from the speakers hanging from the coconut and mango trees, on most days, I got great satisfaction from a spontaneous hello, a hug, or seeing that the kids were having fun playing ball or shooting baskets. It could also be as simple as smiling while waiting to board the bus. I considered a day successful when it appeared that the kids did something they had never done before.

AZUPANE and the city of Maracaibo were welcome changes from IND and San Carlos. My living situation, renting a room, was about to change, too.

Eight

Maracaibo

Maracaibo, the second largest city in the country, was a welcome upgrade from San Carlos. In the 1970s, local officials described Maracaibo as one of the most exciting new cities in the world, a description that fell between fantasy and error. It was nowhere close to the booming metropolis they wanted everyone to believe it was, even though it had electricity, running water, and indoor plumbing, all modern conveniences not typically associated with life in the Peace Corps.

For people with extra spending money, there was plenty to do. They could frequent bars, hamburger joints, pizzerias, and movie theaters; watch professional baseball; shop at a supermarket; attend a symphony orchestra concert; exercise at a sports complex; enjoy a bullfight; swim at nearby beaches; or read the Sunday *New York Times* in the library at the American consulate. While the city offered all the comforts of a large urban area, they were too expensive to indulge on my $220 per month living allowance.

However, I was able to change my eating habits. I drank milk again after a year without it. I opted to limit my intake of hamburgers and pizza and would treat myself to a banana split and shrimp chop suey with a strawberry or chocolate shake at Wily Quink Lunch, a Chinese diner whose name came from misspelling "quick." I ate there at least once a week and got dinner for less than two dollars.

Restaurants could be an adventurous undertaking. Once at a pizzeria, I was biting into a cheese and sausage pizza when a cockroach crawled up the leg of the table, plopped itself on the napkin in front of me and paused before considering whether it was worthwhile to step on my pizza or walk away alive. I did not hesitate, grabbing the menu and, with one swift hit, flattened the little bugger and swept it off the table.

The waiter, watching from the cash register, walked over and, stepping on it, completed the execution.

It was hard to grasp the degree of danger in Maracaibo; on the surface, it appeared safe. Even though not every Venezuelan in the city considered me to be an expert in kung fu as had been the case in San Carlos, I felt comfortable walking the streets, even at night. On the other hand, the houses in the Bella Vista neighborhood where I lived had iron bars on the windows and a dog at either the front gate or in the house barking at each passing human being, suggesting break-ins were a real threat. The media presented a sensationalist view of crime. The back page of the tabloids, the so-called "Red Page," was reserved for photographs of the most hideous and bloodiest misdeeds. Every edition contained color photos of the latest victims, usually in the form of a car accident with no survivors following a chase or the bloodied corpses of alleged criminals gunned down by the police or rivals. The accompanying descriptions omitted details of what happened.

Tory, one of the three remaining Volunteers in Maracaibo—Jeff and I were the other two—had his house broken into three times in twelve months; he lost a flute, some clothes, and a pile of money. He invited me to join the group he was putting together to rent either a house or an apartment. But I declined because it meant making a one-year commitment and I wasn't sure if I would be in Venezuela for twelve more months; rumors persisted that the Peace Corps would close by the end of 1975. After a few days, however, I reconsidered, thinking that sharing a house with four others would be a way to meet more people, lower my living costs, and save money for travel. I couldn't worry about Peace Corps' future. Since the day I arrived in Caracas, I'd been hearing it might close down.

Tory found three others to join the group. One was Jeff, who had stayed at AZUPANE after his Peace Corps service. The remaining two were Venezuelans. Rosita, a student at the University of Zulia, was a friend of a friend of Tory's. The final slot went to Fernando, a twenty-eight-year-old artisan whom Tory had met on a street corner in downtown Maracaibo where he was selling his leather handicrafts. Fernando was also Rosita's boyfriend. He would use his room as a workshop to make shoes, purses, bags, sandals, and whatever additional leather items he could sell.

Until a few months earlier, Peace Corps restricted the number of Volunteers sharing accommodations to two. However, they never enforced the rule, starting with the administrators in Caracas who overlooked the Volunteers' living arrangements when adding the rent supplements to our monthly checks, though the attitude we should live alone to get the full cultural experience still prevailed.

Safety and affordability drove our decisions on lodging. For single women, sharing a house with other Volunteers was often the most sensible option. In deciding to live together in Maracaibo, we not only ignored the spirit of the housing policy, but we also dismissed the information we received in Miami that Venezuelan society frowned upon unrelated men and women living under the same roof. When Rosita agreed to move in with Tory, Jeff, Fernando, and me, we assumed she had considered Venezuelan traditions.

Even with five people, finding a place wasn't easy. A penthouse apartment in a high-rise building intrigued us until the owner told us the rent. We then shifted our search to looking for a house for less than $250 a month on the premise that most had gates and fences or walls, affording us a level of safety. The real estate agent assured us there were plenty of houses available in that price range.

In short order, the agent found owners willing to rent to us at an amount we could afford and also give us a nine-month lease. The day before Tory was to sign it, in a development that stunned us, the owners remembered that six weeks remained before their children's summer break from school, making a move impossible, and they canceled the deal.

The agent found another house on the north side of the city, about half a mile from Avenida Las Delicias, a major thoroughfare known for its shopping and restaurants. This time, the owners expressed their displeasure that an unmarried Venezuelan woman would be living with four men. We asked the agent to talk to the owners and explain the situation. When he met with them, he suggested they consider the positive side of having Americans responsible for the rent; he assured them this would guarantee they would be paid on time, because Americans have money. He never told them we were Peace Corps Volunteers, figuring that trying to explain that their future tenants did not hold salaried jobs would have thrown a wrench into the negotiations.

Later, he told us the owners were impressed with "Doctor" Tory. Tory, who taught swimming at the YMCA twelve hours a week, never told people he was a Volunteer unless he saw an advantage in it. As a result, many Venezuelans knew Tory, who had a bachelor's degree in Psychology, as a therapist and a doctor.

With our ability to pay the rent on time clinching the deal, three Peace Corps Volunteers and two Venezuelans moved into a two-story unfurnished house with four bedrooms, three bathrooms, large living and dining rooms, a kitchen, and a second-floor porch. At $250 a month or $50 a person, the rent was $25 less than what I had been paying for a room the last three months.

After we moved in, we learned that the cultural concerns over renting a room to Rosita were real when a woman Volunteer visited us and, afterward, the teenagers in the neighborhood asked how much she cost.

Renting a house with four other people was a significant change in lifestyle, starting with finding something to sleep on. For eighteen months, I had rented rooms that came with a bed. For the rest of my time in the country, I would sleep on a mattress on the floor.

Like every other house on our block, we had a cyclone fence in front with barbed wire on top, making us feel safe. The homes in the city's more upscale neighborhoods had embedded broken bottles on top of the walls surrounding their property. Still, we kept the front gate locked at all hours as a precaution, even if someone was home. We hung laundry in the privacy of a small courtyard in the back so no one had to sit and watch their clothes dry to prevent theft. The ten-foot brick wall separated us from our neighbors on all sides. We fit right into the neighborhood. The entrance or living room became a garage for Tory and Jeff to park their motorcycles, which the Peace Corps forbid Volunteers to have.

For recreation, we turned a square piece of iron we found in the back of the house into a seven-foot basketball hoop and borrowed a rubber playground ball from AZUPANE that Peace Corps had donated to them. Despite the low height of the basket, I was unable to dunk the ball. Each shot had to be perfect, so our shooting percentages were well below average. Across the street, a vacant lot full of bumps, holes, and general unevenness served as a baseball field on weekends. A steep incline in left field led to a wall with Socialist Party graffiti saying the country was in a sports crisis. We drew crowds whenever we threw a Frisbee or tossed a raggedy old football the Peace Corps office in Caracas had sent us when they were disposing of equipment as part of phasing down the program.

The baseball field across the street from the house with a
school on the hill and political graffiti on the walls.
(Photo by Mike Kendellen)

I easily fell into a routine. Each morning I got up around seven, showered, and left for work, skipping breakfast. For lunch and dinner, I ate ham and baloney sandwiches with ketchup and mustard, sometimes swapping in scrambled or fried eggs for something different. When someone bought groceries, they would pin the receipts to the refrigerator, and at the end of the month, one of us would take them and calculate what we owed each other. There was always plenty of grapefruit, watermelon, grapes, oranges, and pineapple to eat.

In the first weeks, Tory would make eggs. Once, an omelet splattered on the floor when he missed catching it while flipping it over. Uncertain what to do, we stared at the mess before looking at each other in disbelief, wondering whether we should eat everything anyway or throw it in the garbage. Shrugging, we scooped up the damaged breakfast before the five-second rule took effect—food on the ground less than five seconds would supposedly not be contaminated—and put it back in the pan. A minute of heat should burn off the bacteria, we figured. We were Peace Corps Volunteers, Americans, strong and capable of fighting off any bacteria. We enjoyed the meal and lived.

One evening, I returned home from work to find a paper bag, a dish of moldy leftover spaghetti, a butter wrapper, a half-dozen frozen eggs, and three empty water pitchers in the refrigerator and, mysteriously, an empty ashtray in the freezer. What was going on? A few days earlier, the General Electric refrigerator had stopped working. The GE office in Maracaibo told us they no longer made the part we needed for our ten-year-old model, so we thought it made sense to use the freezer as a refrigerator, and someone had seen the need to store an ashtray in it. We called a meeting and resolved everything. The next day the fridge was clean, the water pitchers were full, and the ashtray was back in Fernando's room.

Ana, Tory's Venezuelan girlfriend, remarked after watching us sort matters out that we had established house rules in an ad hoc democratic fashion. Well, maybe. But I was certain we did not have an ounce of Jeffersonian thought in our head when doing it. Instead, all we wanted was to avoid confrontations and live together without annoying each other. We presumed if each of us staked out a part of the kitchen with the food we bought, it would lead to anarchy. Sharing food would eliminate accusations of eating or stealing someone else's vegetables, lunch meat, or milk. The scheme actually worked.

We stumbled our way through housekeeping and home maintenance. On our first night, the dog disappeared. The neighbors figured it had been stolen, though with the front gate well-secured and impossible to slip through, we didn't understand how that could happen. It was a mystery how he got away. A few weeks later, we lost another dog, a black mix, part Belgian German Shepherd and part Doberman puppy, named Carota, meaning "bean" in Spanish; he was also stolen. Over time, we would add two parrots, a Siamese cat, and try again with a dog we named "Chicha."

Two weeks after we moved in, we called a plumber to fix a leak in one of the bathrooms. When I met him at the door, he was holding a handsaw and said someone had called him to come to the house.

Although seeing a man with a handsaw claiming to be a plumber seemed weird, I let him in. I didn't ask what he planned to do, figuring he was the expert. A few minutes later, he asked for twenty bolivars ($5) and said he would return the following day with the proper tools to fix the dripping shower head. Suspicious, we didn't expect to see him again. But then he showed up a few days later, fixed the leak, and asked for another twenty bolivars.

One Saturday morning while reading in my room, I heard a loud scream. I ran to the kitchen and found Fernando holding his legs and rolling across the floor in agony. He had stepped barefoot into a puddle of water that formed from defrosting the refrigerator. When he opened the fridge door, an electric current shot up his leg, dropping him in agony to the floor. Down for a few minutes, he got up slowly and ate his usual breakfast of corn flakes.

Our jobs—or, in Rosita's case, studying at the University of Zulia—kept us busy. We didn't see much of each other except on weekends. After a few weeks, I came home one evening to find Rosita alone in the kitchen pouring a glass of water. Without saying hello, she started talking.

"I have a big problem. I just received this from the doctor. Here, look," she said as she handed me a piece of paper written in Spanish. Knowing I couldn't read the doctor's note, she translated it. "It says I'm pregnant."

I didn't know much about her. She studied business at the university and came from eastern Venezuela. Congratulations seemed out of order. We talked for an hour and a half; about what, I don't remember. Her English was far worse than my Spanish, so I asked short questions and she followed with brief answers. She made it clear she did not want the baby. Even though she was more of a stranger than a friend, I said everyone in the house would give her whatever support she needed. But I wasn't sure about her friends.

The mystery was answered the following day when a classmate dropped by the house. She didn't stay long. All I heard was "*Ay, Dios mio!*" ("Oh my God!") when Rosita told her she was pregnant. She hurried out the door, never to return. Fernando, the father, did not agree with her decision to end the pregnancy and refused to help her find a doctor. She stopped talking to him, and a few days later moved out.

She found a replacement to rent her room before leaving, a gesture we didn't expect. Daniela, the new tenant, was twenty-two, not much younger than the rest of us, and just under five feet tall. She never spoke about being a javelin thrower on the University of Zulia track and field team or of her two-year-old daughter. Instead, she talked about going to Peru and Ecuador to buy drugs. As dangerous and criminal as her plan looked, we ignored it, thinking it too preposterous to take seriously. Even so, we never considered asking her to leave, wanting to avoid confrontation. We hoped she would leave on her own. Whatever potential problems might occur, we figured they would go away once she moved out.

A few days later, Jeff asked if anyone had seen Daniela. No one could recall seeing her for the past few days and hadn't noticed that she had put a lock on her door, but we all somehow assumed she would be back. Before the month was over, she reappeared, and suddenly strangers were hanging around the house, smoking marijuana while listening to *Al Kooper's Greatest Hits* at full blast. Fernando reported the neighbors gossiped about the loud music and strange odors.

We did not wish to be the focus of gossip in the neighborhood. With Jeff in the U.S. and Tory in Caracas, Fernando and I were left to tell her she had twenty-four hours to go. She nodded in agreement and then disregarded the order. When I saw her in the kitchen later in the week, I asked why she hadn't left. She was waiting for her boyfriend from New York before leaving for their trip to Peru, she told me. Coincidence or not, he arrived the next day, and without saying goodbye, they were gone.

The following week, Fernando surprised us by announcing he was marrying nineteen-year-old Cristina. I congratulated him, though not without wondering what her father, a college professor, thought of his daughter marrying a street peddler.

Harry Morgenstern, a fifty-five-year-old self-employed scrap dealer from Seattle who had been living in Maracaibo for twenty years, asked about moving in with us, an idea no one liked. The differences in age and lifestyle would lead to problems, but we welcomed him at the house as a visitor anytime. He lived in a shed near a junkyard out on the outskirts of the city, once owned a fleet of taxis but was forced to quit the venture when Venezuela passed a law limiting the number of cabs a person could control to one, making taxi companies obsolete. Now his battered 1960 pickup truck provided the means to transport trash, cardboard, boxes, tin, tiles, and other junk he sold. I avoided asking him about selling scrap, partly because he was the same age as my father, but also because I was afraid he was struggling. In retrospect, we were too young to appreciate him and so never probed or challenged him on his amazing stories and right-wing politics. When or why he came to Venezuela remained forever unclear. We just let him talk and entertain us. And that, he did.

Harry liked to indulge in recounting his World War II adventures. "Let me tell you what happened. I was there," was his preferred introduction. "There" meant Europe in the 1940s. He enjoyed telling stories about spying on the "Reds," as he referred to the people in the Soviet Union. My personal favorite incident occurred in Minsk, the capital of present-day Belarus, where he photographed "people of interest." He often had trouble operating his camera, allowing his target to get away before he could take a photo. Once, in broad daylight, while trying to focus it, a Russian woman, who he described as "gorgeous," approached him and in perfect English invited him to her apartment, where she kept Harry hidden for two weeks to protect him from German agents and save him from the dangers of the spy trade. At least that's what he told us. No matter how much we badgered him that the woman in all likelihood worked for the KGB and had prevented him from snapping photographs, he stuck to his story that a beautiful lady saved him in wartime. Harry thought the idea that she was a KGB agent was crazy.

He liked telling the story of the time he rode a German World War II-era BMW R75 motorcycle and sidecar combination belonging to an unnamed German general off a ship in New Jersey. He drove the BMW straight to storage, parked it, walked away, left the U.S., and didn't return for years.

He never said very much regarding Watergate and Nixon's resignation, the major U.S. events of the time, though he had plenty to say about Communism, which he hated with a passion. With the mere utterance of the word "Communism," Harry would go off on a reactionary, profanity-laden, commie-hating tirade. Once, after finishing a few small repairs at the home of the American nun doing social work, he came over and ranted about a political argument he had with her. "She is 90 percent Communist and 10 percent Catholic. I'm just as religious as the next guy, but Jesus Christ, the fucking Communists are up to no good."

When I said she was doing great things in the barrios, he cut me off, saying, "I don't care, and she's a commie."

Harry and his truck in front of our house in Maracaibo
(Photo by Mike Kendellen)

To humor him on the current state of American culture, I showed him a cover of the satirical magazine *National Lampoon* depicting a Russian woman athlete with a penis protruding from her gym trunks. It shocked Harry. "This is what the American people want?" he asked, assuming the story authentic. "Those commies are even worse than I imagined," he grumbled while grabbing the magazine on his way to the kitchen, looking for anyone to show the cover and berate the Soviets. When he found Ana having coffee, he fumed about the despicable Soviets.

I tried to tell him the publication was poking fun at politicians and that it was satire, but he wouldn't listen. So I told him another story I had read. A woman who once spent a night with disgraced Attorney

General John Mitchell afterward confided to a friend, "I thought John was a sap until I found his tap in my tush." Expecting at least a smile, Harry shrugged instead. "Just a typical guy."

If Harry believed what I said was true, it was a waste of time trying to explain the *National Lampoon*, which some newsstands in Maracaibo sold.

At fifty-five and not looking a day younger, he once wondered aloud if he should have done something else with his life, mentioning that maybe he should have been a doctor. He didn't see much of a future for himself in Venezuela—or for Venezuela either. After twenty years in the country, he still held Venezuelans in low regard. "They are just like Southern niggers," was one of his many one-liners, which said as much about him as his spy stories did. Harry was resigned to die alone in Venezuela. I felt sorry for him and often refrained from making wisecracks on whatever he was raving about at the time. Instead, I reminded myself of his favorite line: "Just remember, Harry told you."

After five months, I had adapted to AZUPANE. I enjoyed working there and liked my colleagues. But the future of Peace Corps remained precarious. When Volunteers finished their two-year service, they were not replaced. In the past eighteen months, only one new group of Volunteers had arrived. Peace Corps was planning to shift from urban education and agriculture programs to school gardens, home economics, and nutrition, with eighty-five Volunteers projected for 1975, down from 245 when I arrived in January 1974—but those plans, announced a month ago, were fading fast.

Washington insisted that training programs for new Volunteers could not proceed unless Venezuela agreed to provide some financial support for them over the next two years, a scenario not much different from the one Caracas faced a year prior when Washington first raised the idea of host countries increasing their contributions. Each time Caracas broached the subject with the government, they came back with their standard reply: "We will discuss this and give you our answer in a few months." A staff member confided over dinner in Maracaibo that the future of Peace Corps in Venezuela was all about money.

Caracas, not giving up, cabled Washington to emphasize that the Peace Corps, an American asset, showed support for national development by its mere presence. Various ministries that might benefit from Peace Corps assistance agreed in principle, they told headquarters, but they were unwilling to provide financial assistance despite the request being the equivalent of forty minutes of oil drilling. While the embassy was pleased to hear the Minister of State for Economic Planning Gumersindo Rodriguez say he wanted a long-term strategy whereby programs would fit into Venezuela's overall planning and priorities, they were stunned when Rodriguez expressed the most interest in a home economics program.

Despite the pleas from Caracas, by the end of August 1975, Washington had cancelled all future trainings and programs, leaving fewer than seventy Volunteers in the country; most would leave over the next five months. With money scarce, staff were laid off, and a few of the Americans transferred to other countries or left Peace Corps altogether. While closing a program has its share of trauma and drama, it was not unusual. From 1961 through 1973, Peace Corps closed sixteen offices, all but one for political reasons. After receiving the dismal updates, I wondered if I would be able to complete my two years of service.

I had been thinking of staying for a third year, but now was wondering if I should drop the idea. If I left, I could travel before returning to the U.S. and enrolling in graduate school, a typical scenario for many Volunteers after completing their service. Seeing South America was my priority. I would begin in Colombia and make my way to Ecuador, Peru, and Bolivia, followed by Chile, Argentina, and Brazil and then maybe Central America. Or maybe I should first fly to Buenos Aires, or to Rio de Janeiro, and head toward Chile, then up to Colombia before flying home. I considered various routes through South America, but the final choice would depend on money and my plans once I returned home. With ten months to go, nothing was definite.

I continued to stay apprised of Peace Corps matters from newsletters, occasional memos, and staff visits. I also received first-hand updates when the director came to Maracaibo. On one visit, he mentioned that the new U.S. ambassador in Caracas was Harry W. Shlaudeman, who had had a long career in the Foreign Service. Before being an assistant to Secretary of State Dean Rusk from 1967–69 during the Vietnam War, he had been the State Department desk officer for the Dominican Republic when the Marines invaded in 1965. More intriguing, he was stationed in Chile when the military toppled Allende in the 1973 coup.

Caracas Peace Corps staff pondered how Shlaudeman, with his background, would make his time in the country noteworthy. Venezuela wondered, too. The political parties opposed his appointment because of his presence in Chile and the Dominican Republic in the midst of political upheaval in those two countries. What problems could occur with him as the ambassador? Peter Stevens, the director, thinking out loud over dinner, said it wasn't evident what sort of mischief could happen in a country like Venezuela, which at the time was a friend of the United States and considered one of the most stable and wealthy countries in Latin America. As it turned out, Shlaudeman put most of his effort into backing and monitoring the nationalization of the oil industry. After a year, he returned to Washington to be the assistant secretary of state for inter-American affairs.

Venezuela's concern over possible U.S. entanglement in its domestic affairs was not unfounded. In December 1974, *The New York Times* published an article by Seymour Hersh, who had earlier won a Pulitzer Prize for his reporting on the massacre by American soldiers of as many as five hundred Vietnamese civilians in the My Lai hamlet. He also detailed covert operations involving assassination attempts on foreign leaders and interference in local elections. The following year, the Senate Select Committee to Study Governmental Operations with Respect to Intelligence Activities, better known as the Church Committee after its chairman, Senator Frank Church of Idaho, revealed the CIA had played a role in ousting presidents in Chile, the Dominican Republic, and Guatemala. The Venezuela media reported on the hearings. Around the same time, Farrar Straus & Giroux published *Inside the Company: CIA Diary* by Philip Agee, a ten-year veteran of the agency. The book was an instant bestseller and a sensation in Latin America.

Agee identified nearly 250 people, most of them in Mexico, Uruguay, and Ecuador, who had a connection to the Agency. In his 640-page tome, Venezuela is mentioned just once. As a CIA employee based in Washington, DC in the late 1950s, Agee revealed he had conducted background checks on Venezuelans applying to work at the Creole Petroleum Corp., the Venezuelan subsidiary of Exxon, to root out potential troublemakers. According to Agee, the company wanted CIA assistance in employment decisions, a service the agency provided for U.S. corporations in Latin America. The oil giant later denied any affiliation with U.S. intelligence.

State Department cables indicate that *Inside the Company: CIA Diary* irritated them, as did Agee's post-publication statements and activities, though the CIA limited its public comments to saying he was an agent of the Cuban government. *The Economist* called the book, "inescapable reading," whereas William Colby, the CIA director at the time, said it was "terrible." A more neutral assessment came from the former CIA station chief in Cairo, who said the book was "as complete an account of spy work as is likely to be published anywhere."

In 1996, the CIA declassified an internal review of the book that ends with a personal attack on Agee: "Like other adolescents of the 1960s who have vented their impatient and frustrated idealism in destructive acts, Agee, out of touch with his deeper feelings, vents his rage and displays a towering arrogance. By virtue of the trust placed in him, he damages more than himself."

David Atlee Phillips, a twenty-five-year CIA veteran in the clandestine division operations, wrote in *The Night Watch* that Agee's book was accurate in the people and organizations it revealed, and the CIA was forced to make changes.

Peter Stevens, the Peace Corps director, did not like the book. He once advised a Volunteer not to read it, but if he already had, he should burn it rather than give it to someone else or donate it to the Peace Corps library in Caracas. This was a dinner conversation that spread across the country. The director's opinion of *Inside the Company*, and whatever suggestions he made about sharing or destroying the book, had no influence on what the Volunteers did. However, a week after Stevens made his critical comments about the book over dinner, the Volunteer he'd spoken with concluded that Peace Corps should not be in Venezuela and resigned.

On one of my few trips to Caracas, I bought the book in a second-hand bookstore for half price. It was not as awful as Colby suggested. While reading it, I found the hundreds of names, organizations, and acronyms to be repetitious and tedious. Forty years later, though, I thought it was a fascinating read on CIA operations.

In response to the book, Congress passed the Intelligence Identities Protection Act in 1982, which made it a federal crime to intentionally reveal officers involved in covert operations. For the rest of his life, Agee was entangled in legal matters with the CIA and constantly addressing accusations he worked for the KGB and the DGI, the Cuban intelligence agency, *Dirección General de Inteligencia*. The FBI never arrested him, despite his frequent visits to the U.S. from Cuba, where he lived. In January 2008, he died after ulcer surgery in Cuba. *Granma*, Cuba's Communist Party newspaper, described him as a loyal friend.

When I arrived in Venezuela in January 1974, the Vietnam War was in its ninth year, unless you began counting in 1950 when the United States Military Assistance Advisory Group (MAAG) was established in Saigon or 1961 when a hundred Green Berets arrived, or March 1965, when President Lyndon Johnson sent 3,500 Marines. By 1974, no American troops remained in Vietnam, but the war dragged on until April 30, 1975, when North Vietnamese tanks burst through the gates of the presidential palace and South Vietnam surrendered. At the time, I was having a beer with Jeff and Brian. Brian, listening to the nightly BBC radio broadcast outside on the porch where the reception was better, ran into the house and proclaimed, "Saigon has fallen. Saigon has fallen. It's over and good riddance. We finally have Vietnam out of the way."

During the Vietnam War, the military met its recruitment goals through a draft. When I turned eighteen and registered with the Selective Service, an independent government agency, there were 380,000 American troops in Vietnam. I expected swift disqualification because I could not use my right arm. So I was surprised when I received my draft card and saw I had been classified 1-Y, making me eligible for service in the event of war or national emergency. Really? They would draft me into the military? I did not contest the decision. If the Army wanted to draft me, let them.

A year later, Nixon issued an executive order that called for a lottery as a means to determine who was selected to serve, replacing a system that seemed random and easily avoided if one had the right connections or could attend college or join the National Guard. At one time, Peace Corps Volunteers could receive two-year deferments— though not automatically, which led to the problem of Volunteers being drafted in the middle of their Peace Corps assignment, disrupting programs and commitments to foreign governments. The deferments ended with the lottery, a nationally televised event that took place on December 1, 1969. My number, based on my birthday, was 96 out of 365, meaning tens of thousands of eighteen- to thirty-five-year-olds were ahead of me, making it almost certain I would not be drafted even if I had been classified 1-A. A few weeks later, my new draft card arrived. This time, I was classified 4-F, which disqualified me from military service. I never heard from the U.S. Army again.

Far away from American domestic politics, adjusting to a new job and living in Maracaibo occupied my time. Ambivalent about the end of the war, my reaction was less exuberant than Brian's. All I could muster on hearing the news was, "Oh, yeah?" If a pollster had called me for my view, my answer would have been, "I have no opinion." In a letter home, I asked about the response to the war ending and remarked, "The Vietnam War is not over yet," adding that refugees coming to the United States would be the next phase of the war.

My mother related that people were not happy that Washington planned to resettle tens of thousands of Vietnamese who had no skills, no friends, and a language barrier. Nevertheless, the resettlement program continued. Since 1975, more than one million refugees from Vietnam have resettled in the U.S.

The fall of Vietnam was of little importance in Latin America. Stories with more local interest involved Cuba and Fidel Castro; the revelations of the CIA involvement in the 1973 coup in Chile; nationalizing the oil companies in Venezuela; and most important of all in Maracaibo, the various predictions of how well the Zulia *Aguilas* (Eagles), the local team in the Venezuelan winter baseball league, would do.

Although I read *El Panorama*, the major Maracaibo newspaper, I kept up with U.S. and world events through weekly visits to the Venezuelan-American Cultural Center (CEVAZ) library to read *The New York Times, Sports Illustrated* and *The New Yorker*. One story not reported in the Venezuelan papers was that Jimmy Hoffa, the former head of the Teamsters Union, was missing, presumably murdered by the Mafia and buried in a landfill in New Jersey. *TIME* published a piece on a new rock star named Bruce Springsteen, whose music they described as "primal." I had never heard of him. The article did not inspire me enough to order a tape at one of the several stores that made cassette tapes of whatever music you wanted, a common and cheap way to buy albums at the time. Many decades later, however, I became a fan. My wife Barb and I went to his concerts, the first one being in Washington, DC one a year after September 11, 2001, when he released *The Rising*.

The 1976 U.S. presidential campaign was already getting underway with announcements and preparations for the primaries. On the Republican side were President Gerald Ford, the incumbent, and Ronald Reagan. Polls showed Hubert Humphrey led Henry Jackson and George Wallace for the Democratic Party nomination. Wallace was famous for his "Segregation Now, Segregation Tomorrow, and Segregation Forever" speech at his 1963 gubernatorial inauguration. Jimmy Carter had yet to enter the race. Wallace would later drop out of the race when he failed to win a single primary.

The local media reported members of the Venezuelan Congress complaining that the U.S. had secret plans to seize the oil fields to prevent Venezuela from nationalizing them and setting higher oil prices, mirroring similar reports in the United States that also included options for dealing with Saudi Arabia if a Middle East war broke out and OPEC raised oil prices again.

I thought Venezuela was being excessively paranoid. The talk of an attack seemed like nothing more than a derivative of a phantom CIA plot, and the making of an anti-American conspiracy fantasy. But I was wrong. Years later, a classified Congressional Research Service (CRS) report from 1975, released in 1996, confirmed Venezuela's concerns. The CRS had concluded troops could occupy the oil fields in Venezuela, Nigeria, and Libya without much of a fight if the United States could surmount European objections. The rationale was that the Marines and Navy only had to defeat a small Venezuelan army and sink their fleet of three submarines.

But as we know, the proposed attacks never occurred. No one panicked, and unlike the lack of post-invasion long-term planning for Iraq in 2003, the CRS warned that the biggest concern about the plan was whether Washington had the will and capacity to capture and take control of the underwater petroleum sources after sinking Venezuela's navy.

As I did in San Carlos, I went to a lot of movies in Maracaibo, averaging about a one a week. I saw *Citizen Kane* at the university theater along with the nine other film buffs that night who bought a ticket. Other movies were Sam Peckinpah's *Bring Me the Head of Alfredo Garcia* starring Warren Beatty; *The Passenger* by Michelangelo Antonioni with Jack Nicholson; and *Harakiri*, a 1962 Japanese film about the samurai and suicide in the seventeenth century, which I thought was a good movie. In

2012, film critic Roger Ebert put it on his list of the greatest movies ever. Others films I saw included *Chinatown* with Jack Nicholson and Faye Dunaway; *Airport 1975* with Karen Black, Charlton Heston, and George Kennedy; *Maracaibo Petroleum Company*, a Venezuelan documentary; *Godfather Part II*; and *Tommy* by Ken Russell.

It had been months since I'd heard allegations of Peace Corps/CIA connections when *El Vespertino*, an afternoon tabloid, reported the CIA was operating in Maracaibo and that the Peace Corps and the Maracaibo Symphony were infested with spies. At the house, we rolled our eyes and chuckled at the preposterous theory; the same old bullshit. I assumed many, particularly university students, believed it. No one at AZUPANE mentioned the article.

The same paper criticized President Carlos Andres Pérez for his lack of progress in putting the country on the path to prosperity as he promised during his election campaign two years before. The list of complaints began with the quality of care at hospitals. It continued with bad mail service, too few police patrolling the streets, and criticism that law enforcement preferred to shoot first and ask questions later. The schools were getting worse, and the cost of living had risen 20 percent in Maracaibo in the last year, resulting in demands for a raise on top of the 10 percent wage increase Pérez had decreed twelve months earlier.

Despite the dissatisfaction and legitimate criticisms, he remained an attractive politician. He had near unanimous backing for his plan to nationalize the petroleum industry, a development Venezuelans had no doubt would improve their lives. In less than six months, Venezuela would own all the oil in its territory and would control the accompanying infrastructure to extract, process, and ship it around the world. The future looked bright, with billions of dollars expected in new revenue. Pérez didn't seem concerned about the complaints of lost letters and packages and trigger-happy cops. When asked about the problems at a press conference, he said, "I can't perform miracles."

The Maracaibo Symphony Orchestra, an international collection of players and an alleged CIA front, played every Thursday night from October to June at the Symphony Hall, a welcome change from the standard array of movies shown in the theaters. Poles, Americans, Russians, French, Italians, Chileans, Uruguayans, and Hungarians worked twelve hours a week and earned $675 a month, the same as a teacher at the American school and more than three times the pay of a Peace Corps Volunteer. It was an excellent salary for the time.

Boris Pergamenshikov, a cello player from the Soviet Union who had won the Tchaikovsky Prize at twenty-six, gave a guest concert. *Maracuchos* (the term for people born and raised in Maracaibo) were a tough crowd for any event, so it was impressive when they gave Pergamenshikov a standing ovation—only the second one I witnessed in Venezuela, the first being for a matador killing a bull at a bullfight. He showed his appreciation by returning to the stage for an encore. Two years later, Pergamenshikov defected to West Germany, where he lived for the rest of his life.

The biggest musical event of the year was the Elvin Jones concert sponsored by the Venezuelan-American Cultural Center. With tickets going for $1.25, the show sold out. The American Consul in Maracaibo acted as the master of ceremonies. As the concertgoers entered the theater and chatted in the aisles, waiting for the performance to begin, he greeted them with, "How's it going with you folks tonight? Can't complain? Hot enough for you? Drinks are available in the lobby. Take your time."

Weeks earlier, I had met him when I renewed my passport. He asked me what Peace Corps was doing in Maracaibo, which surprised me. I had expected the U.S. government representative to know about the country's own projects in the city where he worked, if not the whole country. After briefing the Foreign Service officer on the Peace Corps, he mentioned a former Volunteer he knew in the Andes Mountains near Merida, who was operating the first commercial mushroom farm in the country. The consul said Venezuela used to import mushrooms from Ecuador, but thanks to the former Volunteer, it was now able to export them.

I recognized a lot of familiar faces in the crowd. The bald director of the Maracaibo Symphony stood near the refreshment table talking to a woman I often saw at the Cultural Center reading room. I wasn't sure if they were married, but they seemed to make a delightful duo. Ann and Chris, a British couple, who with their dog Spot had arrived in Maracaibo three years earlier after they shipwrecked north of the city while sailing around the Caribbean, were chatting away in the aisle. Chris was employed by a computer firm and Ann taught primary school. They didn't like Tory for reasons never explained, and told him in no uncertain terms to stop coming over to their house. Jim Larson, who worked for a Texas-based petroleum parts company, was there with his wife, Laura, and nodded hello to me. Anita, their daughter, attended the American school on Bella Vista Avenue along with other children of oil industry employees.

Steve, from the Maracaibo Symphony, who I hadn't seen in months, was standing near the exit. The Symphony had recently suffered a 25 percent budget cut, and several of the Americans, whose approach to their job was "No Pay, No Play," quit and went home rather than take a salary cut. Steve was one of the few who stayed, despite hating Venezuela, Venezuelans, and Maracaibo, in that order. He wanted to buy dope, or as the *El Vespertino* called it, "the damn herb," for himself and other symphony members, and was hoping his contact might be at the concert. A French woman, who I often ran into at the symphony, was already seated near the front. Behind her sat the librarian from the American-Venezuelan Cultural Center, whom I'd met earlier in the day when buying concert tickets. It was no surprise to see Nerva, the daughter of a millionaire who at one time volunteered at AZUPANE, at the concert. Full of energy, I watched her run to the other side of the theater when she had spotted a friend. I was amazed at the number of people I knew.

An hour after the concert was to begin, the audience, about an even mix of expatriates and Venezuelans, woke up when they heard, "Ladies and gentlemen, Elvin Jones." Five musicians walked out on the stage as the crowd whistled and applauded. I knew next to nothing about Jones, except that he once bested Ginger Baker, the founder of the British group Cream that included Jack Bruce and Eric Clapton, in a drum battle. But I did not expect a fifty-year-old man to walk out wearing Bermuda shorts and a plaid shirt. I assumed he was younger and better dressed. I guess no one had told him shorts were worn only at the beach in Venezuela, or maybe he was aware and just didn't give a shit. You can't always tell with people. He fiddled with the wires and cords that connected his drums to the amplifiers and then played for two hours. Elvin Jones died in 2004, and the 2012 *Beware of Mister Baker* documentary on Ginger Baker, much to my surprise, included scenes of the two in a drum-off.

So much of living abroad is about understanding culture, including your own. After eighteen months, I still struggled with

American and Venezuelan cultural differences. In one letter home, I described my complicated feelings on Venezuelan culture:

> If you're down and out and singing the blues, pack your bags and come on down to exotic Venezuela. Yes, here in a world dominated by men, where the women refuse to lead the revolution, and where they prefer to sit at home and paint themselves up in the hope Don Juan would soon arrive and propose, sealing an unadventurous life. That isn't all. It also has Los Llanos, the Plains, where cowboys roam; the jungles where the animals wander; and the Andes Mountains where life is quiet and peaceful. Venezuela is urban, and Maracaibo is a distant second to Caracas, the cultural and political center of the country.
>
> The oil industry, run by Texans in the state of Zulia with Maracaibo as its capital, provides the revenue to keep the economy moving. The tall Texans stand out with their ten-gallon hats driving their flashy convertibles down Bella Vista Avenue often find themselves at traffic lights behind donkey carts and their owners, who earn less in a week what the oilmen spend for lunch. It ain't Houston.
>
> After living in Venezuela for almost two years, I have come to respect the culture. They just do things differently. Sure, the public services are inefficient and poorly maintained. Nothing runs on time even though everyone wears a watch. Life revolves around a siesta (nap) and a fiesta (party). There is baseball, bullfighting, beer, and a lottery. Despite being the hottest city in the country, Maracaibo is more known as the coldest city because the air conditioning is on full blast in hotels, restaurants, offices, and shopping centers. I never sit near the air conditioner in a restaurant so as not to catch a cold and sometimes I wear a sweater to the movies. Venezuela is expensive but has its benefits, so bring money if you come.

The men were rude and arrogant, and the loud, vocal, and social aspects of the culture were not my cup of tea. Francois de Pons, a representative of the French government in Caracas in the early years of the nineteenth century, was close to the mark when he wrote in *Travels in South America*, a memoir of his time in Venezuela, that men from Maracaibo, known as *Maracuchos*, lacked character:

> After allowing the inhabitants of this city to possess activity, genius, and courage, we have nothing further to say in their praise. They are accused of violating their promises, and even of attempting to break through written engagements. Their character, in this respect, is so notorious, every stranger whom business induces to visit Maracaybo, (sic) affirms, it would be much better to enter into commercial speculations with the women, because they appear themselves to possess the sincerity and good sense that are everywhere else considered as belonging mainly to men.

I loved the tropical fruits, such as coconut, guava, mango, melon, papaya, and pineapple, and was shocked at the amount of sugar people consumed, which I associated with the number of overweight people I saw. The problem has persisted. In 2014, the World Health Organization reported that 68 percent of Venezuelans over the age twenty were overweight, the highest rate in South America; ironically, they attributed this to the food shortages caused by the faltering economy. In response, President Nicolas Maduro's government announced they hoped to cut in half the 40 percent rate of obesity among Venezuelans by 2019.

A friend wrote to ask about consciousness-raising in Venezuela, an uncommon question about a foreign country. After Venezuela, I worked and traveled in thirty countries, and no one ever again asked me if I met people who had raised or were on the road to raising their consciousness. But I liked the question and considered it in the Venezuelan context before replying. I wrote:

> Venezuela needs consciousness raising. They are shit upon all the time by the authorities. The people are like robots. They are conformist. I wish just once someone would raise their middle finger to an authority figure.

Now and then I would spot Mormon missionaries wearing their ubiquitous white shirts and black ties pounding the pavement in search of converts while never appearing to sweat. Though I never met any

Mormons, I did meet the Children of God—also known as Jesus Freaks—when two young Venezuelans came out of nowhere and jumped in the backseat of a taxi with me, introducing themselves as members of the cult. After a quick hello, they announced they loved me and I was welcome to their home anytime. I groaned to myself. They wrote their names and address on the front of the pamphlet containing Bible verses and predictions by the group's founder, David Brandt Berg, that America would have an apocalyptic end.

A few weeks later, I ran into the same couple at a movie theater. They again pushed their way into the taxi I had flagged. Upset that I had not visited them and their six housemates, they began reciting what I had read in the pamphlet. I raised my hand, saying, "Wait. I'll talk to you if you don't bring up religion." The man switched gears and said he had lived in Southern California and that his father was wealthy. I couldn't tell from his tone if he was being critical of him, or if he was just bragging that his daddy was rich. The conversation stalled and thankfully the taxi arrived at my destination. I said goodbye and never saw them again.

I was always curious to hear what Americans thought about Venezuela and how Venezuelans viewed the United States, other than their assessments of our foreign policy. One of the AZUPANE staff members received a letter from a friend who was teaching political science at a high school in the U.S. The students, he said, while providing no explanation, assumed Venezuela would be the next Latin American country to go Communist. The conclusion perplexed the teacher. Didn't they know Venezuela had a healthy economy based on free-market principles, unlike Communist countries? Why did they think Communism was a threat to Venezuela?

El Nacional reported that members of the Socialist party attended the Third World Writers and Thinkers Symposium at Sacramento State University in California and afterward traveled to other universities. The importance of the article is what Americans were telling their guests. Americans surprised the touring socialists with their peculiar misconceptions about Venezuela and their general ignorance of the country, starting from the fact that nearly every American they met was unaware that Venezuela even produced oil, much less was a founding member of Organization of Petroleum Exporting Countries (OPEC). More insulting still was the total lack of awareness during the Socialist

Party's cross-country trip that Venezuela was a democracy that debated freely and passed legislation before nationalizing the oil industry, a process which ended with a bill the president signed into law, one of the proudest moments in the country's history. The oil companies were not seized illegally. The visit was quite a shock.

I wrote in my journal that September and October 1975 were the most amazing months of my life up to that point. I don't know why. Forty years later, my wife corrected me, saying that the most amazing month of my life was May 2001, when we got married.

I cannot recall what made me write that at the time, but I am certain watching the World Series between the Boston Red Sox and Cincinnati Reds on a twelve-inch black-and-white television in Tory and Ana's room was not the reason. Besides, nine months into the job, I was in a funk over it, especially since I regretted transferring from the Recreation program to Social Conduct at AZUPANE.

Nine

The Grind

After five months in Recreation, I transferred to Social Conduct as part of an overall reorganization of the program. At the same time, AZUPANE hired Carlos Sanchez, a psychologist from Uruguay, as the head of operations. One of his first acts was to change the schedule to a regular Monday to Friday 8-11 and 3-6 routine, which eliminated Wednesday afternoon excursions. My days at the pool, dunking on a seven-foot hoop, swinging from trees or playing on a swing, were over. Under the old timetable, we changed groups every two hours, but now we worked with the same kids all day. It was a bigger adjustment than I expected.

Under the new plan, the occasional two-hour field trip to the city was dropped leaving only the excursions to the beach as outside activities. It was unfortunate, because the city field trips were good experiences for the kids. The type of city excursions we'd been doing had varied. Over the past few months, the older kids came over to the house one afternoon to practice cooking, and we took the younger kids to the supermarket and to the airport to expose them to a wider world than their home and AZUPANE. At the supermarket, we put three-year-old Nerio in a shopping cart while six other kids hung on to it as we rambled up and down the aisles filling the cart with food while "The Pusher" — "goddamn the pusher man" —by Steppenwolf blasted over the speakers. Nerio suffered from severe epilepsy and had difficulty walking. After a few steps he would lean forward, lose his balance and fall face down, increasing the possibility of an epileptic seizure. His family considered him an embarrassment. Yet, Nerio liked to run and took advantage of the sizeable AZUPANE grounds where he could fall on soft grass. But he looked happy in the shopping cart, having fun with the other kids.

We also took the kids to the airport, which was open to the public back then, unlike today's airports. It was common to see families at the departure gates bidding farewell to loved ones or welcoming siblings and parents home. With the kids, we ambled through the terminal as if it were a shopping mall. They loved the commotion and activity. We generated lots of stares as a dozen developmentally disabled kids hobbled and limped past passengers and airport employees.

On one excursion to Plaza Bolívar in central Maracaibo, a policeman mistook me for one of the kids. Apparently, the combination of my arm and my beard made him stupid; he told the staff to get "Fidel" back on the bus. The new schedule eliminated these outings, and instead, we stayed inside AZUPANE's lush grounds all day, every day.

In Social Conduct, we taught the kids everything from greeting people to table manners to toilet training, which seemed worthwhile, as once a week without fail, one of them would fill their pants in the middle of an activity. But their parents needed to follow up at home in order for them to really learn the necessary life skills. My Spanish was insufficient to teach them how to comb their hair, brush their teeth, eat at the table, and act appropriately in front of others. I missed our days at the pool and playing games in Recreation where informality, a lack of structure and having fun, were the rules. Social Conduct was too much about getting the kids to follow orders or getting them to listen to you. Teaching personal hygiene to seven- to ten-year-olds was not my cup of tea, even if I had spoken better Spanish. I felt like a babysitter, sitting on the lawn or a swing or indoors on the floor while trying to teach manners. It wasn't my kind of work. Less than a month after I transferred I realized I had made a mistake.

I worked with two Venezuelan women. Johanna, the coordinator of the section, was thirty-three-years-old, attractive, single, and the oldest of eight children. She ran Social Conduct with authority and got things done, never afraid to issue an order. A stylish dresser, she would wear a wig to parties. Whenever I saw her in one, I would stare in disbelief and ask myself, "Why?" Mila, her friend, was proficient at ordering me around when Johanna was absent and did whatever she instructed her to do. Though I liked Johanna, too, and got used to working with her, she issued too many orders for my liking.

Johanna and Mila needed a man in the group to teach the older boys about grooming and oral hygiene. But I suspected the real reason they wanted a man was to help with two of the older boys in particular. Roberto Jose and Ramon Eduardo were active and aggressive teenagers, both severely mentally disabled but physically strong, and two of the most challenging kids to work with; they needed full-time attention. All the men assigned to Social Conduct before me had transferred out. The men were replaceable the two women believed, and I was the latest replacement.

Roberto Jose could be aggressive and disruptive. He made sounds of varying decibels and pitches, unable to enunciate a word. Because he was blind, couldn't speak, had a temper, and was unpredictable, most staff were uncomfortable working with him. He was our biggest challenge. Without warning, he would throw whatever he got his hands on and strip down to his underwear. In terms of his family situation, though, we had less of a challenge to deal with, because Roberto Jose was the son of the co-founders of AZUPANE. Unlike most other parents, Roberto and Elsa Lara took their 16-year-old son shopping, to the beach, on family visits, and all around the city, even though he created a scene wherever they went. His mother accompanied him to functions and proudly stood with her son. From what I observed, many of the other parents never did that. Many, too embarrassed to be in public with their "problem" children, kept their disabled child in the house unless they were going to AZUPANE. Meanwhile, Ramon Eduardo, because of epilepsy, could not control the movement in his arms and hands. He would disrupt snack time by grabbing food from the table, where the kids sat during breaks, and throwing it across the room. At home, his father sat and watched him, afraid that at any moment he would destroy furniture or accidentally hurt his mother or siblings. Dario assigned him to me one day at the YMCA pool. We always first treaded water at the shallow end before working our way to the deeper end. That day, with ten minutes remaining before we returned to AZUPANE, I left Ramon Eduardo alone, assuming one of the staff would keep an eye on him, and went to the other end for my informal session of water aerobics, a routine I followed every time I was at the pool. Suddenly, someone was yelling he couldn't see Ramon Eduardo. I climbed out of the Olympic-sized pool and ran along the side, looking under the water for him. The lifeguards, who had been standing around in tracksuits chatting, dove in and found him, face down. They pulled him out, and delivered CPR, and an ambulance took him to the hospital. When I visited him the next day, he was out of danger. He was back at AZUPANE the following week. Even now, forty years later, I realize Ramon Eduardo almost drowned because I left him unsupervised, thinking another staff member would watch him.

Johanna assigned me to keep Roberto Jose and Ramon Eduardo from disrupting the other children during activities, which meant taking them outside and away from the group. Whenever they created a disturbance, I would hear, "Hey, Mike, take them for a walk," which I considered babysitting. Though unhappy, I was reluctant to express my concerns to her or the chief of operations or even offer suggestions to improve the situation; I didn't have many, anyway. I lacked the Spanish to be subtle and diplomatic and the maturity to accept that management might rebuff my ideas.

During this time, I sat around too much, especially cross-legged in the lotus position on the floor. When I worked in Recreation, I was at the pool three days a week, and most of the rest of the time I was walking, running and stretching. In contrast, working in Social Conduct required no physical exertion. As a sign of how bad things were, I wondered if I would be better off coaching baseball back in San Carlos rather than staying in Maracaibo. Feeling miserable, in a letter to a friend I wrote,

".... I sit on my ass and am bossed around by a couple of women."

At the time, I was reading *Siddhartha*, a tale about the quest for peace and understanding, by Herman Hesse, the winner of the 1946 Nobel Prize for Literature, a favorite author on college campuses in the 1960s, and one of the most read and translated European authors of the twentieth century. At the house, we had collected most of his novels from poaching copies from the Peace Corps libraries in Caracas and Barquisimeto. One book reviewer suggested reading *Siddartha* at a slow pace, preferably late at night when no one else was around, and I could understand why. The book made me think of my situation at AZUPANE. Siddhartha's son searched for answers to life on his terms, but realized that a threat met with another threat can cause violence, accomplishing nothing. And, if war results in death and nothing can be achieved after death or killing others what purpose does conflict serve? I saw a parallel with my situation with Johanna and Mila. They were raised in an environment where people looked at the world in a different way than I did, so conflict was inevitable, if I understood Siddartha correctly. So, what would direct criticism of Social Conduct accomplish? Johanna would probably take it the wrong way. Even though I might feel better if I criticized what we were doing in Social Conduct, if I went too far, I might be out of a job.

It wasn't just the bad situation in Social Conduct that bothered me; the entire working environment at AZUPANE had changed. Morale had sunk to its lowest level since I started six months before. The staff seemed weary and strained. The vision the Padre had set out for AZUPANE was very different from what now occurred every day. It was a little like the Peace Corps: the jobless and under-employed Volunteers did not match the ideal espoused in Washington, DC.

Health matters caused absenteeism among both the staff and the kids to rise to nearly fifty percent. The ailments among the staff varied from a dislocated ankle to back pain and kidney problems to a stretched tendon to a cyst that had to be removed. One woman was pregnant. Another missed a week of work with a cold. The recreation coordinator was on his honeymoon though staff who lived near him reported seeing him painting his house. Others complained about the difficulties of working with developmentally disabled kids and about their various issues with the kids' siblings and mothers. Nothing much was going right.

The days dragged on, and it seemed like everyone, including me, was just going through the motions. The new schedule, which had us spending three-hour blocks of time with one group, was not well-received. Adding to the problem, fundraising efforts by the Padre and the Board lagged, resulting in a shortage of money to buy even the basic materials needed to conduct classes, lessons and activities.

I fell into a funk and slept away weekends. Once to relieve some stress, I went out in the rain to throw a Frisbee with Tory. Afterward, I felt better. One morning waking up irritable and tired of babysitting I stayed home from work. If the job didn't improve in my remaining time, I would consider leaving before next March. I should have been taking part in community development in an impoverished country rather than working at a private institution in an oil-rich nation in the initial stages of an economic boom. On the positive side, I was helping the underprivileged: the developmentally disabled and people with other disabilities. As usual, there were pros and cons to what I was doing.

The Grind

When Jeff was in Maracaibo, I rode on the back of his motorcycle. But when he was in the U.S. trying to get a visa so he could return and work at AZUPANE as a paid employee, I took the bus to work. I left the house by 7:15 and walked eight blocks to the bus stop to wait for the unreliable Route Six bus. Without a schedule, it was impossible to know when it would arrive, making my arrival time at AZUPANE a guessing game. I would often wait for twenty minutes, and frequently, two buses would arrive at the same time, one following the other. I stood most of the way, holding onto the nearest seat. The bus stopped whenever a rider clapped or whistled, signaling they wanted to get off. Most of the time, as far as I remembered, the driver ignored my waving and drove right by my stop, or he wouldn't notice or would pretend not to hear the claps and whistles from passengers because the music he was playing was too loud. My alternative was a three-mile walk.

The Padre could be petty. At the weekly staff meeting, when morale was at its lowest, he reported that the kids lost eight hours of activities each week preparing to board the bus to go home. This could be an ordeal because most of the kids needed help getting on the bus and each had a lunch box or a change of clothes. The staff, though, did not like hearing they were wasting time, and they were in no mood for criticism. One fired back at him, "Don't worry about it, you will get your time when we are on 24-hour duty at the beach for three days straight." Touché! The Padre, hating confrontation, did not reply to the jab at his resistance to changing the policy on compensation time after the weekend excursions.

The Padre ruled like a dictator. He seldom delegated and didn't like to be criticized or to openly disagree with staff, but he loved to engage at an intellectual level on any topic. For all his faults, he was intensely charismatic, always positive, and upbeat and never admitted to a problem he couldn't solve. He raised money to keep AZUPANE open and advocated for people with disabilities. Unfortunately, he spent an inordinate amount of time fundraising and not enough on the program of daily activities, which he left to the chief of operations.

From his decade in the U.S., the Padre adopted the habit of being punctual, the antithesis to the Venezuelan convention of being late. Schedules and punctuality mattered to him. One afternoon I arrived at three sharp. The Padre was alone at the entrance, a rare occurrence. I wondered what was wrong. He told me, with uncharacteristic disdain, that when the kids arrived at two-thirty, no staff was present to help them off the bus, so he'd lock the gate to remind us that arriving at three o'clock was unacceptable. He wouldn't open it to let me in, making me enter the grounds from the office which took me ten minutes to do. At the next meeting, he introduced timesheets, which struck everyone as contrary to his anti-institutional views. I was exempt because AZUPANE did not pay me.

The Padre had his quirks. He berated Brian for pouring a drink for himself after bartending all night at the seventh-anniversary party. He told him to pay a dollar for it like the guests did, implying AZUPANE could not afford to give away something that could be sold, even one glass of soda with a shot of rum for a staff member as recognition for his effort. Once, he asked a couple how it was possible, despite having been married for five years, that they didn't have children.

In one of his more bizarre moments, he reprimanded Jeff for dating one of the women at AZUPANE. At the end of a weekend beach excursion, they did not return in time from a walk on the beach to catch the bus back to Maracaibo. The bus left without them because the driver wanted to get home for dinner. Jeff and Betty had no other choice than to walk the five miles to the nearest highway to catch a bus. The Padre heard about this, and the next day he called Jeff to his office to explain what happened. He had certain suspicions. "Did the two of you engage in foreplay during your walk?" he asked.

Jeff wanted to fall off his chair laughing, but instead just chuckled and saved the laughs for when he re-told the story at the house that night. "Look, Padre, your staff abandoned us," he began, "The only thing on our mind was getting back to Maracaibo before dark. We were not thinking of foreplay." The Padre did not comment except to say that if Jeff continued to date women on the staff, he would fire them. "Then you must fire me, too," Jeff retorted. The Padre ignored the comment and told Jeff to return to work.

In the 1970s, programs for the developmentally disabled changed, placing an emphasis on the individual and identifying long- and short-term goals, including quantifiable and measurable behavioral benchmarks as the disability world moved away from institutionalization and its dehumanizing impact. The aim now was to improve people's quality of life and foster happiness, vague goals which few agreed on how to define, much less how to measure progress towards achieving them. AZUPANE's planning was beginning to reflect these challenges and developments.

Today's crazy world of big data being used to make sense of and interpret most everything was decades away in the mid-1970s. The AZUPANE motto *"Queremos Realizarnos"* ("we want to realize ourselves") was both a goal and a principle about the development of one's abilities and talents. Attempting to achieve these aims through social interaction, music, recreation and learning to perform basic daily tasks was not conducive to collecting data, which presented a quandary for the Padre. He needed some way to measure progress and success in the program for a presentation he was preparing to give at an upcoming conference in Mexico City on how AZUPANE could be a model for working with the developmentally disabled. At a staff meeting a month before the November symposium, he got right to the point: "We have no statistics, and I will need some for my presentation. How can we measure the progress the kids are making?"

No one suggested any ideas for how to collect data or what kind to gather. At that point, we didn't even take notes of what we observed while working. What could be documented from simple every day activities? Because the majority of the kids were under twelve, some of their changes in behavior could be attributed to simply growing up, but without testing or some form of measurement that provided data, personal development would be difficult to assess. We assumed the kids progressed, even if it was slow and sometimes, barely discernible but what role did AZUPANE play in that progression? The social workers interviewed the parents, visited homes and wrote qualitative evaluations, but they never shared their findings either in meetings or informally. If each child had goals to achieve, the staff were not aware of them.

Given all the headaches, and assuming that nothing would change in the coming months, I drafted a request to move my termination date forward thirty days, which was permissible within the rules. There was no point in staying longer than necessary. What did one less month of service matter with six to go? But did I want to quit before the end of two years? I enjoyed AZUPANE; it just happened to be in a bad phase at the moment.

I almost chose not to send the letter. Instead, I thought about my future. I reasoned that with a firm departure time, I could plan my post-Peace Corps days in a more serious manner. My latest itinerary had me flying to Buenos Aires and making my way back to the U.S. by bus and train on two thousand dollars. I had no idea if this was feasible. But it sounded appealing, so I mailed the letter asking to leave next February instead of March. The Caracas office approved my request without asking questions.

I also pondered what it would be like to go home. I assumed that a few weeks after I returned I would miss the Venezuelan lifestyle. Those first weeks would be fun, and then I would find a job and get back into an American routine. Graduate school looked like a better choice. Living in Venezuela had made me more interested in the United States and the American way of life and its values. As a student, I could further explore what made America tick. Or, if that didn't work out, I could become a journalist. My plan was so flexible that at any moment, day, or week, it could change.

I had already received an application form for an American Studies program and was having difficulty completing it. The admissions office required a one-page essay on my professional goals and how my particular interests related to what I planned to study. I suffered from writer's block, possibly because I didn't have any long-term goals, and I wasn't going to invent them. I considered telling the school that working in the urban jungles of Venezuela consumed so much of my time that sorting out the rest of my life was not in the cards. Besides, writing a ten-year personal plan impeded my thinking through the logistics of travelling to La Paz from Argentina five months from now.

My second draft was more whimsical than the first one. "Dear Mr. Dean," I began, "I am struggling with envisioning life in the United States after two and a half years outside the country. If all goes according to plan, I hope to be the resident intellectual at a technical college and win literary contests by writing sonnets in Esperanto. After three decades of that, I would examine Zen and the art of motorcycle maintenance, having been a frequent passenger on motorcycles in Maracaibo. At fifty-five, when I retire I will become a tour guide." I stopped at that, wanting to sleep on it and re-think the whole essay in the morning.

The next day, I composed a more banal and traditional letter, telling the school that my experience living overseas had made me more inquisitive about American culture and that rediscovering America through the windows of history, literature, and the arts piqued my interest in journalism as a profession. I posted the letter, along with the fifteen dollar application fee and waited to learn my fate.

I skipped the conference on disability in Mexico. The estimated cost for the two weeks, including a week of being a tourist, was equivalent to three months of travel in South America, a trade I wasn't willing to make. When AZUPANE closed for the duration, with most its staff in Mexico, I stayed in Maracaibo, glad to be away from work, only to face on-going drama at the house.

Money problems and the related tensions at the house resurfaced after a period of calm. Fernando, whose craft business always seemed on the verge of collapse, was behind on his rent, yet again. He spent more time at the house than out on the street peddling his products, which made me think he should put more effort into his work. Daniel, his assistant, quit and enrolled at the University of Zulia, leaving Fernando alone to produce and market the sandals, purses, bags, and key chains he designed. When Daniel flunked the university entrance exam, Fernando declined to hire him back, admitting he'd never liked the quality of his work, using the resignation as a way to get rid of him. Fernando then hired a teenager in the neighborhood as a replacement but fired him after a week for showing up every day with a hangover and sleeping it off in the workshop. After he left, Fernando discovered the kid had stolen a few tools and some clothes. Next, he found two other boys to assist him. It made no difference, as sales continued to lag, and Fernando still owed Tory his rent.

Yosera, our latest tenant, lost her job soon after she moved in. Her sister sent funds every month, which always seemed to arrive after the rent was due, and so she wound up owing us money. She did not help her cause when she traveled to Cúcuta, a free trade zone on the Venezuela-Colombia border where most items were cheaper than in Venezuelan stores, to shop for new clothes. She also was disrupting the system we'd created to share the cost of food. Each time one of us bought groceries we attached the receipts to the refrigerator, and at the end of the month Jeff, Tory, or I would calculate what each of us owed. When I calculated the expenses for October, I found Yosera's receipts didn't match the kind and quantity of food in the kitchen. Over the past two months, the amount of money we spent didn't correspond to what was in the refrigerator.

Fernando suspected she was trying to cheat us. When I told him about the latest food costs for the month, he flew into a rage and ripped the expenditure list off the refrigerator and threw it away, which suspended the food sharing plan. When he confronted Yosera on the discrepancy between what she claimed to buy and what was in the refrigerator, she denied even knowing about the system. But, if that was true, why did she attach receipts for sixty-one bolivars ($15) for the month? She couldn't explain it. We called a meeting to reduce the tension and discuss the food scheme. She agreed to pay off her debts and Fernando cooled down. He put the list back on the refrigerator door, and we resumed buying groceries to share and recording the purchases. It was the only way to manage the house.

Yosera caused us concern in more than just buying groceries. One of the Maracaibo newspapers reported that police had arrested three men in a local restaurant after a server overheard a conversation at a table about a pending drug sale. The server called the cops, and a short time later they turned up and arrested three individuals. As Yosera told us the next day, the police missed grabbing the person they were really seeking: her marijuana supplier.

In the fourteen months that I lived at the house, we received a steady, but not overwhelming, flood of guests. The latest was Juan, from Argentina, who appeared without warning. He had been traveling throughout South America for two years and in Colombia, his most recent stop, had been living on a farm near Santa Marta, a favorite destination for world travelers. He sold leather crafts on street corners much like Fernando did in Maracaibo. Looking for a business colleague, Fernando invited him to stay with us. He promised Juan's presence wouldn't interfere with paying off his debts—the last thing we needed was another non-paying tenant. We were skeptical that he could make much money from selling crafts on the streets of downtown Maracaibo. There weren't that many street vendors or pedestrians in the city. The climate might have had something to do with it; people preferred shopping in air-conditioned stores. The partnership got off to an ominous start when they went out together one evening and Fernando "lost" 100 bolivars, more than half of his rent. He didn't explain what happened. Restless, Juan didn't stay long and left for Colombia.

Work got better after the break, and I found I was enjoying myself again. I asked the Peace Corps to change my termination date back to the end of the March, as originally planned. Thanksgiving passed, marked by a dinner hosted by Sister Theresa, the American social worker at AZUPANE. Christmas was a few weeks away, which meant cooler temperatures, seasonal foods, and music. The radio played both local and traditional carols. Gaita music, which originated in the state of Zulia and sounded similar to a steel band, dominated the bars and discotheques this time of year. The neighbor kids roller-skated up and down the street in front of our house in pairs and threes. People painted their houses, a Christmas tradition in Venezuela. Wreaths adorned most doors and "Noel" signs hung from windows. The bank where I had a savings account, put up a tree in the lobby, shoppers packed the stores, and the local staff warned me that even with sales, everything was still overpriced.

The Christmas concert at the Zulia State Cultural Center included a chorus singing carols in English, Spanish, French and German. Among the highlights were a young girl singing "White Christmas" in English followed by the audience and chorus joining together to sing "I'm Dreaming of a White Christmas." A solo of "Holy Night" in Spanish by one of the oldest men in the chorus, capped off the night. It was so beautiful that people in the audience and chorus members alike cried, and if he had sung it again, maybe I would have cried, too.

I got into the Christmas spirit by trimming the orchids in front of the house which covered the telephone wires and enveloped the front gate. Six months prior, we had pruned the orchids, Venezuela's national flower, when our next-door neighbor had claimed the overgrown orchid bushes were the cause of her bad phone connection. It was only a matter of time before she would complain again. The phone company wouldn't cut back the bushes for us, so I resorted to using a machete, the one gardening tool we had. I hacked away while listening to Chilean protest music. Afterwards, I hung lights on the bushes.

We also lined the second-floor porch with green lights and put a red bulb in the entrance room where Tory and Jeff parked their motorcycles. We concocted a tree from a coat hanger and hung it from the ceiling along with a ring of lights suspended from curtain rods. In the middle of one wall was a picture of Suzanne, the Babe of the Month, taken from the back page of *El Vespertino*, the same newspaper that alleged the Peace Corps was a front for the CIA in Maracaibo. Next to her hung a leaflet from the Socialist Party called "The Anatomy of Christmas." On the other side of Suzanne was a map of Venezuela. A poster of Mick Jagger filled most of the opposite wall. Off to the side, stood a bookshelf with a statue of Buddha perched on it. A few ornaments hung from the dining room light.

At AZUPANE, we exchanged gifts. I was surprised they even considered the idea because several staff members were saying everyone complained about it last year. The Padre's secretary, who was new, had proposed the exchange, and as with other ideas discussed over the past months, there were no objections. Originally, the gift exchange would have excluded Jeff and me because the staff thought we couldn't afford it. We didn't own a car, wore t-shirts most of the time, and lived in a sparsely furnished house, all of which they interpreted to mean we were poor. Unlike the gift exchange I still have with my siblings today, where no one whispers a word about whose name they've drawn, at AZUPANE, everyone knew who had their name within minutes of the drawing. I drew Rosa, one of the five local volunteers. It was suggested I buy her a silk scarf, and that I shouldn't pay more than 15 to 20 bolivars (around $5). The next day, Rosa told me the Venezuelan volunteers didn't want to take part in the exchange because they didn't have the money to buy a present. "So don't get me anything," she said. When I asked one of the staff what I should do, he recommended I ignore her and get something for her anyway.

When I went shopping for a scarf, it was raining harder than it had in two years, according to the local paper. I stopped and took cover in a storefront on Avenue Cinco de Julio, a major shopping street, waiting for the rain to stop for a bit before venturing out again. After about an hour of running and taking cover every other block, I spotted the sign I was looking for: "*Pañuelos se Vende Aquí*" ("Scarves Sold Here"). I walked in the Fin de Siglo (End of Century) department store and asked where I could find the scarves. The salesperson in the rudest *Maracucho* manner possible, abruptly said, "*No hay.*" ("There aren't any.") Just as abruptly, I turned around, marched out and hurried next door and found one for three dollars. On the counter in front of the cash register was a jar of Snickers and Milky Way candy bars, which seemed like excellent Christmas gifts to myself. After the clerk told me they cost sixty cents each, an outrageous price, I didn't buy them. I paid for the scarf and took a bus home.

AZUPANE had two Christmas parties. One was for the kids which was disappointing —only half attended, because the office, inexplicably, did not inform all the families. The other was for the staff, where everyone arrived in a festive mood after receiving their annual bonus, two weeks' salary, earlier in the day. I arrived at 9:30 and stayed past midnight. After dancing, wine and champagne, the traditional Venezuelan Christmas dish, *hayacas*—beef, pork, chicken, raisins, capers, and olives folded into cornmeal dough and wrapped in banana leaves— were served. After eating, we exchanged presents. I received two t-shirts, the usual garb I wore to work and so I was most appreciative. Gifts that others received included cufflinks, the ubiquitous necktie, and a transistor radio. Most of the women received perfume. Johanna gave each of her staff in Social Conduct a gift: I got a Parker pen with my name engraved on it. After the exchange, the party was over and everyone went home. The following night Quinto Crillo, a popular local band, performed for the staff, parents, donors, and "Friends of AZUPANE."

My birthday was the day before the Christmas concert. Ana invited ten people for a dinner of rice, black beans and wine. Earlier in the day at her office, she baked a cake for dessert. While making it, Ana's American boss walked back to see what all the chatter in the kitchen area was about. When he noticed the bowl of cake mix on the counter, he walked over, put some on his finger and licked it clean. "Tastes good," he said. A few hours later in the middle of the afternoon, he apologized to his staff and went home early. Ana couldn't recall a time her boss had ever left the office before anyone else. He would never know the cake mix he'd licked from his finger contained marijuana.

The next evening, I was still feeling the effects of the wine and cake and wound up missing the concert at AZUPANE. At work the following day, the Padre asked me why I wasn't at the concert. I said I was too exhausted and had gone to bed early, which seemed lame, even if true. Jeff skipped the concert for more plausible reasons. He had returned to Venezuela the previous week on his Peace Corps visa, after waiting three months for the Venezuelan embassy in Washington, DC to issue one allowing him to work as a foreigner. But the visa had expired a few days earlier, meaning he was in the country illegally. He didn't go to the concert because he feared that if the police pulled him over, they might arrest him. The Padre agreed.

On Christmas, we had our own party at the house, starting with drinking Cuba Libres (rum and Coke) on the afternoon on Christmas Eve afternoon while listening to carols by Johnny Mathis, the Mormon Tabernacle Choir, and Hawaiian Don Ho from a tape a Volunteer had received from his sister and left behind after he terminated. In the background of "Silent Night" and "Jingle Bells," we could hear his sister crunching potato chips. Tory gave each of us a jar of peanut butter as a gift. After midnight on the morning of December 25, we sat in front of our tree made of coat hangers, candles, and plastic cups. I felt like we were part of a cult, waiting for the coat hanger tree to change into our leader or disappear in a puff of smoke. Tory tied plastic bags together, constructing something called a zilch bag—perhaps the strangest new thing I learned in Peace Corps—with a bucket of water underneath them. We set the bags on fire and watched the lightning-like reflections in the water. After a few games of Ping Pong, we lit sparklers, wished each other a merry Christmas and called it a night.

As my second year came to an end, I looked back at the eventful times. I had resigned, un-resigned, changed my termination date twice, switched jobs and moved to Maracaibo. At AZUPANE, I transferred work areas, and before the holiday break, Sanchez, the chief of operations, had approved my move from Social Conduct to Expression. He said if that's what I wanted to do, I should do it without question. The Peace Corps approved my request to revert to my original termination date, the end of March, even though my request perplexed the director.

Our lease would expire in three months, about the time I expected to find out about graduate school and start packing for my big trip through South America. In the more immediate future, though, my parents were coming to visit, and Venezuela was about to nationalize the oil industry.

Ten

Let's Get to Work

During my first year and a half in Venezuela, the future of the petroleum industry was the talk of the country. In 1973, Carlos Andres Pérez ran for president, promising to nationalize the oil companies as soon as possible after he was elected rather than wait until 1983, the date Venezuela had originally set to take over the industry. Venezuela would reap the benefits of higher oil prices through nationalization and use the revenue to reduce, if not eradicate, poverty.

While it was a smart campaign strategy, the government could not dismiss the expertise the American, Dutch, and British firms contributed in extracting and marketing the oil. *Forbes* magazine considered American technology and resources so superior that "if there had been no perfect illustration of what the United States' technical and capital resources could do for the world's underdeveloped areas, it would have been necessary to invent the Republic of Venezuela." Beyond that, the government needed a stable revenue stream to enable national planning; the U.S. market, its largest buyer, would play a critical role.

Pérez, needing to calm everyone down, particularly the oil companies, said he would not seize the oil fields and assets as other countries had done. Instead, the government would purchase the international companies through negotiation and legislation, and then contract with foreign firms for whatever technical assistance was needed to safeguard a smooth transition.

And that's more or less what happened.

Because AZUPANE was located on the former grounds of the Creole Oil company offices, which included the former home of the CEO, now the administrative office and the Padre's residence, working there reminded me every day of the petroleum industry and the wealth it could produce. Oil in Venezuela goes back to the time before Columbus arrived, when the native people used it for medicinal and illumination purposes. In 1535, Gonzalo Fernandez de Oviedo y Valdes mentioned Venezuelan oil leaks in his *General and Natural History of the Indies*. He called it "the nectar from Cubagua," saying it was useful for treating gout. In 1783, King Charles III decreed that the mines on Spanish territory in the Americas belonged to Spain. Thirty years later, Simon Bolívar reversed the decision when Venezuela declared independence and announced that oil and other natural resources belonged to the country, and not to another state—or, as occurred in the twentieth century, to foreign oil companies. The principle, though, would not be applied until 163 years later when Venezuela took ownership of its oil.

For most of the nineteenth century, Venezuela had no roads or bridges and an economy based on sugar. It was so underdeveloped, they had no choice but to allow foreign companies to mine for natural resources. In 1865, Jorge Sutherland, the president of the state of Zulia, gave the first contract for exploration to the American Camilo Ferrand, but nothing came of it. A decade later, Antonio Pulido founded "Compania Nacional Petrolia del Tachira," the first oil company in Venezuela. Using a rig imported from Pennsylvania, they dug holes and extracted oil with buckets, but the output was disappointing—hardly enough to provide kerosene to local towns.

More promising was asphalt, a sticky, black liquid form of petroleum found in 1,100-acre Guanoco Lake—the largest pitch lake in the world, also known as Bermudez Lake, located in Sucre state in the eastern half of the country. The asphalt had an estimated value in the hundreds of billions of dollars. The find was so large, *The New York Times* reported in 1901 that the supply would last until "the end of the world." Over the next thirty years, Venezuela granted concessions to several companies to explore the tar pits and oil fields throughout the country.

It was not until Juan Vicente Gomez, a barely literate general, assumed power in 1908 and ruled for twenty-seven years that oil became important in Venezuela. While credited with establishing Venezuela as a leading oil producer, Gomez had an atrocious human rights record and jailed or killed his opponents as he saw fit. One murder involved one of his sons killing Gomez's brother, the vice president. He also allegedly fathered ninety-seven children.

During World War I, global manufacturing concentrated on supporting the war effort, causing a pause in exploration. After the war, demand for oil grew and Gomez, astute enough to realize Venezuela needed international companies' technology if it hoped to find the oil long suspected to be in the Lake Maracaibo region, granted new permits to foreign companies to explore for and extract oil.

By the end of 1921, Venezuela was producing 1.4 million barrels a day, despite such obstacles as the lack of roads and maps and the abundance of malaria-carrying mosquitos near the oil fields. As a result, Gomez became a wealthy man, which he often stated was his primary goal in life. He turned the country into his personal fiefdom, which his opponents referred to as *La Hacienda* ("The Farm"). The dictator also launched an extensive public works program, for which the Venezuelan Congress rewarded him with the title *El Benemérito* ("the Meritorious One"). His political adversaries, less generous with titles, preferred to call him the "Tyrant of the Andes," a reference to his Tachira mountain area roots and the tactics his secret police used against his rivals.

When Gomez died in his sleep in 1935, Venezuela was the second largest oil producer in the world. Technology had advanced, and commercial mining of asphalt had ended, making Maracaibo the cornerstone of the country's economic development. Bermudez Lake was relegated to a natural wonder with an interesting history. In 1993, the airport in Tachira was renamed the Juan Vicente Gomez International Airport. Venezuela remained an important oil producer through the 1940s. By the beginning of World War II, though, the Soviet Union had become a petroleum-producing country, pushing Venezuela to third place behind the United States and the Soviets. During the war, Venezuela was a major energy supplier for the U.S. war effort. After the war, global demand for oil surged, and the Middle East became a new source.

In the 1950s, the Middle East, led by Saudi Arabia and Iran, transformed the global oil markets. By 1959, Venezuela accounted for only a third of the world's output, down from near 50 percent in 1948, and the foreign companies were selling oil from the Middle East at a lower price than that produced in Venezuela and the United States. President Dwight Eisenhower, under pressure from the U.S. companies, imposed import quotas to protect U.S. domestic producers who sold oil at a higher price than international rivals. The higher prices and decreased demand forced Venezuela to alter its national development plans to accommodate the loss of revenue. Needless to say, Venezuela was not happy.

The U.S. and Venezuela each had their interests to protect. Keeping in mind the importance of the Venezuelan market to the American economy, Washington negotiated a trade agreement to ensure an oil supply to the U.S. that, in turn, would keep American exports including food, electronics, and automobiles affordable in Venezuela.

When it came to the oil industry, the last straw for Iran, Iraq, Kuwait, Saudi Arabia, and Venezuela was in August 1960 when the international oil companies imposed a second price cut without consulting them. They banded together and met in Baghdad, where they formed the Organization of the Petroleum Exporting Countries (OPEC) with the purpose of stopping the ad hoc pricing system. OPEC stabilized prices for thirteen years. Then war broke out.

In October 1973, the same month the Peace Corps offered me a job and weeks before Venezuela elected Carlos Andres Pérez as its next president, Egypt and Syria launched a surprise attack on Israel on Yom Kippur, hoping to regain territories they lost in the June 1967 Six-Day War. Taking a lesson from the foreign oil companies, OPEC raised the price of oil 70 percent, to $5.10 a barrel, and changed global politics forever. To keep prices steady and high, they cut production quotas by four million barrels a day. In announcing the new prices, Saudi Oil Minister Shiekh Yamani exclaimed, "The moment has come. We are masters of our own commodity!" Venezuelans cheered.

To help defend Israel, the United States sent arms and considered sending more than $2 billion more in military assistance. In response, OPEC halted its exports to Canada, Europe, Japan, and the United States, causing chaos at the gas pump and a recession. An angry Saddam Hussein wanted further sanctions and called for complete economic warfare against the U.S. When his petroleum partners, looking at a larger world than the Middle East, rejected his demand, he threw a tantrum, calling the other OPEC countries American lackeys. Iraq, determined to earn as much money as possible from the crisis, then unilaterally raised its output so it could increase income.

In late December 1973, with the Yom Kippur War over, the OPEC members bordering the Gulf met in Tehran to discuss oil prices; Venezuela attended as an observer. Iran, the world's second largest oil exporter and a close U.S. ally under the Shah, advocated for a hard line on prices. He argued it was time Western countries paid more for the commodities they needed, as they had no qualms about selling their assets to poorer countries at prices they couldn't afford. "They will have to realize the era of their terrific progress and, even more, terrific income and wealth based on cheap oil is finished," the Shah declared. Iran wanted to raise the price of a barrel to as high as $23, but without the majority of his colleagues behind him, OPEC set the compromise price at $11.65. Six months earlier, it had been $2.73.

Letters from home confirmed the panic I had been reading about in the *Daily Journal*, an English newspaper, as well as *TIME* and the local media. A gallon of gas in the United States cost 64 cents ($3.22 at 2014 prices) compared to 36 cents in 1972. Food prices doubled, and people talked of embracing the radical idea of starting vegetable gardens. Gas stations required appointments to avoid fights at the pump; unemployment was on the rise and the U.S. economy fell into a recession. In Venezuela, no such economic problems existed; most people had jobs and gas was less than 25 cents a gallon. With the government preparing to take ownership of the oil companies, optimism reigned. Most Venezuelans saw better days ahead, except for the unhappy man on the front steps of the house where I rented a room; he insisted months ago that President Pérez had put his country on the road to disaster. It was too soon to say if he was right.

January 1, 1976, is one of the most important days in Venezuelan history. On that day, Venezuela took ownership of fourteen oil companies, which put the production, refining, and marketing in the hands of the government. A pop song, "Manos a La Obra" ("Let's Get to Work") celebrated national pride in the takeover of the petroleum industry in the spirit of Simon Bolívar, the Liberator. Each time the radio played the catchy tune, we turned up the volume and blasted it throughout the house.

Celebrations took place in Cabimas, the site of the Barroso No. 2 well that in 1922 produced 100,000 barrels of oil a day, making world headlines and marking the beginning of Venezuela's modern history as a major oil producer. On New Year's Day, President Carlos Andres Pérez delivered a long, sober, and restrained televised speech in which he told the country that nationalization brought new responsibilities: "We have not accomplished a heroic act, but rather an historic act of responsibility and national dignity." Pérez added he would not use oil as an economic weapon.

In a now declassified cable, the U.S. Embassy described the speech as "statesman-like" and lacking the typical embellishments heard in most political speeches in Venezuela. Nationalization would mean less rhetoric and more responsible spending meant to improve the lives of Venezuelans, reported the embassy. In an interview in 1993 as part of the State Department's Oral History Project, Harry W. Shlaudeman, the American ambassador to Venezuela in 1975–76, recalled he had advised Washington to stay calm because a government takeover of the industry was inevitable. He said, "There was nothing we could do about this; they were going to do it anyway, and they were going to take this property." Shlaudeman called the two years of negotiations "a long struggle."

Washington followed Ambassador Shlaudeman's advice and accepted nationalization as a *fait accompli*. Venezuela signed technical service and export contracts with Exxon, Shell, Sun Oil, Texaco, Gulf, Amoco, Phillips, and Mobil to ensure that production and marketing continued without major disruptions. Robert Morley, the economic officer at the U.S. embassy who arrived six months after nationalization, said in an interview with the Oral History Project that U.S. interests were two-fold. One, to keep Venezuela as a reliable source of petroleum; and two, to take advantage of the new wealth to sell U.S. goods and services." As far as he was concerned, mission accomplished.

Venezuela used its billions in oil revenue to modernize its military, purchase American F-16 jet aircraft, Italian warships, and British radar systems. Wanting to bolster its image of a modern country, it began a foreign aid program in 1974, earmarking 1.88 percent of GDP for multilateral agencies, a percentage point more than double the highest rate in 2015, when Sweden led the world with 0.99 percent. Most of Venezuela's bilateral assistance went to Andean nations, Central America, and the Caribbean.

However, it was not without controversy. In 1976, a month after nationalizing the oil industry, Venezuela also contributed one hundred million bolivars ($25 million) to Guatemala in the form of food, clothing, blankets, tents, troops, and firemen after an earthquake killed more than twenty-five thousand people and left one million homeless. Soon after President Pérez announced the aid, I was at a fruit stand buying a *batido* (a cold smoothie-like drink made of papaya or banana, milk and sugar mixed in a blender) when a customer complained the government gave too much in humanitarian assistance. "We have needs in this country and better ways to spend a hundred million bolivars. I don't understand how we could give so much money to Guatemala," he griped.

The oil revenue was also used to build a subway in Caracas, improve the ports, build hospitals and a new international airport, subsidize housing, and expand the social security system. The government enlarged the Guri Dam, officially the *Embalse Raúl Leoni*, the hydroelectric project and reservoir on the Caroní River in Bolívar State in eastern Venezuela. It would become one of the largest and most productive power stations in the world. Over ten years, the government would invest more than $38 billion in the electric grid, leading to 95 percent coverage, one of the highest rates in Latin America.

Yet political and business leaders doubted the country could manage its wealth over the long term to benefit the country. In 1976, they did not believe that oil at $12 a barrel was sustainable. A lower price would sink the economy and obliterate the national development plan. Venezuela was fragile, and its known oil reserves were estimated to last twenty more years. The petroleum industry employed thousands, directly and indirectly, through American companies like Allis Chalmers, Black and Decker, Briggs and Stratton, Exxon, First National City Bank, IBM, Sears, and Shell Oil, many of them in the Maracaibo area. Parts of Maracaibo resembled a bastardized version of America, except everyone spoke Spanish. The economy was about oil and nothing else.

Still, in January 1976, Venezuela was calm, good times and prosperity were ahead, and my parents were coming to visit.

Eleven

My Parents Come to Visit

The planning started four months earlier with an exchange of letters covering itineraries and logistics. Based on Venezuela's comfortable temperatures in January and the cold weather in the Midwest, my parents, Bob and Helen, chose the second week in January for their one-week visit. We could fit Caracas, the Andes Mountains, the city of Merida, and Maracaibo into eight days, though it might be tight.

I suggested three itineraries. The first one was to spend a few days in Caracas before flying to Merida, then finishing the trip by driving to Maracaibo and staying three days. In Maracaibo, in addition to AZUPANE and the house, there was the Guajira Indian market, a shopping destination for tourists a few miles north of the city. Also, boat rides across Lake Maracaibo and a visit to the oil rigs were possibilities. I dropped the idea of driving straight from Caracas to Maracaibo because it would be long, hot, and monotonous. After a while, the flat landscape would look the same, and we would be driving after dark on unfamiliar roads filled with bad drivers. Equally undesirable and impractical was driving from Caracas to Merida to Maracaibo over eight days. I had some planning to do.

We also considered going to Angel Falls, the highest waterfall in the world—nineteen times higher than Niagara Falls. We would be taking a big chance, given the cloud cover in Canaima National Park, the mountainous jungle territory in southeastern Venezuela where Angel Falls was located, as it would probably obstruct our view. The Falls, named after the American aviator James Crawford Angel, who

164

discovered them in 1935, were seven hundred miles from Caracas in what is now Canaima National Park, an area six times the size of the Grand Canyon. UNESCO declared it a World Heritage Site in 1994. That trip would be more of an adventure than we wanted, so I crossed it off our list of possible places to go.

After my parents arrived, how would we get around? I advised them to forego coming with a group, as we didn't need a guide telling us when to look out the window of the bus, or that we had to be back on the bus in ten minutes. Instead, I recommended they buy plane tickets to Caracas, where I would meet them at the airport. In Merida and Maracaibo, we could either rent a car, take taxis, or a combination of both. Putting them on a local bus seemed cruel.

But I hadn't driven in two years and didn't want to resume driving in a city like Caracas, which appeared to be one big traffic jam with vague rules of the road. Plus, the police often demanded bribes and threatened drivers with jail time for minor infractions. We could rent a car in Maracaibo, where the streets were less congested, but not in Caracas, where taxis were widely available. I suggested we take a drive from Merida to Maracaibo through the Andes and enjoy the magnificent scenery. Flying over the mountains was pointless if you could drive and had the time.

Hertz and Avis had deals. Avis offered $70 for five days plus thirteen cents per kilometer to rent the best-selling Maverick, a car Ford manufactured in Venezuela and marketed as a cheaper alternative to the Volkswagen Beetle at a time when gas prices were soaring because of the oil embargo and OPEC price increases. I estimated we would drive seven hundred kilometers, for which we would pay $160. My father, who was paying, thought the price was right.

The Kristoff and the La Lago were the two five-star hotels in Maracaibo. The La Lago, with rooms for thirteen dollars, would be a major upgrade compared to the places I stayed when I traveled. I did not know the Kristoff, other than its location in downtown Maracaibo. I was certain we could arrive without a reservation, doubting the two largest and best hotels in a city where tourism was not big business would be booked solid. We needed flexibility in our itinerary, and I didn't want hotel reservations to control our schedule.

It had been two years since I had been home, so I was not surprised when my parents asked what I would like them to bring. My short list included a pair of Levi's blue jeans with a youthful 32-inch waist and length; the latest edition of the hometown newspaper; three jars of peanut butter; a Frisbee; and a money belt I could wear while traveling in South America. I added that it was just as important what they took back with them than what they brought me. The perfect scenario would be if they packed a suitcase with gifts and requests, which I would fill with my belongings for them to take home and put in storage.

Fernando asked for three or four books with illustrations of patterns for sandals, shoes, bags, hats, and other items to give him ideas for designs and whatnot for his business. Jeff was less grandiose and only asked for a Bic pen, being tired of buying pens that ran out of ink after a few hundred words. Tory didn't ask for anything. I also asked for ten rolls of film for the flat Kodak Pocket Instamatic 110-camera I owned. But wanting more than 3x5 prints from their visit, I wondered if they could bring a movie camera.

The unpredictability of customs agents at the airport worried all travelers. How closely would they look through my parents' luggage, and at what cost? I had heard stories. One visitor from the U.S. avoided a $50 duty on his brother's bike when he told the agent he owned it. Or you could simply speak English and hope the non-English-speaking officers would let you through without applying a duty rather than try to make themselves understood.

Venezuelan customs had rules, but they were enforced erratically. If they asked you to pay the tax, the first option was to play the dumb American tourist and express surprise at such regulations, hoping they would shrug and welcome you to Venezuela. If they made life difficult for my parents, I planned to flash my Peace Corps identification card, which said I was working in the interest of the Venezuelan people at the request of the government. Surely that must mean something.

But I knew it sometimes meant nothing. Once, the police stopped a Volunteer for making a left turn on his motorcycle without first sticking his arm out to signal. The Volunteer handed the officer his Peace Corps ID. After glancing at it, the officer arrested him. It appeared that working for the people did not exempt you from following the laws of driving. The ID card, however, carried weight with the Marines at the U.S. Embassy, where Volunteers liked to go for a decent hamburger in the cafeteria. Some two- or three-star hotels in Caracas offered 10 or 20 percent discounts to Peace Corps Volunteers, but you needed the ID card. If necessary, when my parents arrived, I would use the Peace Corps card at the airport. Otherwise, my Venezuelan ID card, called a *cedula,* was more useful in most situations.

Although a coat was unnecessary unless we went to the mountains—and even then, coming from a Midwest winter, the cooler mountain temperatures might seem mild—I advised my parents to bring light sweaters for the chilly January nights in Caracas and to keep warm in the air-conditioned hotel in Maracaibo. I suggested they also bring sunscreen, because the hotels would have swimming pools and standing outside or walking a short distance would expose them to the tropical sun, not to mention how expensive suntan lotion was in Venezuela.

In my last missive before they drove from Wisconsin to Miami for their flight to Caracas, I said the pace of life was slower than in the U.S., and people were seldom on time. They should arrive with no expectations. They should bring cameras and not worry whether they might get stolen or they might get robbed. The odds were against it. Venezuela was a safe place. American Express and Diner's Club cards could be used in restaurants, hotels, and with car rental agencies. For reading, I recommended *The Zinzin Road* by Fletcher Knebel, a work of fiction revolving around Volunteers in Africa that he dedicated to "Peace Corps Volunteers—Kennedy's children."

I organized a week of activities with plenty of flexibility and time to move from place to place. If I loaded the schedule with too much sightseeing, we would end up disappointed. The one cultural practice I ignored in putting together the itinerary was the Venezuelan custom of eating a dinner-sized meal at midday rather than in the evening. Despite two years in Venezuela, I still preferred eating my main meal of the day after dark.

My parents arrived without any trouble or incidents at customs. For the first couple of days, we exchanged news about people we knew, starting with my seven siblings and followed by nieces and nephews before catching up on friends, neighbors, and other relatives. My mother said few of their friends were familiar with the Peace Corps; most thought I was a missionary, making me wonder if I would rather have people think I was a CIA operative.

We stayed at the Macuto Sheraton Hotel on the Caribbean Sea in La Guairá, forty-five minutes from Caracas and close to the Maiquetia International Airport, now called the Simon Bolívar International Airport. La Guairá is one of the country's oldest cities and largest seaports. Parts of the city had narrow cobblestone streets from colonial times, with Spanish-style homes painted in bright blue and yellows with bars on the windows. An old Spanish castle overlooked the harbor.

In the 1960s and 1970s, the Macuto Sheraton was considered one of the best hotels in Venezuela. American magazines carried ads with a picture of the beachfront with the Avila Mountains in the background. Its facilities included swimming pools, tennis and volleyball courts, a bowling alley, a shuffleboard deck, billiard tables, and a jogging track. Room service offered the *Hamburguesa Sheraton* (the Sheraton Hamburger) for $3. Yachts could be rented, and a nine-hole golf course was down the road. The hotel theater was showing *The Eiger Sanction* with Clint Eastwood and George Kennedy. One morning at the pool, a man seated in a lounge chair sipping a Bloody Mary while reading a newspaper caught my father's eye. My father turned to my mother and me and grumbled, "He's on vacation, does he have to read *The Wall Street Journal?*"

The Macuto Sheraton closed in December 1999 when thirty-five inches of rain fell on the north central coast over a 48-hour period, causing floods and mudslides that killed tens of thousands, leaving 150,000 homeless. Before he died, President Hugo Chavez promised an eight-hundred-room hotel to replace the shell where the five-star hotel once stood, but nothing happened. In August 2017, the shell was still there.

My mother kept a journal during the trip, a habit she began when she vacationed in Cuba in 1939. I didn't know she was writing short and succinct impressions on the trip until she passed away. Among her possessions was an envelope full of travel brochures, receipts, airline tickets, menus, and letterhead from the Macuto Sheraton and La Lago hotels, all of which now seem like museum pieces. Her journal on Venezuela was among her belongings.

My Parents Come to Visit

January 7: Beautiful day! Arrived at the airport around 10:30; parked the car for a week; had breakfast; checked in. The plane left at 3:30 and arrived in Caracas about 7:00; went through health, passport, and customs inspection. Good to see Mike. Long ride to the Macuto-Sheraton Hotel. Nice room on the ocean.

January 8: Left early for Caracas, which took almost an hour. Beautiful day. Very large city; busy, noisy and a lot of pollution. We walked miles; took a bus within the city; had a sandwich (very good) and juice. Interesting people. Beautiful buildings; hovels; beggars; outdoor cafes. Before boarding the bus for the hotel, we had a delicious Venezuelan meal. The bus trip took over an hour—couldn't have seen what we did without Mike and we needed an interpreter.

January 9: Our 33rd wedding anniversary and it was raining when we woke up. When it stopped, we walked down the beach for breakfast in the hotel—very good juice and melons. The afternoon turned sunny and we spent it around the pool. Very relaxing afternoon. After dark, we walked into Macuto and had dinner in a Chinese restaurant. Amazing walls with broken glass cemented on top so no one could get over it.

After two days in Caracas, we flew to Mérida on Aeropostal Airlines, Venezuela's oldest airline. Our big adventure in Mérida was taking the *Teleférico de Mérida* cable car to Pico Espejo; at nearly 15,000 feet, it was the highest cable car in the world. My father and I went up the mountain, while my mother, being acrophobic, waited at the bottom. On the way, we met a Canadian woman and her son; her husband feared heights so much he would not even leave the hotel. My mother felt better when we told her that story.

January 10: Had a wake-up call for 6 a.m. so we could get to the airport for our flight to Merida at 8:30. We left at 9:30 and arrived in Merida forty-five minutes later. Stayed at Hotel Chama, named after an Indian chief. A beautiful day—this town has a university called Los Andes (University of the Andes). We walked around the town all afternoon—narrow streets; marketplace; plaza; Cathedral; Mass at 5:00 p.m. We had lunch and dinner at really nice restaurants with good food and service. Café con leche grande is strong but good.

My father had borrowed a 16mm Bell and Howell movie camera from his brother-in-law for the trip and used a roll and a half of film on the ride up the mountain. I looked forward to seeing the movies of the cable ride and the ones my father would later shoot at AZUPANE. After returning home, my mother wrote that they loved the movies and watched them every week for a month. As it turned out, I did not see them until thirty-five years later when I digitized them.

Like the Ford Maverick and the Macuto Sheraton Hotel, the cable car has since vanished. In effect, it died of old age. In 2008, the government closed it down based on a study that concluded the fifty-year-old system had reached the end of its service life. When it was built in the 1950s, twenty-five European companies needed three years to construct and connect the towers and wires at three different levels.

The government and its international partner, which specialized in manufacturing aerial lifts, began rebuilding a whole new system in 2010. Videos available on YouTube show the difficulties in working on a 10,000-foot mountain: weather, lack of oxygen, steep mountainsides, and transporting materials and equipment were some of the obstacles. It reopened in April 2016. The new cable car was renamed "Mukumbarí," meaning "resting place of the sun," the name the first settlers in the Sierra Nevada gave to the highest mountain.

January 11: Got up to rent a car to go to Maracaibo and couldn't do it. So we decided to go on the cable car up the Andes. I only went to the first level, but Bob and Mike went to the third level. Beautiful day. The Andes are green and lush, full of trees, and there are houses scattered here and there. I waited at the first stop (8,000 ft.) sitting in the sun but too hot to sit directly in it. Afterward, we walked around the town—Sunday afternoon seemed to be visiting time, date time, and family time. Almost everything was closed and everyone was dressed up—the children are very appealing. Had a nice dinner at the hotel because we could relax as we had a car rented for the next day to take us to Maracaibo.

After two nights in Merida, we hired a taxi to take us to Maracaibo because the single car rental agency in the city had rented out its entire fleet. We arrived after a seven-hour drive and my parents checked into the La Lago Hotel. The following morning we went to the YMCA with a group of kids from AZUPANE for swimming class. In the afternoon, we drove to the beach where a camping excursion was underway.

My father took slides and shot a few minutes of movies. My mother's journal ended with our arrival in Maracaibo. I never got to ask before she died in 2008 why she stopped writing about the trip. This was her last entry:

January 12: Left Merida at 7:00—cool but the sun wasn't up over the mountains all the way. A nice driver and away we went through the Andes—around curves, through little towns; had to slow up because part of the road fell off the edge; we drove through a landslide and water with the help of logs. It was quite an experience stopping for food, gas, buses, and taxis. There were local people, travelers, Indians, and I'm sure we were the only Americans. We went through oil towns—saw such poverty. We didn't reach Maracaibo until 1:15—a long ride. The bridge over Lake Maracaibo is immense. Mike had made reservations at Hotel del Lago—very, very nice. There we rented a car, and Mike took us to the old port of Maracaibo and the Indian (Guajiro) market—quite an experience. While resting, we had a giant glass of cold juice—their juices are very different, and I love them.

Robert and Helen Kendellen with me in Maracaibo

Over a dinner of *pabellón*, the national dish consisting of shredded meat, black beans, white rice, and fried bananas, I told them I would be leaving in two months after completing my two years of service and travel in South America. How long I would be on the road would depend on whether I enrolled in graduate school for the fall semester, which would mean a return to the U.S. by July. I expected to hear whether I had been accepted to school before I left Venezuela. The other factors that could influence the time of my return would be how much I was enjoying myself and how my money was holding out.

If I didn't go to school, I would be on the road as long as I had money. I hoped to go to the Inca ruins at Machu Picchu in Peru and continue to Chile and Argentina. But I don't think my parents were listening to my travel plans. They were more interested in the part about leaving Venezuela in two months and being home soon after. Leaving the door open to staying longer, I mentioned Volunteers who had remained in the country after they left the Peace Corps and found jobs at universities and government ministries earning more than they did as Volunteers. They didn't ask if I was serious about staying.

My mother and I in front of our house in Maracaibo
(Photo by Robert Kendellen)

A week after they returned home, my mother wrote a letter to me on La Lago Hotel letterhead saying they had a wonderful time, and a few weeks later, my father sent me an envelope containing 260 bolivars buried inside newspaper clippings. They could not exchange them at the airport in Maracaibo because the money changer had run out of dollars.

"Can you give us a date when you'll be home?" my father asked. Everyone wanted to see me home and hear of my plans. He wondered if I had considered working for the federal government, where he worked as a postal inspector, or joining the Foreign Service. If not the government, what about returning to the bank where I had been working since I was seventeen? None of those suggestions interested me.

My travel plans were no more certain than a job. Every few days I juggled them between seeing South America and fighting off the urge to go straight home. What would it be like to be in the U.S. again? How would I function? While it would be nice to be back home, I knew the emotions surrounding my return would dissipate in about a week, and the routine of American life would begin. The truth was, deep down, I was not ready to leave Venezuela.

I had been on vacation for a month. It was time to return to work. On my first day back, I learned a lot had happened while I was away.

Twelve

Back to Normal

The latest economic indicators showed the cost of living in Maracaibo had risen faster than any other part of the country, including Caracas. According to the government, prices had gone up the past six months by 13 percent, which seemed low because most things seemed to have increased four or five bolivars—in most cases, that would be over 13 percent. The month before, the president had doubled the price of wheat, forcing the bakeries to charge more for bread. When sales subsequently declined, the bakers went on a nationwide strike. In response, the president decreed a reduced price and the shops reopened. However, they, having the last word, sold eight doughnuts for a bolivar instead of ten.

In other economic developments, the president announced in late 1975 that Venezuela would not have color television throughout the country during his administration because it was not a national priority. As a result, the government postponed the debate on choosing between the NTSC or the PAL system, the two color encoding systems for analogue television. West Germany lobbied for PAL, while U.S. manufacturers favored NTSC, the system Venezuela adopted a few years later. Country-wide color TV became available in 1979.

Several personnel changes occurred over the month I was gone. Johanna, the Social Conduct coordinator and my former supervisor, shocked us when she abruptly quit, saying she was going to study English at the Venezuelan-American Center and go to the United States for further study. Other staff reduced their hours because of heavy course loads at the university. One returned to work full time after months of working for the family business. As we had agreed before my break, I changed areas for the third time, moving to Expression, where we worked with the kids through music, art, and theater.

The AZUPANE beach house on Lake Maracaibo
(Photo by Robert Kendellen)

After a week, I went on a beach outing. By eight o'clock that Friday morning, the thirteen children under ten years old who had paid the twenty-bolivar fee sat on the AZUPANE driveway, each with a suitcase, waiting while Victor, the bus driver, put their luggage underneath the bus. Sharon, an AZUPANE volunteer whose neighbor worked for an oil company and who was an acquaintance of a Board member, was late. I never got used to the Venezuelan sense of time. Being late annoyed me, particularly when the person was not Venezuelan. When she finally arrived, she said she had fainted the previous night, forcing her and her husband to cancel a dinner date with friends. Why she volunteered for the campout was a mystery because she always seemed uncomfortable around the kids. This one would consist of seven- to ten-year-olds, most of whom needed help getting dressed or eating—and for a few, walking. It wouldn't be a holiday. Seven adults would live under one roof with the thirteen kids.

As the bus pulled away, the kids waved while their mothers cried and waved back. The kids were all smiles as we drove off. We bought fruit, vegetables, and meat in the Mara municipality north of

175

Maracaibo, just a roadside stop in 1976. Years later, though, it had changed, as had Venezuela. In September 2015, President Maduro declared a state of emergency in Mara and sent three thousand soldiers to protect the people from paramilitary groups, drug traffickers, and extortion.

While some of the staff shopped for food, others, including me, unpacked the breakfasts of empanadas, *arepas*, juice, and soda the kids brought. They were well-behaved, ate quietly, and didn't spill any drinks. Trips to the bathroom were limited to only one.

When we arrived at the beach, Italo, the Italian groundskeeper whom the Padre had hired to keep the beach house clean, met us. His first question was whether we brought him any music. We didn't. Rafael apologized for forgetting to pack the cassette player and an ample supply of D-size batteries. So for three days we would be without music, and Italo would have to wait another week for cassettes.

The unloading of the luggage and setting up the house went without a hitch. We knew the routine: get the kids into their swimming suits, stack the suitcases in the two bedrooms, and put the food in the refrigerator. The rule for the beach excursions was one piece of luggage per child. On this trip, eleven-year-old Julio Cesar set the record for the amount of clothing stuffed into a suitcase for a three-day excursion, thanks to his mother. We all chuckled at the two pairs of long pants, eleven pairs of shorts, thirteen pairs of underwear, two blankets, and one hammock he brought.

The beach on Lake Maracaibo, often shallow and filthy, was warm as bathwater when the tide was high on a windless day. That day, the water was over seventy degrees and blue, rather than brown. We swam for an hour and afterward had a lunch of meat, soup, rice, empanadas, and salad, followed by a nap. Late in the afternoon, Isabel asked for a show of hands on whether we should have eggs or meat for dinner; everyone except Sharon wanted meat. Not only did she want something more substantial to eat, but she also wanted to eat the main meal around six, not at midday. Outvoted, she retreated to a room in anger, slamming the door, and spent the rest of the afternoon there. Close to sunset, she reappeared. She laid down in a hammock where she proceeded to faint.

She recovered, but skipped the egg dinner. After the kids had gone to bed, the staff sang around a bonfire, which brought Sharon out of her room; she pointed at the fire and asked me what time everyone went to sleep. At first, I considered it an innocent question; then I realized she wanted peace and quiet so that she could sleep. She also asked if the mouse turds she insisted she saw in her room meant the beach house was infested with rats or mice. Never having seen any myself, I was dubious. The Padre had hired Italo to keep the place neat and clean, and he had been living there for weeks; the least we should expect was a rat-free weekend. Not wanting to risk waking up to a rat lying on her, she slept in a hammock above the floor and out of reach of any rodents. The next morning when the bus arrived with supplies, she jumped at the chance and returned with it to Maracaibo. Minutes after it left, the tension diminished, and the rest of the outing was quiet and uneventful.

On the ride back to AZUPANE on Monday afternoon, the kids slept. It had been a long weekend. It was funny and revealing to see the kids welcomed home. The whole household of nine-year-old Lourdes greeted her as the bus pulled up in front of her house. She took it all in stride and strutted to the door like a queen, as if she did this every day. Paco's grandmother and mother met him at the door. As they were about to give him a kiss, he stopped, motioning with his hand for them to wait; he turned to wave goodbye before kissing his mother. Martín's parents warmly welcomed him home, too, but I was never sure what, if anything, Martin comprehended. His mother asked if everything was all right.

At our house, the five of us continued adapting to living together. Occasionally, we had to sort out whose turn it was to wash the dishes, agree on an acceptable volume when the radio was on, and remind each other to clean up after taking a shower. When any of these lapses occurred, we either dealt with them quietly or ignored them, which we did most of the time. No one wanted a confrontation over mundane incidents. We believed or hoped irresponsible conduct would rarely happen, and if it did, would never be repeated. If the radio was too loud, we assumed someone was in a good mood or was listening to their favorite song. If the bathroom was a mess, we figured the last person to use it was late or in a hurry. All was forgiven. Being in our mid-twenties, we were too naïve to consider that bad behavior could become a habit. There was no reason to call anyone out on it.

One evening, Fernando knocked on my door wanting to talk. I never knew what to expect when he initiated a conversation. Often he sought advice or just wanted someone to challenge him on his latest idea, looking for clarity on some philosophical question with which he was grappling. Though lazy and lacking motivation, Fernando enrolled in night classes to give his life some direction and planned to earn a high school diploma at twenty-eight. But he suffered from an inferiority complex, a trait I noticed in many Venezuelans, particularly when comparing themselves to Americans. One Volunteer said his host family in Los Teques considered him to be superior to them solely because he was an American. How do you respond to that? Natalia, the head of the household where I lived during training, gave me the impression she was inferior to no one. Americans behaved in ways that only made her laugh.

On this evening, Fernando seemed depressed; something was restraining his ability to concentrate on his studies. His mind wandered when reading, something he considered abnormal, and it worried him. After the long introduction, he got to the crux of the problem. Cristina, his girlfriend, had been in Europe for three months and was expected back any day. The waiting, the expectations, the unknown—all were becoming intolerable. Their sole communication was a phone call when she told him she might be pregnant. He struggled to become a part of her close-knit family, which included seven children. Cristina's father, a history professor who once sent Spanish dictator Francisco Franco a congratulatory telegram after he executed two members of the Basque Homeland and Freedom (ETA) party and three Revolutionary Antifascist Patriotic Front (FRAP) devotees for killing policemen, did not like him. His possible son-in-law did not have a high school diploma, had no career path, and faced an uncertain future. Fernando, not wanting to lose Cristina, knew he needed to improve his relationship with her siblings and mother, but especially her father. Her return from Europe would be interesting.

A few nights later, Jeff and Tory were involved in one of their surreal and absurd philosophical discussions, which Fernando found both amusing and thought-provoking. Jeff mocked Tory's theory of life, saying it was what Jerry Mathers as the Beaver, a popular television character in the 1960s, represented. He put his idea into a mathematical formula on the blackboard we had in the living room.

Back to Normal

URI/U = Dios = Jerry Mathers as the Beaver.

The formula read: "URI, (a political party representing the country's business interests) divided by U (the universe) equaled God, which was equal to Jerry Mathers as the Beaver." Jeff and Tory nodded as if the equation had opened their minds to the meaning of life. On the other hand, the equation puzzled Fernando. He wondered what it all meant. Jerry Mathers? The Beaver? Who were they? What did they mean? Did the Beaver have the answers to universal questions? He stared at the blackboard without saying a word. Adding to the absurdity, I picked up a newspaper from the floor and pointed to the headline, "Fernando El Zorro," (Fernando the Fox), which confused him even more. What did it mean, he wondered, and equally puzzling, what was my intention?

Fernando didn't sleep well. The next morning, he knocked on Jeff's door, wanting to know the meaning of God and more about Jerry Mathers as the Beaver. Jeff, trying to refrain from laughing, told him the whole thing was a joke. They were only having fun. Jerry Mathers was an actor on television who played a kid named Theodore whose friends called him Beaver. It meant nothing. *Nada*. Nothing. Don't worry about it.

Fernando often took things we said or did too seriously, if not literally. He considered Tory and Jeff gurus because they practiced yoga and discussed *The Teachings of Don Juan: A Yaqui Way of Knowledge* by Carlos Casteneda and Zen philosophy late at night. He remained flummoxed over the idea that Beaver and God were connected and wondered how anyone could trivialize God. "Okay, but what about Fernando El Zorro?" he asked. That, too, was meaningless and just a headline in a newspaper, Jeff explained. Fernando left the room staring at the floor, looking depressed.

The next day at breakfast, Fernando said he was thinking of killing himself. Maybe we should have taken a suicide threat seriously, but we didn't. He had already concluded we were crazy for coming to Venezuela to work for peanuts and enjoying it, which he found incomprehensible. Throw in Jerry Mathers and the Beaver and we looked even nuttier, but killing yourself over it? Fernando, a master of not dwelling too much on one topic, put the Beaver and his relation to a higher being behind him and never spoke about them or his own death again.

Perhaps due to Jeff and Tory's influence, Fernando tried yoga, still a new form of exercise in the mid-1970s. His first class was at six o'clock in the morning. In an attempt at self-discipline, he decided he would wake up without using an alarm clock. The next morning, he got up as planned and caught a taxi in front of the house. After ten minutes, the driver turned on the radio and to Fernando's shock, he heard, "*El tiempo es la dos en la manana*" (The time is two o'clock in the morning.) Shit. It was supposed to be 5:30, not two o'clock! He ordered the driver to turn around and take him back to the house. Before going to bed, he set the alarm, postponing his start at a new self-discipline regime. At 5:30, the alarm woke him up. He dressed and left. But like night school, yoga proved to be an insufficient difference maker. He quit after a few weeks.

Waking up without an alarm clock and going to yoga class were small steps, but Fernando's poor business acumen was the real obstacle to feeling better about himself. His self-awareness helped motivate him, but it was not enough to offset the time he wasted thinking about what could go wrong in every scenario he considered for improving his life.

He kept trying, though. He volunteered at AZUPANE, teaching arts and crafts in the afternoons, hoping it would ease some of the guilt about his failing business venture. He lasted only a few weeks. Whenever he moved on to his next undertaking, he would create a set of expectations that led to overanalyzing the situation, which exhausted and overwhelmed him, resulting in more disappointment, inaction, and depression. Basically, Fernando tried too hard. All this noise came to fruition when he realized that above all, he missed Cristina. If she returned from Europe and her family welcomed him, maybe all the sideshows would disappear.

He couldn't wait for her to return, but he didn't know when that would be. She had been gone three months and he hadn't heard a word from her, which was driving him crazy. Then, on the same morning he remarked about the lack of news, a postcard arrived saying she would be home that exact day. He changed clothes and ran out the door looking for a taxi to take him to the airport. When the last scheduled flight landed and she wasn't on it, he called her mother, who said she knew nothing about it.

A week later, in the middle of the day, he walked in the front door drunk. Unbeknownst to us, Cristina had already returned from

London. She told Fernando she'd had an abortion and never wanted to see him again. In a drunken stupor, he asked me how much he owed for rent and food because he planned to leave Maracaibo in a few days.

He stayed.

One night I attended a rally of the *Movimiento al Socialismo* (Movement for Socialism) or MAS Party. With my dark complexion and full beard, part of my Black Irish heritage, I blended reasonably well into the Venezuelan crowd. Socialist Party leader Jose Vicente Rangel, who would serve in the Hugo Chavez Administration more than twenty years later, and local leaders Freddy Munoz and Pompeo were the featured speakers. The gathering attracted mostly young political followers, wearing t-shirts with the MAS fist on the back and holding large posters; they stood in front of the stage shouting various slogans and waving their signs. I bought the special edition of the *Voz Socialistica* newspaper for a bolivar; it included the Socialist Manifesto. The vendor asked me if I often read it. Not sure whether he was conducting a poll or just being curious, I said, "I never heard of it" He stared at me, looking confused, and walked away.

The first speaker walked onto the stage to a thunderous ovation as the political groupies, who were just a few feet away, screamed as loud as they could. He raised his left arm in the MAS salute of solidarity and went on a fifteen-minute diatribe lambasting the Zulia state government for not assisting the poor, laborers, and Guajiros, and for not fixing potholes.

The speaker was the exact image I had of a South American politician: passionate, verbose and fiery. The crowd loved it and so did I. Every few minutes, they would shout, "*Si podemos*" (Yes, we can.), which thirty-two years later, U.S. presidential candidate Barack Obama used as his campaign battle cry. The speaker finished by citing President Pérez as the real problem in the country, not the oil companies, a recognition that Pérez had taken the steam out of the Socialist Party when he nationalized the industry in January, a decision they had supported and encouraged for years. The words were borderline disrespectful. The unprecedented public personal attack on the president, however, went unheeded.

From the back of the room, a man yelled that the Guajiro Indians were lazy, and because of that, they didn't have jobs and were impoverished. Two men standing near me, one wearing a hard hat—

perhaps an oil worker—and the other in a straw farmer's hat, cracked jokes in such loud voices that one of the trusted Socialist Party supporters pushed his way through the crowd and told them to be quiet, or else they should leave. "Listen. Maybe you can learn something," he admonished, pointing a finger at them.

I saw a couple of familiar faces in the crowd. One, a medical student who'd started as a volunteer at AZUPANE a week earlier, was hanging around with a Bolivian folklore vocal group that had been playing in various locales in Maracaibo for the past month. The other was one of the original five tenants in the house, Rosita, who I ran into while leaving. As we were talking and waiting for taxis, a man sitting in a car stuck his head out the window and asked Rosita why she was leaving if the rally was not over yet. "It's just a bunch of talk, nothing more," she shouted at him, which was pretty much my sentiment as well.

By now, I had taken enough taxis and buses to wonder about a photograph I saw on every dashboard of a guy wearing a fedora. While Peace Corps advised us about being in taxis with sleepy drivers and no seat belts, they never mentioned the ubiquitous photograph of a man with a thick drooping mustache wearing a dark suit and a high-peaked black felt hat that was found in most vehicles. Who was he?

Dr. Jose Gregorio Hernández, born in 1864 in the town of Isnotú in Trujillo, in western Venezuela, committed his life to teaching, medicine, and treating the underprivileged while writing books on science and philosophy. He became a legend after he was hit by a car and killed on his way to visiting a patient. Dr. Hernández is the unofficial saint for protection during overland journeys and caring for the sick. Out of respect, honor, and superstition, a prayer card with his picture on it can be found in most every bus, car, and truck in the country. A statue of Hernandez has surpassed the sixty-foot-high monument of the Virgin Mary Mother of Jesus as the most popular tourist site in Trujillo. Souvenirs such as postcards, penholders, figurines, and statuettes are available. Three decades after returning from Venezuela, I created my own souvenir when I put a magnet on the back of a laminated picture of him and attached it to our refrigerator.

In 1986, Pope John Paul II declared Dr. Hernández "venerable," a first step toward sainthood. The Vatican announcement mobilized the Archdiocese of Caracas into action. They sent representatives to Rome with stories of miracles, a requirement for all saints, and continued to collect more statements. In 2014, the *New York Times* reported that the office in Caracas pursuing Dr. Hernández's sainthood had received more than eight hundred letters describing miracles he performed. As of December 2016, Venezuela was still waiting to hear from the Vatican.

Dr. Jose Gregorio Hernandez 1864-1919

Meanwhile, the Padre continued his quest to open the minds of his staff to new ideas. His latest attempt, made possible through a donation from a Board member, was arranging for a late afternoon showing of *One Flew Over the Cuckoo's Nest* starring Jack Nicholson, the film based on the novel about institutionalization and authority by Ken Kesey. It smashed all attendance records for Maracaibo, despite the ten-bolivar ($2.30) admission—at that point, the most ever charged for a ticket in the city's history.

The Padre wanted to use the movie as a teaching tool and hoped it would stimulate reflection and connect it to AZUPANE's mission of a humanistic approach to the developmentally disabled, an uphill battle under any circumstances. However, the version we saw was different from the one I had seen in Caracas a few weeks earlier. The theater owner in Maracaibo cut two scenes from the 135-minute film, allowing for one additional show a day, a half-assed way to generate more revenue. Thanks to the cut scenes, one of which was Nicholson's failed attempt to lift the bathroom sink early in the movie, the ending didn't make sense.

A few days later, we met to discuss the movie. Though Jack Nicholson won an Academy Award for his portrayal of RP McMurphy, the staff's favorite character was the Chief, who, in the end, fled the institution. One staff pointed out his action expressed self-realization, a principle captured in AZUPANE's motto, *"Queremos Realizarnos"* (We Want to Realize Ourselves). The Padre contrasted the conditions, the inhumane treatment at the hospital, the lack of respect toward the patients, and the patient movements in the institution with the openness at AZUPANE, with its unlocked doors, constant encouragement for the kids to explore, and relaxed environment.

While getting the staff to think and develop new programs was forever a challenge, the Padre still questioned why we couldn't arrange a boat ride, a fishing trip, or a card game like the ones depicted in the movie. We were divided on whether he was joking or if he really wanted us to organize them.

While in Caracas in March 1975, I overheard a secretary in the Peace Corps office say, "We'll be lucky to last until Christmas," and then added they would be selling office equipment as part of downsizing. When I heard this, I asked if I could borrow a typewriter to use in Maracaibo. A few weeks later, I received an Underwood 21, a standard model at the time. It became my most prized possession in Venezuela. In my room at the house, I put one foot on a stool and the other on the floor, with the typewriter on one chair while I sat on another, pecking away writing letters and journal entries. I would not have written as much as I did without the typewriter, making me wonder what kind of record I might have had with one in San Carlos. It was possible, maybe likely, I would have kept everyone awake at the *residencia,* and the noise from the typing might have made the other tenants and the owner suspicious.

My source for acquiring typewriter ribbons was Tory's girlfriend, Ana, whose American employer had recently switched to electric typewriters that used cartridges, making ribbons obsolete. So I spent some Saturday mornings shopping for typewriter ribbons. One Saturday, on the way to look for ribbons, I stopped in Smiling Faces, the local head shop, to see if they carried posters of Che Guevara, something I thought would look cool hanging in my room. The store smelled of incense and was well-stocked with puzzles, games, and knickknacks such as the "Dr. Frankel quick abortion clinic:" a stick of dynamite and a guillotine representing French birth control methods. Corny figurines of "the world's best grandpa" and a man carrying the world on his shoulders, with an inscription at the bottom in English that read "A desk job would be easier," filled the shelves.

The store did not have Che Guevara posters. However, they were playing the Rolling Stones and the Allman Brothers over its stereo system with two speakers mounted on opposite walls. Radio stations played such music all the time. Months before, the portable cassette player at the house died, and we opted to replace it with a radio. "Let's Do the Twist Again" by Chubby Checker was one of the big hits at the time; in Spanish, it translated to "Vamos a Bailar a Twist Nuevo." Radio stations also played Elton John, the Bee Gees, the Who, Joan Baez, Diana Ross, and Cat Stevens, among others. Hearing the music in the store reminded me how much I missed a good sound system. When a friend wrote and asked me what I missed most in Venezuela, I said music. I browsed a bit longer so I could listen to more tunes.

When "Sympathy for the Devil" finished, I exited and walked fifty feet down the street to a store that sold typewriter ribbons. Before buying some, I stopped to look at the paperbacks and magazines. I missed having a good bookstore and never passed up a chance to browse in one. Our primary source of books was the Peace Corps office and the American Bookstore in Caracas. A store in Maracaibo sold used paperbacks for two dollars, mostly science fiction and romance novels, reflecting the reading habits of the expatriates working in the oil industry. The book exchange at the Venezuelan-American Center was another source. The quality and quantity of available reading material in English was much better than I expected.

Venezuelans who liked to read had a problem of cost rather than choice. An editorial in the local paper said the people of Venezuela did not have good reading habits, partly because books cost too much. Books in English should cost more than ones published locally, I thought, but works in Spanish should be affordable. I wanted to read *One Hundred Years of Solitude* by the Colombian writer and, later, Nobel Prize winner Gabriel Garcia Marquez in Spanish as a way to improve my grammar and vocabulary and was encouraged when one Volunteer, fluent in Spanish, said the novel read better in Marquez's native language than in English. Despite the claim, I was skeptical. For an English speaker, could any book be more enjoyable in Spanish? It seemed odd.

When Marquez died in 2014, literary critics of the day said the English translation was not only an outstanding one, but the novel also read better, contradicting the opinion I heard forty years earlier. Hmmm. My difficulty in 1976, though, was not whether one of the world's great works of fiction was better in Spanish but that it cost twenty bolivars or five dollars, which was way too much for a book. I would have to read something else to improve my Spanish.

On the rack next to *TIME* magazine and *Vision*, a Latin American weekly, was *The Gentleman's Bathroom Companion* by the National Lampoon. After paging through it, I decided five dollars, the same price as one of the greatest novels ever written, was too much. Then, after picking up two typewriter ribbons a few aisles over, I proceeded to the checkout counter where the manager was throwing out a bundle of the *Miami Herald*. I asked if I could take one of the week-old newspapers. He was more than happy to oblige, and he didn't ask me to pay for it.

With six weeks to go until the end of my two years of service and no specific plans on what to do next, I received a letter notifying me that my application to graduate school had been rejected. I was more relieved than disappointed, and rationalized I could learn more by staying in Venezuela. With the unemployment rate in the U.S. at 7.5 percent and expected to rise, finding a job would be a challenge.

Back to Normal

With graduate school out of the picture, I though more seriously about continuing at AZUPANE or teaching English at the Venezuelan-American Cultural Center (CEVAZ). They paid 1,400 bolivars ($350) a month for ten hours a week of teaching, better than a Peace Corps Volunteer salary, but when I included the extra I received for rent and the $75 monthly readjustment allowance, I would come out ahead staying with Peace Corps. When comparing medical benefits, Peace Corps won hands-down with its free and better care. On one level, working at AZUPANE was a forty-hour a week job, with comp time and weekends off in an urban setting and the modern conveniences of running water and indoor plumbing, not the typical situation portrayed in Peace Corps advertisements and memoirs. Caracas considered it one of the top four Volunteer jobs in the country. I never knew why, but I suspected it was a combination of the Padre's cooperation, zero on-the-job problems with Volunteers, and little monitoring required from Caracas.

Though it was not unusual for Volunteers to resign before they completed two years of service for a variety of personal and professional reasons, including being disenchanted or concluding that the program represented a dark side of foreign aid, I had no such qualms. I wasn't going to resign over some U.S. policy I didn't like. I hadn't exploited anyone, nor did I feel like a foreign policy tool as some political activists in Venezuela and the U.S. believed. Peace Corps had been an excellent opportunity. Every day I saw and learned something new. Remaining in Venezuela had its appeal. Further thinking it through, if I stayed past June, I could make a two-month trip back to the U.S. and then return to work for an indefinite period. My sister was expecting her first baby around the beginning of September, and she had asked me to be the godfather. I wanted to be at the baptism rather than have a stand-in.

While I compared the pros and cons of potential employers, an equally important factor in deciding whether to stay on after Peace Corps was whether we could remain in the house beyond September. It already looked like everyone had plans to leave and I would have to find someplace else to live. The lease expired at the end of June, and Jeff and Fernando were talking as if it was time for them to move on. Renting a room with a family again was out of the question. While Tory planned to stay in Venezuela, Ana wanted them to rent an apartment of their own as soon as they could. Also, I had to consider that maybe I had been in

Venezuela long enough, having soaked it for all she was worth. Perhaps I should go home, recession or not.

First, however, I needed an extension. I called Caracas and asked to stay until June, my third request to change my termination date—not including when I resigned while in San Carlos, only to un-resign a few weeks later. I realized asking to change my termination date again might set off mumbling in Caracas: Can't Kendellen make up his mind? But I wasn't too concerned about whether my indecisiveness bothered anyone as long as they granted the extension. I never heard of them not approving one, so I remained optimistic.

The simplicity of the process amazed me. All a Volunteer had to do was write a letter. Peace Corps did not conduct interviews or ask questions about motivation. I assumed my latest request would surprise my program officer, but I expected he would support it. Not knowing the country director well, I was less certain what he would do.

As I considered my future, I wondered if I wanted to get entangled in money, contracts, and personnel matters at AZUPANE. They had their problems and challenges, ranging from financial to human resources to training to activities for the kids, always the priority, despite the management and organizational issues that often superseded everything else. The Peace Corps might have had budget problems, but at least I got paid on time.

At AZUPANE, though, like everywhere in Venezuela, salaries were another matter. Staff earned only a little more than I did. Like most employees I would hire, meet, and supervise over the years, AZUPANE employees complained they were underpaid. I lacked the experience and perspective to conclude if their gripes were legitimate or simply typical of what any group of low-paid employees would say. The Padre, not sympathetic and facing challenges in balancing the budget and raising money, believed their salaries were commensurate with their education and limited experience. As I would learn, this dynamic exists in every institution, company, business, firm, and organization.

AZUPANE's fiscal woes did not bother the staff even though a shortage of cash could mean a late paycheck. No one seemed interested in the Padre's fundraising strategy or was curious enough to ask if he even had one. Occasionally, we would see him showing visitors around, explaining AZUPANE was the only center in Latin America for the developmentally disabled that offered an "open classroom" environment. Most seemed impressed, but few gave money. Visiting government officials responsible for special education in Venezuela, a UNESCO officer, and the Minister of Interior expressed awe but did not open their wallets. Receptions featuring local politicians resulted in nods during the Padre's presentation, showing they were captivated, but they donated nothing. Other than Exxon giving some of its property in the 1960s, the oil companies stayed away. A night of music, food, 130-bolivar tickets and ten-bolivar drinks also raised needed funds. The National Karate Championship contributed ten thousand bolivars, the largest single contribution while I was at AZUPANE. A different donation came from the youth choral group, Up with People. Between performances at the La Lago Intercontinental Hotel, they sang for the kids one afternoon. Unlike today, when nonprofit organizations and private institutions make public their donors, AZUPANE never released a list of its supporters, which didn't seem to bother anyone.

The Board of Directors paid the Padre 5,000 bolivars a month ($1,250) and gave him free use of a car. He lived rent-free in the former residence of the last American CEO at Exxon, which also served as AZUPANE's offices. No one considered the amount outrageous, or, more accurately, I never heard anyone comment on it. Besides, grumbling about executive pay was not part of the culture. It helped that everyone liked him as a person.

Staff turnover increased in the first half of 1976. Dr. Gonzalez, who had been the physician at AZUPANE for more than five years, resigned. He told the Padre the workload of his private medical practice had become too much to manage along with his responsibilities at AZUPANE. Rumors persisted he had resigned because the Padre wanted him to work more hours, which he refused to do. When there was no official announcement of his sudden departure, and the Padre did not hold a *despidida* (farewell party) for him, a Venezuelan tradition, we knew the separation had probably been as ugly as rumored.

Two other staff resigned over salary. The Padre paid his secretary less than $200 a month. As a result, he was hiring a new one about every eight weeks; refusing to pay more money for a job he thought required little effort and few skills. He held a similar attitude about Victor, the bus driver who didn't miss a day of work in three years. The Padre considered him underworked—a perception that no staff member understood—even though he ran errands between transporting the kids three times a day and drove them around the city on excursions and to the beach on weekends. While always polite, he seemed unhappy. I never saw him smile. But he was reliable, a scarce commodity in Venezuela, and he never had an accident. When his contract expired, the Padre offered him another one, but without a raise. Victor quit, loathing his boss for his lack of appreciation, a development that shocked us. Sometimes it was hard to reconcile the Padre's humanitarianism regarding people with disabilities with his attitudes about his staff, most of whom he believed underperformed. The Padre replaced Victor with three women drivers and their borrowed mini-vans and station wagons.

A week after Victor quit, a minor crisis occurred with one of the new drivers. While taking a group of kids home for lunch, the driver looked in the rearview mirror and did not see fourteen-year-old Edgar in the back seat of her station wagon. She didn't remember dropping him off. Somehow, he got out of the car without her noticing. This never happened when Victor drove the bus. It was not clear how it could. Meanwhile, his mother called the office to report her son was late. After the Padre and others had made a few phone calls, they discovered that University Hospital had admitted Edgar with a broken leg, arm, and collarbone from being hit by a car. He recovered but did not return to AZUPANE for three months.

Once, Alex, a teenager, went missing at the end of the day. We broke into small groups and rushed to search bushes, backyards, and stores. I jumped in Neil Volkmann's car. He was the Peace Corps program officer from Caracas, in town on a monitoring visit. I hoped that in his car, we'd be able to cover the area faster and find Alex. Jeff and Joe, a physical education teacher at the American school volunteering at AZUPANE, took their motorcycles to look for the boy. Others tried the Victoria Supermarket, where we had gone on a field trip and pushed eight kids around in a shopping cart, startling the other shoppers and bringing looks of "Who brought the circus?"

Alex, however, was nowhere. Thirty minutes later, we were back, worried and wondering what else to do. Then, to everyone's relief, Señora Paredes, the Padre's housekeeper, turned the corner holding Alex's hand. A neighbor had found him looking for pigeons in front of her house and got him to say "AZUPANE." She then called Señora Paredes, who went to get him.

It was a challenge identifying an activity suitable for all the kids, considering their broad range of mobility and mental capacities. There were times when I would wrestle with them. I started first with two or three, and when the other five or so in the group realized wrestling looked like a lot of fun, they would join in. A few minutes later, the situation would be out of control and I would have to stop. I had to be careful because some of the kids were so fragile they could hurt themselves from the slightest bump or fall. I introduced volleyball as a safe alternative, but it was more physically challenging for most of them, so they stopped playing. Today, forty years later, we have the mobility-challenged playing sitting volleyball. In 1976, however, the concept was new and had yet to catch on. At the Paralympic games in Toronto that year, it was just a demonstration sport.

The kids did not always cooperate. Once indoors, they bounced a ball off the floor until it hit the ceiling. Their game ended when the ball hit the lights and splattered glass over the room, but no one was hurt. We swept the floor in silence, knowing we dodged a possible calamity.

Typically, I read stories or played with building blocks and modeling clay before moving on to an activity requiring more physical exertion. The kids were of varying ages and developmental capabilities, and not all seventeen of them liked playing games; some preferred more sedate activities. Two of them were eleven-year-old twins, obese and with limited physical ability and energy. Unable to take part in games requiring a lot of movement, they sat together and watched, enjoying the socialization, until they started fighting. One day, while I was trying to organize fun on the basketball court for thirteen kids, they were off in the corner hitting each other. Since neither could beat up the other, I let them punch each other until they tired of it while the rest of us continued playing basketball.

One Friday afternoon, only five kids were in Expression. The others were out sick, or their parents had kept them home for a family function, or the family had left early for a long weekend. With fewer kids to look after, we took them to the Lake Maracaibo Club. The guard stopped us at the entrance, asking what we wanted. We told him we had called ahead and whoever answered the phone said we were welcome.

But he wouldn't budge. We waited while he went inside to check with his supervisor.

Ten minutes later, he returned and said we could not enter the club. He did not give a reason, nor did he apologize. We left and walked a few blocks to the La Lago Hotel, where the security guards again denied us entry, saying we did not have clearance, presumably because five developmentally disabled children seemed threatening to them. Since when did you need permission to walk into a hotel lobby? Despite the mid-afternoon heat, we continued walking down Milagros Avenue to the Marina only to find the park closed for cleaning. After resting on the benches, we walked the mile back to AZUPANE, arriving hot and thirsty at break time but feeling good because the kids had enjoyed the excursion. I grabbed a half a pitcher of water and gulped it down.

That night while lying in a hammock on our second-story porch going over the day, I realized an important issue had emerged from the outing. Belkis, the oldest girl at AZUPANE at twenty-one, was not happy with what she witnessed when she accompanied us. She demanded a meeting with Sanchez, where she declared the older kids would no longer go on excursions with the younger ones because it was embarrassing when strangers stared and made comments such as, "Look at them, they are mentally retarded." She asserted she was not like them. I would like to believe being at AZUPANE encouraged that statement and her recognition of her own individuality.

Caracas responded to my request to extend my stay by wanting it in writing. Wasting no time, I wrote a short letter asking for the longest possible extension, since Peace Corps had not made an official announcement about its future. In fact, the most recent communication from Caracas appeared upbeat and optimistic, saying talks with the government regarding more financial assistance were going well, though it could have been the Peace Corps' way of believing the glass was half full rather than half empty. When the program officer called the Padre to inform him they had approved my extension through June, he wanted to know, half in jest, if it meant I was staying until mid- 1978, two years from now. No, I would be in Venezuela two more months. And maybe I would remain even longer.

President Carlos Andres Pérez had been aggressive in moving Venezuela forward. He nationalized the oil industry, established a foreign aid program, developed a national plan to spend the projected billions of dollars from oil, rejected criticism about questionable law enforcement practices, claimed he couldn't fix every problem, and told the people that color television was not a priority. But he shocked the country when he announced he would reduce the number of holidays. He said if Venezuela wanted to show the world its work ethic had improved and continue on the road to modernization, the country could not have twenty holidays that included a week at Christmas, several Catholic holidays, and national days such as Simon Bolívar's birthday, Independence Day, and Labor Day.

While the ruling only applied to government offices, the president encouraged all employers to follow his lead. Because of the timing of his announcement, the first holiday he abolished, Carnival, was just two weeks away. The AZUPANE staff did not know what the Padre would do. He always wanted us to work more. Would everyone have to cancel their plans for Carnival?

Thirteen

Holiday Time

The staff grumbled over the possibility of losing time at the beach, the traditional way of celebrating Carnival. Still, they didn't complain too much; it wasn't their style. They shrugged and said it was up to the Padre, who surprised everyone when he went along with other private institutions and businesses and announced that AZUPANE would observe the holiday as usual. The president would have to find another way to reduce the number of work days lost to holidays. In the end, only the government did not declare Carnival a holiday.

It was my third Carnival in Venezuela, the first being during training when I traveled to Punto Fijo with Natalia and her family. The prior year, with the few flights to Trinidad already full, another Volunteer and I took a fishing boat from Guiria, the farthest eastern point in Venezuela, to Trinidad around midnight and snuck, into the country for a few days of steel bands, parades and partying. There was no other way to get there. The seven-mile boat journey avoided immigration, but it was not uncommon. Once there, I experienced one of the best festivals in the world. Then we snuck back into Venezuela. This year for Carnival, I would go to Bogotá by bus.

The night bus for San Cristobal left at 9:30. I was glad to be on the road again, it having been over a year since my last trip. I slept most of the way. When we arrived at 4:30 on a Sunday morning, I caught a taxi to San Antonio del Tachira, a town Simon Bolívar passed through in his quest for independence from Spain; there, Venezuelan immigration would stamp my passport with an exit stamp. But when I got there the immigration office was closed.

I sat down on a concrete bench in front of Simon Bolívar Bridge. A police officer strolled over, eyeing my beard and backpack, mumbled "hippie," and walked away without questioning me about my plans. He didn't bother the drunks sprawled out in the street or the three guys babbling on the other side of the plaza. The cop also ignored a couple of teenagers smoking cigarettes in front of the taxi stand. Maybe the others were regulars at the bridge. Presumably, the drunks, like me and the kids, were waiting for the visa office to open. Otherwise, why hang out at the border before dawn on a Sunday morning? Well, maybe because the bars had just closed. I had arrived after all the fun and was witnessing the sequel: drunkenness, sleeping in the street, and waiting. More men who had too much to drink arrived. They stumbled over the other drunks, waking two of them who, after getting an apology, went back to sleep.

An hour later, a car pulled up to the immigration office. A foreigner got out and pounded on the window as if he had an emergency. To my surprise, the window slid open and the man placed his passport in a hand. A few minutes later, the window opened again and a hand extended the man's passport. The foreigner grabbed it, and after paging through it looking for his exit stamp, got back into his car and sped across the bridge to Colombia. It was 5:30, meaning I had not quite three more hours of waiting ahead of me.

I asked the police officer who had called me a hippie when immigration opened for business while also inquiring about the guy who just drove off. The cop didn't know anything about him, but he suggested I knock on the door to see if I could get an exit visa, too. When I tapped on the window, it slid open. I placed my passport in the palm of a hand that jutted out. I stood there waiting. All was quiet. The drunks were sleeping. After a few minutes, I, too, had my exit stamp from Venezuela. I walked over to a taxi and woke the driver, saying I wanted to go to DAS (*Departamento Administrativo de Seguridad*), the security agency responsible for immigration, in Villa del Rosario in Colombia. DAS opened at 6 a.m., so my wait there would be short.

As we approached an area crowded with bars and nightclubs near Villa del Rosario, we picked up three men who wanted to go to the next town. They asked the driver to stop along the way if he saw the police so they could report they had been robbed. A few minutes later, we came to a screeching halt, and seconds later two officers were in our faces. The drunks told their story, and the cops scribbled in their notebooks. After listening, one of the policemen said, "Don't expect us to get your money back for you." The three amigos did not appear perturbed at hearing the bad news, feeling fortunate they were alive after a wild Saturday night in Villa del Rosario.

A few more kilometers down the road they got out, and we continued for a quick stop at the DAS before the taxi dropped me at the bus terminal in Cucuta. The driver asked for twice the regular amount, charging me having to wait while I got a visa. I didn't argue, since doubling the rate meant I would pay sixty cents instead of thirty cents.

I bought a ticket for the 10 a.m. bus to Bogotá. As I was boarding, the person behind me said in English, "Are you going to Bogotá?"

Surprised to hear English, I turned around and saw a gaunt man in his mid-twenties who needed a haircut. "Yes, I am," I said.

"Are you an American?" he continued.

"I am. I've been in Venezuela a couple of years."

Instantly, I realized I made a mistake giving him that information, which could lead to more questions I was not interested in answering. He surprised me when he changed the subject and asked what I knew about a magazine in his hand.

"Have you ever seen this?" he asked as he pointed to the cover of *Back to Godhead,* the official magazine of the Hare Krishna movement. I admitted I'd seen it at newsstands in Caracas but had never read it.

As we waited to board, he continued making small talk. "Hey, I am from Caracas. *Soy Venezolano.* I'm Venezuelan. What's your seat number?" Hare Krishna Man was speaking in a tone way too friendly for a stranger who'd introduced himself ten minutes ago. I started to realize this might not go well.

"Seat three, across from the driver in front of the door," I said.

"What seat do I have? Twelve or fifteen? I can't read the ticket."

Already suspicious, I said it looked like a twelve and suggested he double-check with the driver, feeling bothered and irritated by a question to which I was sure he knew the answer. If I could make out the seat number on my ticket, so could he.

After we boarded, the bus left in a cloud of fumes. I had an excellent view of the road and the scenery in front of me. While most of the passengers put their luggage on top of the bus, I put mine underneath my seat because it often rained in the mountains, and it was safer there, too. I heard stories about the baggage handlers opening backpacks and suitcases when loading them and removing whatever they could. On my previous trip to Colombia, I'd met two German tourists who accused two baggage handlers of stealing their cameras and the coins they had been collecting from each country on their world travels. When they got into a screaming match in German and Spanish, I walked away, doubtful the Germans would get their cameras and money back.

We rode through the mountains, picking up and dropping off people along the way so they could shop, go to church, or visit family and friends, the usual Sunday activities. From my front-row seat, Andean life seemed quiet and peaceful as well as simple and hard. Bus travel was slow in the Andes. We must have stopped every ten minutes between Cúcuta and Bogotá. Despite the long waits and frequent stops, the passengers, mostly women and girls, as well as small children with their parents, almost all carrying bags full of food, always appeared to be in a jovial mood. One woman waved at each passenger and laughed and joked with the driver, not a very common scene on a Greyhound bus in the United States, but apparently perfectly normal here.

In fact, once while traveling from the Midwest to California on a Greyhound bus, I experienced the complete opposite of what I was seeing in Colombia. On the overnight ride, I kept nodding off, my head falling on the shoulder of the man sitting in the seat next to me. After the third time, he said, "If you do it again, I'll knock your fucking head off." I stayed awake all night. When we stopped for a break, I ended up standing next to him in the bathroom. Trying to make small talk while pissing, I asked him where he was going. "It's none of your fucking business" came the curt response. An hour later, a few of the passengers got off and I changed seats.

Looking out the window in the Andes, all I could see was green and abundant farmland. During one stop to fix a flat tire, I had nowhere to go, so I stood on the side of the road and listened to the wind. The weather was beautiful, partly sunny and nearly sixty degrees.

We arrived in Pamplona in time for the Sunday midday concert in the plaza. The band played better than The Veterans of the Battle of Carabobo, a music group in San Carlos that included no veterans, as the battle occurred in 1821, who entertained the city's denizens on Sunday nights. Pamplona was cold enough that I had to rub my hands to keep them warm, though not cold enough to cause the musicians' lips to stick to their instruments.

After re-boarding the bus, a woman shouted that someone had stolen her radio. She had left it on her seat as we got off for lunch, and when she returned, the radio was gone. Since the doors were locked as we ate lunch, her explanation made little sense. The police arrived and began their investigation. "Okay, lady," one inquired, "how did you lose your radio?" He sounded a bit rude and impatient.

"Someone took it while I was eating lunch," she told them.

The officers ordered us off the bus so they could search it. The driver counted the passengers as we got off and came up short one, but no one could remember what the person looked like. After the police completed their search without finding the radio, the driver ordered us back on the bus and we continued to Bogotá.

Three hours later, as the sun was setting, we stopped in the middle of nowhere on a narrow stretch of road. All I could make out in the fading sunlight was a large crowd and two armed soldiers looking at a body. I stared out the window along with the other passengers at the dead man lying on his stomach who had either had been hit by a bus or a truck or shot to death. No one said a word. If any of the passengers knew what happened, they weren't saying. The body could have been from one of the guerrilla groups the army had been fighting for years. As we moved closer to the corpse, a woman broke the tense silence, yelling, "Hey cousin," and waving at an elderly gentleman standing on the side of the road. With a look of bewilderment, he tipped his hat as the bus passed him.

In today's post-9/11 world of heightened security, a state of siege might warrant law enforcement departments to ban travel to certain areas and embassies to issue alerts. But the U.S. Embassy had issued no such warning in March 1976, despite Colombia having been under a state of siege for almost a year. This was a time characterized by labor unrest, an expanding drug trade, arbitrary arrests, criminal cases tried in a military court, torture, forced disappearances, executions, and massacres by government troops and their paramilitary allies. Yet with tourism flourishing, the lack of travel advisories, and two hundred Peace Corps Volunteers in the country, Colombia appeared safe.

Not long after passing the body in the road, we stopped to change a flat tire. Everyone got off the bus. I sat on the side of the road and waited. Hare Krishna Man and his Colombian friend used the stop to smoke a joint. I walked a few hundred feet to a farm to look around and savor the scene and tranquility. A couple of kids were filling buckets with water from a well behind the barn, where I could see a few garden tools and animals. Off in the distance, a group of teenage girls was out for a walk. A man, who I took to be the father, wearing a drab poncho, sat in silence watching his two sons in the field. I suspected the brick house, not far from the barn, was more impoverished than the outside suggested. Everyone I met in Venezuela and Colombia told me that the outside condition of a building was misleading. While the homes looked fine on the outside, the inside often reflected a difficult life.

We stopped every two hours for a break. During one, Hare Krishna Man asked me if I ate meat. "Yes, a little," I said, not ready to blame my small living allowance from Peace Corps for my low consumption of it. I wondered what game he was playing.

"Did you know that when you eat meat, you are eating your brother? Like that pig over there, he's your brother in a different way."

"I didn't know that," I said, thinking, what a load of crap.

"Do you eat fish?" Hari Krishna Man asked me.

"Yes, I do," remembering the one time I had seafood in Venezuela—a lobster I bought on the beach on Margarita Island for fifty cents while visiting Volunteers there.

"Fish are your brothers," said Hare Krishna Man, who admitted he smoked marijuana and practiced yoga and had now found the way to nirvana with a meatless and fishless diet. I was skeptical.

The more I listened to Hare Krishna Man, the more I disliked him. I sensed he was looking to sponge off me as much as possible and would at some point ask for money, meaning trouble unless I ditched him. When he laughed upon hearing I was traveling alone, I suspected he considered me an easy target for his manipulations. When I overheard him tell his Colombian companion they needed a place to stay in Bogotá, I worried they'd want to share a room with me, for which I would pay. In the middle of the night, I theorized, they would rob me or ask for a donation to the Hare Krishnas. During the rest of the ride, I plotted a way to get rid of them.

I first became suspicious of freeloaders while traveling in the western U.S. after graduating from college. An ex-college football player from Philadelphia living in Berkley, California, wanted to borrow ten dollars so he could send a telegram home and ask his parents for money. In return, he would give me fifteen dollars, a 33 percent interest rate, when he received the cash through Western Union. With fifty dollars remaining of my own money, I declined the offer because I didn't believe he would pay me back.

On the same trip, I arrived at a street corner in Las Vegas ready to hitchhike at the same time a teenager from Idaho walked to the curb and stuck his thumb out. He suggested we try to get a ride together. I had little choice other than to say, "Okay." A few hours later, while entering Yellowstone National Park, he informed the driver he had seven cents in his pocket and could not contribute gas money. The driver, who was going to Green Bay, Wisconsin, ordered him out of the car at Old Faithful; he could try his luck hitching a ride from more sympathetic tourists. Ever since, I'd decided not to befriend any more moochers while traveling.

Meanwhile, Hare Krishna Man from Caracas wanted to know my plans. "Where are you staying in Bogotá?" he asked. I needed to tell him and his friend to get lost—or, better, I needed to disappear into the crowd at the bus station as soon as we arrived in Bogotá.

Besides keeping alert for thieves on the trip, I had to deal with cooler weather and the lack of toilets. After being acclimated to extreme heat from living ten degrees or about 725 miles north of the equator for two years, I was cold from sitting by the door, which opened several times an hour to let passengers on and off. I was wearing a light wool jacket, the first long-sleeve garment I had worn since arriving in Venezuela, a pair of calf-high socks, and boots, but still my feet and ungloved hands were freezing. We made pit stops but not anywhere near indoor bathrooms. Instead, everyone would hurry off and head to the nearest bush or tree, with the women walking to the furthest bush with the most foliage. The men who couldn't wait relieved themselves a few feet from the bus; once, they even did so as two nuns looked the other way.

Fernando had told me the bus from the border to Bogotá would take sixteen hours, so when I read that the official travel time was twenty-one hours, I was not pleased. However, it turned out to be neither. We arrived at five in the morning after a nineteen-hour ride, even though it seemed as if we were stopping every few minutes to pick people up, drop someone off, or take a snack and piss break.

When we finally arrived, I hurried over to the taxi stand and jumped into the first one in line, telling the driver to take me to the Hotel Nuevo York, one of three hotels I knew in Bogotá. Just before I closed the car door, Hare Krishna Man, wearing a scarf over his head and looking cold, tried pulling it open. I grabbed it from the inside and said in English, "I'm going alone," and slammed the door. Hare Krishna Man looked shocked. I never saw him or his friend again.

Hotel Nuevo York was in the southeastern part of the city, near the intersection of Avenida Sixteen and Calle Twenty-three—except it wasn't. The taxi driver had never heard of the place. However, he did find my next choice, The Miami, nine blocks away, with little trouble. A room with a bed and a bathroom at the end of the second-floor hall was five dollars for a night. Despite the thin walls and the chattering women in the next room, I soon fell asleep. Five hours later at ten o'clock, I woke up to people belching, blowing their noses, slamming doors, children screaming, someone scrubbing clothes, and lots of chatter at the front desk. I dressed and checked out to look for the Hotel Aleman, where I'd stayed eighteen months earlier, hoping they had a room with a bathroom and a towel rather than only a bed and a noisy hallway.

I walked more than a mile to the intersection of Sixteenth Avenida and Calle Sixteen. Knowing the hotel had to be close, I stood on the corner of the intersection in front of the Copetran Bus Depot and did a 360-degree turn but saw nothing. Where did it go? I repeated the turn more slowly, peering at each building. It had to be here. Squinting to make sure I studied every building before moving on to the next one, I finally saw it, just a few buildings from where I was standing. Feeling like an idiot, I entered the hotel.

"Do you have any rooms available?" I asked the man behind the desk.

"Rooms without a bathroom are ninety pesos and ones with a private bath are one hundred pesos; the rooms with a private bath do not have hot water."

He added that breakfast was not included. Without hesitating, I opted for a room with a private bath and cold water. Most places I stayed when traveling did not have hot water, and if I was lucky enough to stay in one that did, I took a cold refreshing shower anyway, being used to them. In Venezuela, where it was ninety degrees most days, I didn't have much use for hot water, so a cold shower came to seem normal. A private bath, even with cold water, was worth the additional ten pesos, about ten cents.

My room at the end of the hall included a bed, a desk, and a bamboo chair that looked as if it would break apart if I sat on it. I sipped warm water from the pitcher on the desk even though I did not know how long it had been sitting there or if the hotel had boiled it. It tasted okay. I mostly followed the Peace Corps advice not to drink tap water except at the house in our middle-class neighborhood in Maracaibo because the real estate agent had said the water was clean. I'm still alive.

The hotel did not have safe deposit boxes for its guests, a standard service offered at reception desks in most hotels before they began providing room safes, leaving me no choice but to carry my cash around in the money belt my parents had brought me. It looked like a regular belt. I had to fold the bills and slide them in before zipping it shut. It was a good belt.

Each morning, I had a breakfast of ham and eggs, bread and jelly, hot chocolate, and a huge glass of orange juice for $1.05 in the dining area off the lobby. For the first two days, while enjoying breakfast, I leafed through an old magazine packed with articles on the Soviet Union that expounded on the advantages of communism. I wondered who had left it. On the third day, I read a 1967 issue of *TIME* with Mao Tse Tung on the cover. One essay described the bright outlook for U.S. foreign policy despite having 400,000 troops in Vietnam. Another expressed optimism regarding Latin America because democracies were blooming in Chile, Costa Rica, and Venezuela. They were right about two of three, but failed on Chile, whose democratically elected president, Salvador Allende, was killed during a coup in September 1973.

One afternoon, I went to see *Alice Doesn't Live Here Anymore,* a Martin Scorsese film with Ellen Burstyn and Kris Kristofferson. The crowd was sparse despite tickets costing only forty cents each. Afterward, I walked the four miles back to the hotel. On the way, a man approached me and asked for directions to buildings he pointed to on a postcard of Bogotá he pulled out of his pocket. "Do you know where this is?" he asked repeatedly. When I replied I didn't know, he asked if I was Colombian—no. Feeling obligated to respond in an attempt to be sociable, I asked him where he was from.

"I am from Ecuador and am looking for these buildings on Carrera Seven," he said as he pointed again to the postcard.

Suddenly, out of nowhere, a man in a long gray coat and dark glasses approached us and asked if he could be of assistance. "I am a tourist policeman. There is a lot of crime in Bogotá, including many counterfeit bills. Show me your passport and money."

What are tourist police? Instead of walking away, or even running away, I foolishly told him I hid cash in different places all over my body, making it inconvenient and awkward to take it out in broad daylight. After saying all that in Spanish, I realized my explanation was too complicated and not clear, actually ridiculous, but I had to say something—he was a police officer. He repeated his request. Standing on the pavement with pedestrians walking by, I fumbled with my belt while wondering why I had to show my dollars and bolivars. How would he know if they were fake or not? Then he darted across the street.

The Ecuadorian, recognizing an opportunity and forgetting about the buildings he was looking for, asked if I wanted to buy cocaine. I said no. Not giving up, he asked about my interest in buying marijuana. Before replying, the tourist cop was back. He handed me his business card, saying he worked with the Bogotá Police Department. "Now I need to see your money," he said once again.

"Why do I need to show you my money and passport?"

"I must be sure you have not been cheated. Maybe you are buying drugs, I don't know. Tourists sometimes put them in the heel of their shoes and other places on their body when they enter the country at the airport." Not seeing the connection, I stupidly said, "I traveled overland by bus, not by airplane."

Unimpressed, he insisted I show him my money. I pulled a one hundred bolivar note from my belt.

"I have to go across the street to check if it is real or not."

"Okay, but I'm going with you," I told him.

He changed his mind after hearing I wanted to accompany him. He noticed I only used my left hand. "What happened to you?" he asked.

"I was sick when I was young," I said, avoiding the precise answer of "polio," which often drew the retort, "What's that?"

The so-called tourist policeman ran off, leaving me and the Ecuadorian drug dealer looking at each other, not sure what to do next.

He said, *"Vamos"* ("Let's go). We walked away in opposite directions, never to see each other again.

Two days later, I saw *Midnight Cowboy* starring Jon Voight and Dustin Hoffman, the only X-rated film to win an Academy Award for Best Film. I had heard Dustin Hoffman played a crazy guy, giving me a reason to see if there was a connection to what I was doing at AZUPANE. As it turned out, it had nothing remotely in common with our work. Afterwards, I walked back to the hotel. Not paying attention to the street signs, I went too far and found myself in the exact spot where the tourist cop had tried to rob me; the Ecuadorian who'd been on a quest to find an office building while hawking drugs was not in sight. I made it back without meeting any other strangers.

Fernando had asked me to buy *The Journey to Ixtlan* and *The Teachings of Don Juan* by Carlos Castaneda, two best-selling books about drug-induced adventures with a Yaqui Indian shaman that had been translated into seventeen languages. Castaneda, considered one of the godfathers of America's New Age movement, once appeared on the cover of *TIME*. Jeff quoted him during the same late-night philosophical discussion that referenced The Beaver and Zorro the Fox. Whatever Jeff said about Castaneda, it impressed Fernando enough that he wanted to read the man's works and learn more about his ideas. The two books cost twenty-five dollars, which was a lot of money at a time when paperbacks still cost less than three dollars. I remembered Fernando still owed me for last month's rent and food, so I didn't buy them.

I was still interested in a Spanish edition of *One Hundred Years of Solitude* by Gabriel Garcia Marquez, Colombia's literary pride and joy, hoping it would cost less than five dollars, as it did in Maracaibo. The Central Bookstore had a hard copy with a mother in a rocking chair on the cover. In the back of the book was a ten-page summary of Marquez's works, plus a picture of him with his big mustache, curly hair, and dark eyes. However, at 225 pesos, or about $15, it was out of my price range.

One morning, I walked two miles from the hotel to the National Park, one of my favorite places in Bogotá. I arrived at 9:15 according to the four-sided clock inside the entrance. Other than the groundskeepers in the flower garden, I saw no other activity. I walked up the asphalt path to Monserrate, the ten-thousand-foot mountain that dominates the center of the city, with restaurants, souvenir shops, and a church at the summit. I passed the military headquarters in the park, then encountered by five teenagers smoking a joint. A signpost on a tree said washing clothes was not allowed in the creek. In the distance, I could see a few houses.

I made my way over to a recreation area and passed basketball, tennis, and handball courts; *bolas carolas*; a soccer field; and a hockey rink where I sat down and read *The Greenhouse* by the Peruvian writer Mario Vargas Llosa, who in 2010 was awarded the Nobel Prize for Literature. After reading for an hour, I walked over to watch a soccer game. It didn't take long to realize that without soccer in Venezuela, I was missing out on an important cultural phenomenon. Of all the countries where Peace Corps had programs, I ended up in one that preferred baseball, boxing, and motocross to the world's most popular sport. Even Venezuelans admitted they stunk at soccer, but saw no end in their national disinterest in the sport. As of 2014, Venezuela was the only country in South America never to qualify for the World Cup.

While watching the soccer game, a man approached me and asked for money. I declined and he walked away. I did not give money to beggars unless they were disabled or noticeably destitute. If the beggar appeared intoxicated or high, I continued walking. However, I made exceptions, such as the time in Venezuela I gave a bolivar to a young double amputee walking on his two stumps at the bus station in Maracaibo and two pesos to an armless man in Cúcuta. In Pamplona, I handed a bolivar to a frail-looking woman who was shouting that Venezuelans were rich. Thinking I was Venezuelan, she asked me for money as I waited to get back on the bus. I put all my change in her hand. The first time I went to Bogotá, I arrived on Christmas Eve and came upon a woman and her three children huddled in front of a doorway, trying to stay warm. I gave her ten pesos.

Also in Bogotá, I was sitting on a park bench enjoying an ice cream when a girl, who appeared to be no more than ten years old, held out her hand, meaning she wanted money. I didn't respond because I could not reach into my pocket for spare change while holding an ice cream cone. Then her friends arrived and demanded I give them money.

"You're rich," said the ten-year-old, with her young friends standing behind her. I denied it. Not surprisingly, they didn't believe me. "We know you are rich, and we are poor." I gave them a peso. A few hours later, while crossing the bridge that separated a poor neighborhood from the downtown business area I heard "*Hola, hola.*" I looked over and saw the five girls waving.

The week in Bogotá was restful. The hotel was quiet except for the few hours in the evening when men I never saw congregated in the adjacent room for a gab session about women. I enjoyed my privacy and the calm. My concentration while reading was better than it had been for months. I didn't miss the disturbances in the neighborhood in Maracaibo such as fast cars speeding by the house or Harry stopping by with his latest complaints about life. When I checked out, the receptionist recommended I take the Berlinas Del Fonce bus to Venezuela. I took his advice and bought a ticket for a ride that, according to the posted schedule, would take seventeen hours. The bus left Bogotá at two in the afternoon, and it rained all the way. Twenty-six hours later, I arrived in Maracaibo.

Returning to work required an adjustment. Even one week in Colombia made everything seem different. Most of the talk in Peace Corps about cultural shock I took with a grain of salt, but if I ever experienced it, it was when I returned to work after that trip. I needed a few days to readjust. It didn't help that on my first day back, rumors about Peace Corps links to the CIA had surfaced yet again.

Fourteen

Crime, Camping and a Coup

It had been months since I'd heard anyone associate the Peace Corps with the CIA. But on my second day back from vacation, I overheard one of the staff tell everyone her friend at the university thought the Volunteers in Maracaibo worked for the CIA. Although some Venezuelans assumed the Peace Corps and the CIA were the same, it was nonetheless jolting to listen to my colleagues talk about it as if it were true. The latest story, both amusing and annoying, was serious enough to consider bringing it to the attention of the Padre. But when interest in the spy story dissipated after the morning break, partly because the apolitical staff either didn't care or knew university students held anti-American views, Jeff and I dropped the idea.

A few days later, I went on a beach excursion with AZUPANE, which seemed like paradise even if Lake Maracaibo was polluted with oil. After the outing, I took a night bus to Caracas for my annual medical and dental checkup. I preferred the ten-hour overnight ride so I could look for a hotel in daylight and avoid whatever dangers were lurking after dark. Immediately after arriving, though, I would go to the Peace Corps office to see if any hotel other than Los Pinos was offering a discount to Volunteers.

The trip got off to an ominous start. Less than ninety minutes after leaving the Las Pulgas Terminal in Maracaibo, the bus broke down. Unable to fix the engine problem, one of the drivers—there were always two on long rides—hitched a ride back to Maracaibo while the other driver sat on the side of the road and waited with me and the other passengers. An hour later, some grew tired of waiting and hitchhiked to Caracas. I opted to wait for the driver to return from Maracaibo with either a mechanic or a new bus. Around two in the morning, a replacement arrived. The baggage was transferred and we continued to Caracas.

The radio had been on since resuming the ride; the driver turned up the volume in the middle of the night. It wasn't that he wanted us to listen to his favorite song, or was warning us a rest stop was near, but it seemed he thought we might be interested in the play-by-play broadcast from Buenos Aires of the military coup underway against Argentine President Isabel Peron. The military arrested her, and the new government soon banned all political and union activity. It would be the most historical event I would hear on the radio until I listened to the live BBC transmission from Los Angeles of the O.J. Simpson verdict. In Caracas, I bought *El Nacional* and *El Universal*, the two major local newspapers, to keep up with the events. Editorials reminded readers that Venezuela was one of two democracies in South America, with Colombia being the other one, and the coup was a loss for democracy. Peter Stevens, the Peace Corps director in Venezuela, had been in Argentina two weeks earlier and reported inflation had so weakened the Argentine peso that his dinner of beef, potato salad, and wine cost a mere eighty cents.

The Venezuelan media was reporting that the U.S. government knew of the plans for the coup. Documents obtained in 2006 by the nonprofit Washington, DC-based National Security Archive verified America's role. According to the released documents, when the Argentine generals were preparing to oust Peron, the U.S. had advised the generals to avoid the Chilean model used in September 1973, when hundreds died at the hands of the police and army, and many thousands jailed and "disappeared." They advised the rebels to keep the number of casualties down. The generals dismissed the Americans' advice, and the coup led to the "Dirty Wars," the disappearance of thirty thousand people, and six years of dictatorship. In December 2010, General Jorge Rafael Videla, who had replaced Isabel Peron as president in March 1976, was imprisoned for life for the deaths of thirty-one prisoners following the coup. In 2012, an Argentine court sentenced him to fifty years for the systematic kidnapping of children while president of Argentina. He died in his sleep of natural causes in prison in 2013. Today, survivors among the disappeared are learning through DNA testing they had been kidnapped as infants and raised by people other than their birth parents.

The next day, I went for a physical exam and visited the dentist. The results found me in excellent health. Not having stepped on a scale in over a year, it felt good to find out I weighed 145 pounds, the same as when I'd arrived two years earlier. My teeth were in good shape, too, except for one small cavity. The dentist asked if I wanted a shot of Novocain or if he should fill the hole without it; the choice was mine. I chose the anesthetic, and fifteen minutes later my mouth was frozen and ready for drilling. He returned to the room empty-handed to tell me something was wrong with the electrical wiring in his office—his dental tools weren't working. He appeared surprised, since he had filled several cavities in the morning. Worse, his regular repairman did not know if he would be available later in the day to fix the equipment.

I had little time for a new appointment, since my bus to Maracaibo was leaving the next evening. He told me to call him in a few hours to check whether the repairman was coming. If so, I would be his first patient in the morning. If not, I should ask the Peace Corps to find another dentist. I left and climbed the steep hill to the Peace Corps office and informed the nurse what had happened. We decided not to wait for the repairman, and she made an appointment for me to visit an oral surgeon within the hour. I caught a taxi to his office, thinking the problem was solved. Before I opened my mouth for the surgeon to take a look on the lower right side, I mentioned that the cavity was small. He stopped searching immediately and announced he couldn't find it. He continued, "If I can't see it, you can wait until you return to Caracas in five months."

I returned to the office and informed the nurse of the dentist's recommendation. "That's the trouble with him," she said. "He's an excellent surgeon, but he doesn't take any other part of dentistry seriously." I opined he probably didn't care about small dental problems because if people waited longer to take care of their teeth, the problem would likely get worse, requiring surgery and his expertise. The nurse laughed at my cynicism while understanding the point I was making: the oral surgeon was not interested in filling cavities. However, whatever he lacked in enthusiasm for basic dentistry, he still cleaned my lower teeth and charged Peace Corps $10 for the work.

When I first arrived more than two years prior, Caracas seemed like a filthy, noisy place. Now, I ignored the traffic, honking horns, and the bottles, plastic bags, and garbage in the streets, and instead looked at the bright spots. It helped that the food in Caracas tasted better than elsewhere in the country, though it was more expensive. For meals, I stuffed myself with *pabellón;* drank fresh pear, apple, orange, mango, papaya, grapefruit, and strawberry juices; and enjoyed a few Golden Delicious apples. I walked for miles, stopping at newsstands to buy more postcards for my growing collection. I also bought cassettes of Bolivian flute music and recordings by the Chilean folk singer Victor Jara, who the army killed during the coup in 1973, and by Inti-Illimani, whose song "Venceremos" ("We shall win!") was the anthem of Salvador Allende's government.

Reading of coups, going shopping, and seeing dentists were minor events compared to the announcement that Peace Corps would close on September 25 and the remaining fifteen Volunteers in the country, including me, would have to complete the end-of-service process a month before that. A combination of congressional budget cuts and a lack of funding from the government of Venezuela forced the Peace Corps to pull the plug. Venezuela was giddy after nationalizing the oil industry, making it difficult for the Peace Corps and the government to agree on what areas Volunteers could best make a difference in Venezuela's march to being a more developed country.

The embassy had cabled Washington to tell them the government favored the continuation of Peace Corps as long as they didn't have to pay for us, making money the issue, not what Volunteers would do. Venezuela claimed they could not afford the $500,000 the Peace Corps requested because a drop in oil production due to a decline in global demand had translated into 20 percent less oil revenue than in 1975. Moreover, the embassy remarked that both countries were up against legislatures claiming impoverishment, and the only way to address high oil prices and a recession was to cut spending. The embassy said it best when it explained: "The ministries are confined to budgets voted by the Venezuelan Congress and are under the same requirements of rigid economy and cost-effectiveness as are our executive departments," putting the blame for the Peace Corps closing on both countries.

Most of the Volunteers believed Venezuela did not care about the Peace Corps, and the lack of money was just an excuse—complete

BS, really. By the end of 1976, Peace Corps would also close programs in India, Iran, and Mauritius as a result of a combination of budget shortfalls and evaluations that questioned the value of what the Peace Corps was doing in those countries.

On the bus ride back to Maracaibo, I reflected again on what Peace Corps meant to me. In a recent letter, my father had commented on how disillusioned I was over my "tour," the word he used to describe my two years of service in Venezuela. Although my letters home had their fair share of negative observations and descriptions of less than fulfilling work, it had nevertheless been a great two years. It was, in a simple and non-altruistic way, a job for which I was compensated, and in return, AZUPANE and IND received free labor. Maracaibo, as a place, fell short of the booming metropolis *Maracuchos* often described it as being, nor did it measure up to a steaming hot Third World location typically associated with Peace Corps service, but it was nothing like an American city, either. With five months remaining, I looked forward to traveling.

When I arrived in Maracaibo at six in the morning, I learned one of the birds at the house had flown away, and a few weeks later the other parrot would die, leaving us with a cat and a dog. I was hungry, but the refrigerator was empty except for mortadella, the house specialty, to make sandwiches.

The house continued to provide drama and variety. Tory's friend Joe visited because his parents went to Europe, his sister was in Canada, and he was dating a woman who wanted to go out with other guys while his friends preferred to hang around and get high—so why not go to Venezuela? Joe worked the overnight shift in an institution for the developmentally disabled where his primary responsibility was to ensure no one ran away. Each morning he got everyone out of bed and helped them prepare their breakfast, at which time he left for the day. Once, he said, an inmate left, unnoticed, in the middle of the night, as the Chief did in *One Flew Over the Cuckoo's Nest*. His absence did not alarm anyone, and no one went looking for him. A few weeks later, the institution received a letter from him saying he was happily married. They let him be.

Most Volunteers did not visit Maracaibo until they terminated. It was isolated from the rest of the country and required too much time and money to travel the 1,200-mile round trip from eastern Venezuela and back, the same reasons I never traveled east of Caracas except during training and to catch a boat to Trinidad. Besides, Maracaibo was considered to be nothing more than a dull metropolis. So, if Volunteers visited, it was after they finished their two years of service and were on their way to Colombia.

While in Caracas getting a health checkup, Ruth, a Volunteer from my training group in Los Teques, said she would visit us on her way to Colombia after she finished her end-of service procedures. A week later at AZUPANE, I received a message from one of the staff that a *yanqui* (slang for "American") was in the office looking for me. I walked over to the main building and found Ruth in a low-cut top, sleeping on the couch in front of the Padre's office. She admitted she might look "scantily clad" in the loose-fitting tank top and told me how she ended up at AZUPANE.

After arriving by bus from Caracas, she had taken a taxi to the house, where our next door neighbor denied a "Mike" lived next to her. The neighbor admitted she knew the "doctor" (Tory) and the "shoemaker" (Fernando), but they were not home. Puzzled on hearing a physician and a shoemaker lived in the house, she wondered if she had the right address. She was certain Tory taught swimming, but she was not aware a doctor lived in the house. Who could that be? She did not understand the reference to a shoemaker, either. Confident the address was right, she left her luggage with the neighbor, found her way to AZUPANE, and asked for me.

One of the men, learning an American woman was on the grounds, inquired about how long she would be staying. When I said a few days, he lost interest in meeting her. He said it was not worth his time to meet her if she would be in Maracaibo for such a short time. As he explained, "I need more than three days to court a woman." Later, I wrote about the attitude and the stereotype of the Venezuelan Romeo in my journal:

They were slickers in the typical Latin lover outfit of tight long-sleeved shirts with stained armpits, wearing platform shoes and smelling of cologne. Be groovy and listen to the sentimental romantic tunes, and maybe before the night was over they would be holding hands. The following day, he would call and perhaps even visit again. Meanwhile, he would have visited the brothel and told the guys in the neighborhood his girlfriend was a gas and had big ones.

I showed Ruth around Maracaibo in a taxi. We went to the Mirador and the Parque Urdaneta before going to the *El Napolitana* on Bella Vista Avenue for pizza. The next day, she extended her Venezuelan visa that had expired a few days earlier, but the Colombian consulate would not issue her a tourist visa. She never said why, but she had to cancel her trip. She returned to the house, struck up a relationship with Fernando, the shoemaker, and stayed for two months.

It had now been two months since seven men in police uniforms drugged and abducted William Niehous, the American general manager of the Venezuelan operations of Owens Illinois Glass Company, a company not well known to the public, from his home in Caracas. The glass manufacturer ranked 87th on the *Forbes* 500 list of companies, with revenues in 1975 of $2.3 billion. Its presence in the country consisted of a manufacturing plant in Valencia valued at about $40 million. The kidnapping captured the attention of the country for my remaining time in Venezuela.

The Argimiro Gabaldón Revolutionary Command (AGRC), a group unknown to the authorities, issued a seven-page communique stating Niehous was an enemy of the people, and insisting the company was plundering the country and interfering in Venezuela's internal affairs. They would put him on trial for his crimes. The manifesto also championed the causes of Vietnam, Cambodia, Laos, and the Palestinian Liberation Organization (PLO) while opposing Yankee imperialism, Soviet revisionism, and Zionism, all typical positions of radical groups in the Seventies. The U.S. embassy called the group communists despite a Communist Party leader disavowing any connection to the kidnappers.

Kidnapping government officials and business executives, a common tactic of opposition groups in other Latin American countries, was unusual in Venezuela. A lot of head scratching occurred when the unknown RCAG claimed responsibility for the kidnapping. What was the RCAG? Who were they? Despite the news coverage, neither the embassy nor Peace Corps issued security warnings or even urged caution. We took no extra precautions. Venezuela appeared calm and safe.

The kidnappers, wanting a ransom, sent pictures of Niehous to *El Nacional* to prove he was alive. They included a letter stating he would be killed in fifteen days unless they received fifteen million bolivars ($3.5 million); they also demanded deliveries of food in poor neighborhoods and insisted the company give each employee a bonus of five hundred bolivars. Owens-Illinois complied with the demands but did not make a payment to the RCAG. Neihous's wife, Donna, however, started talks through intermediaries regarding the ransom even though the government discouraged negotiating, saying it would encourage more kidnappings.

The RCAG wanted their manifesto published in local dailies, but the papers refused, fearing a harsh reprisal from the government. Nonetheless, Owens-Illinois paid the *New York Times*, the *Times of London*, and *Le Monde* to publish it. The Venezuelan government was furious for giving publicity to the "enemies of the state," and, in retaliation, announced it would nationalize the company. However, none of these actions made a difference. After the manifesto had appeared in international media and the demands of food assistance to the poor and better compensation to its employees were met, the RCAG did not release Niehous. Observers speculated the kidnappers were more scared than bold. The media, though, feeling threatened, halted its reporting on the kidnapping. It would be a few months before the story resurfaced.

A few days before *Semana Santa* (Holy Week), Jeff's Venezuelan girlfriend, Soledad, called to say she was hitchhiking from Merida to Maracaibo and planned on joining our camping trip over Easter weekend. The call was unexpected. When she arrived after a five-hour road trip, we welcomed her with Cuba Libres and a spaghetti dinner. After dinner, we went to see *One Flew Over the Cuckoo's Nest*. For the first time in the history of Maracaibo, the theater did not show newsreels, travelogues, or ads before the show. It was the third time I saw the film. After the movie, Jeff and Soledad went to the Easter Week service at the Basilica and I walked home.

On the way, a few blocks from the house, I stopped to buy a couple of hot dogs from a street vendor where a large crowd was gawking at some disturbance about fifty feet away. I couldn't get a clear view and stood back and ate the two sausages, waiting to find out what happened. One of the hot dog vendors said a girl had been raped. Turning to the crowd, I realized the victim, who was screaming, was the center of all the commotion. A few men pushed their way through the swarm of people and carried the woman to a bench where they tried calming her. A car arrived, and they all piled in and drove away. I didn't see any police. I sensed little sympathy for the victim except for the men who put her into the car. Shocked and appalled, I wasn't clear on what had ensued. The teenage hot dog vendors went about their business and seemed indifferent to what had occurred within their sight.

Unreliable crime statistics in Venezuela made it impossible to know the prevalence of rape, which often went unreported because the media would name the victim and publish her address. A news report more than thirty years later said sexual abuse or domestic violence against women in Venezuela was widespread but difficult to prove in the courts. In 2009, the local newspaper *Diario Vea* reported five women were killed each week in gender-related violence, and the data showed an average of one attack on a Venezuelan woman every fifteen minutes.

The next morning, we left for the mountains for three days of camping. I overslept and instead of me getting everyone else up as planned, Soledad woke us all up at 4 a.m. Tory informed us that Pancho, his friend who worked at Avis, had not brought over a tent as he had promised. So we went back to bed until seven, at which time Tory called Pancho to check when he planned to drop it off. The revised plan was to meet him at 8:30 at the Aikido Self-Defense School. We packed our rented car and drove to Marisa's Bakery for donuts and orange juice before meeting Pancho. He arrived with the tent just as we finished. We thanked him, put it in the trunk, and left.

We didn't drive far. After a few miles, a car pulled alongside us, the driver pointing to our rear tire, saying it was low on air. With that news, we looked for a CVP (*La Corporación Venezolana del Petróleo*), the government-owned gas stations found throughout Venezuela. Luckily, there was one a few miles down the road where we filled the tire. When we pulled out of the CVP, we were four hours behind schedule.

"*Mano duro,*" meaning "hard hand," the highway security plan employed during long holidays, was not as much of an obstacle as we expected. The military, selective in choosing their victims, flagged overcrowded vehicles or noisy old cars, leaving everyone else alone. Our car was generally in good shape and they waved us through each roadblock, probably because the police recognized us as foreigners.

As we headed towards Cubiro, the scenery was unspectacular and sometimes just plain dull. In Carora, a small town fifty miles southwest of Barquisimeto, we bought a can opener so we could drink the soda we purchased at the CVP. The town, known for cattle raising produced a remarkable number of musicians, historians, and scientists. In 2009, it became a sister city of Milwaukee, Wisconsin. We struggled to figure out how the opener worked and had to stop again at a roadside food stand to ask.

We arrived in mid-afternoon near Quibor, a small town known for its pottery. Having no idea how to find the campground, we stopped a man walking along the road to ask for directions. He pointed straight ahead. Fifteen minutes later, we passed the Plaza Bolívar in Cubiro where a church bordered one side of the plaza; on Easter, we would hear the bells from our campsite. As we drove through town and continued up the mountainside, hundreds of people in bathing suits were walking on the roadside. There were no signs for a campsite. In the distance was open grassland that looked like a great place for a picnic; we wondered if the people we saw earlier spent the day there.

Not knowing if we were going in the right direction, we stopped a car to ask what was ahead. We were told we should expect to see farms and pasture, along with a dirt track that led to San Miguel, a tiny town we could not locate on a map. However, they didn't know about campgrounds. We drove on until we reached a fork in the road, with a farmhouse occupying one corner. We parked and walked toward the mud house. On the way, we passed a shed which looked as if humans were sharing space with a few pigs and cows. As we approached the front door, a couple came out to greet us and offered us coffee.

We asked if we could stay on their land for a few days and park the car on the property. The farmer had no objections but warned that wild pigs roamed the area. We unloaded the tent and food and walked down a steep incline to a flat area at the bottom that looked like a beautiful place for camping. As we unpacked, someone yelled and waved. Ana went to see who it was. The farmer was trying to tell us we couldn't set up camp in the middle of a path. We looked at each other and wondered what he meant. What path? He pointed to a hill on the left where horses grazed. So off we hiked through a wheat field and up the hill.

After about a hundred yards, the farmer appeared again, shouting that we could not pitch a tent where we were standing. Our attempts at communicating were failing despite our group including two Venezuelans and three foreigners who spoke varying levels of Spanish.

We gave up and resorted to gestures to understand him. He waved. We followed. Hiking around a bend and past a steep hill where we saw cows and horses in the distance, he pointed at a clump of trees fifty feet away and said, "You will find peace and quiet there."

We pitched the tents and relaxed until a group of teenagers perched themselves on a hill and watched us. Tory entertained them with a flute concerto, and when he finished, the teens gave him a round of applause. The teenagers returned the next day with more friends, and Tory played the flute again. Our only other visitor was a man who wandered into the campsite, looking lost. He stopped and stared at us for a few seconds before continuing, never saying a word.

We watched the sunset over the mountains and a full moon rise the first night. In the middle of the second night, after it had rained, I woke up needing to go to the bathroom and crawled barefoot to the front of the tent. Half-asleep, Jeff blocked the exit because, as he later told me, he thought I was a stray cow trying to get into the tent rather than a person attempting to get out. I slid past him and stumbled into a thick fog, plenty of mud, and cold air. I told myself my bare feet could take five minutes of cold mud, the estimated amount of time I needed to walk and take a dump. While staring into the fog and squatting with my pants around my ankles, insects started biting my feet. I was helpless in my compromised position, leaving me with no other choice than to let the bugs bite me while hoping the cold would kill them. When nature had run its course, I pulled up my pants, tiptoed back to the tent through the mud, and went back to sleep.

By morning, the fog had lifted, but the cloud cover was low, making for a dreary day. Hoping it wouldn't rain again, we hung our damp blankets on trees to dry out. In daylight, I saw tiny bites covering my toes, and they itched. Over the next week, a few scabs developed from all my scratching.

Off in the distance, we saw people in a large open area with a beautiful view of the mountains. If the weather had been better, there might have been more campers than the ones we saw squeezed into a single tent. Ana and I wandered over for a closer look. The other campers huddled under a tree, singing religious songs, maybe praying it wouldn't rain. Despite the effort, it rained, raising doubt about the power of prayer, and we moved under a tree, trying to stay dry, swatting flies, and killing mosquitos as we watched others play soccer or slide around in the mud.

Despite the rain, flies, mosquitos, lack of music, and lack of water and beer, we were not roughing it, as we had a car to escape from misery anytime we pleased. On our first morning, we went for breakfast at a restaurant owned by a couple from Brooklyn, New York, where, on the owner's recommendation, we ordered a Spanish omelet, their specialty. On our second morning, when we were looking forward to another hearty breakfast, the Brooklynites informed us a busload of tourists had earlier cleaned them out of food. We got back in the car and drove to the other restaurant in town and settled for ham and eggs with water, as they were out of coffee and hot chocolate. They offered no excuse for their shortage. For the rest of our meals, we survived on ham, cheese and baloney sandwiches, juice, and fruit.

After three damp nights and days, we returned to Maracaibo on Easter Sunday by way of Bocono and Valera. We ate lunch at the Rockefeller-founded CADA restaurant in Barquisimeto, where I had a hamburger and a Coca-Cola, a welcome change after a weekend of cold sandwiches and water. A beer would have hit the spot, but CADA, joining the national campaign to limit the number of drunken drivers on the roads during the holidays, was not selling alcohol until the Easter holidays were over.

Fifteen

Change

Adjustments at the house dominated the next few weeks. Ana, never comfortable living with the Venezuelans tenants, and Tory, were moving out at the end of April, so they could have their own apartment. With their departure, we needed to find new boarders to cover the rent and to re-equip the kitchen with a refrigerator, plates, utensils, and pots and pans—all of that belonged to them.

Finding responsible young Venezuelans tenants might take time, and we assumed the pool of people who lived on their own was small. The unmarried staff at AZUPANE all lived at home with their parents, siblings and extended family. To nobody's shock, we didn't receive any responses from the ad we placed in the newspaper. Even though we had learned during training that unrelated Venezuelan men and women did not live in the same house, we ignored that insight and didn't even discuss whether we would rent the room to women. We needed tenants.

We immediately considered Juliana and Marta, the two women taking part in a three-month training program at AZUPANE. They were from La Grita, a town in Tachira state, 250 miles from Maracaibo near the Colombian border. They once mentioned in passing that they wanted a better place to live than a *residencia*, the kind of place I stayed for seven months in San Carlos. Juliana came from a family of nine girls and three boys. She married at sixteen and by twenty, already had three children. As far as we knew she was still married, though she never mentioned her husband. The other woman, Marta, wasn't married. We invited them to see the house. They found the hundred-square foot-room too big for the two of them so they asked if they could invite a third woman to stay with them, thinking she could sleep in a hammock. We didn't object as long as they paid the rent on time.

With Tory leaving, we would have to address Fernando's late rent payments. When he first moved into the house, he worked hard to make money from his leather business. After he broke up with Cristina, he lost motivation, and his productivity plummeted to a level that his revenue from selling sandals and crafts did not cover the rent. Tory advanced his share, allowing Fernando to run up a tab. Jeff and I, having no intention of continuing that arrangement, told him that unless he paid his rent on time, he and Ruth would have to leave. The news was not as surprising or devastating as we thought it would be as they had already made travel plans. However, before they left, Fernando had to take his high school equivalency exam.

Ruth tutored him every afternoon for two weeks. On the evening of the test, we waited with great anticipation for him to return home. We were all rooting for him. When he walked in the door with a smile, looking exuberant, we knew the result right away. Not only had he passed, but upon hearing he had received a perfect score, I burst out laughing. How was that possible? It seemed absurd. But I didn't ask. We congratulated him, poured him a glass of wine, and gave a toast to his success and future. A week later, he and Ruth left to live with his sister near Caracas. I planned on visiting them the following month, but I never did. Months later they left for the U.S. where Fernando found work as a chauffeur in Pennsylvania and Ruth taught physical education, the same job she had in the Peace Corps.

After Fernando and Ruth had moved out, we rented their room to two other women, making five Venezuelan women and two American men in the house. Andrea, an acquaintance of Tory's, had wanted to move into the house for months, but Ana had always objected. We never knew the specific reason, though Tory once commented, that Ana just didn't like her.

Andrea and Luz, the new tenants, worked as typesetters at *El Panorama*, the local newspaper. They once described their job as formatting, making sure every article fit properly on the page while ensuring that words at the end of columns were broken according to spelling rules, not convenience. Andrea said placing ads caused the typesetters headaches because they took up so much space on the page.

They always knew the number of pages ahead of time as if this mattered in our lives. These days the size of the paper wasn't a concern although when I was delivering papers while in high school, the number of pages the next day could matter. If the station manager announced the paper would be over seventy-five pages, we could bring an extra canvas bag or even a wagon to carry them.

A week after Andrea and Luz moved in, we canceled our subscription to *El Panorama* because they brought us a copy from work. Still, I would miss the middle-aged man who delivered the paper by throwing it at our front gate while riding his bike, always getting within ten feet, which impressed me. After reading the paper before I went to work for nine months, reading it in the afternoon took some getting used to. We no longer received the Sunday edition so every Sunday morning I walked to the *bodega* on the corner and competed with the neighbors for the limited number available. If they were sold out, I would walk up the hill to Bella Vista Avenue to buy *El Nacional*, the Caracas paper that arrived in Maracaibo around ten o'clock.

I spent a lot of money on magazines and newspapers, in both Spanish and English. Once in a while I would have a beer after work and read the afternoon tabloids, which were heavy on sports and crime. Sometimes, I bought *Vision,* the Spanish-language *TIME* of Latin American, or even *Esquire,* but when I started going to the Venezuelan-American Center almost every week, I stopped buying them. I didn't renew a subscription to the *Sporting News* when it expired. I occasionally bought the Sunday edition of *The New York Times* for $3.50.

When Tory and Ana moved to their apartment, they left us with an empty kitchen. We perused the ads in the newspapers to see the available items to re-equip it. A couple who were teachers at the American school was leaving and wanted to sell "everything." We jumped on the opportunity and bought a refrigerator, a coffee table, a few dishes, silverware, and some chairs, which allowed up to six people to sit at the Ping Pong table for dinner, removing the need to sit on the floor to eat. Being able to sit together changed the whole atmosphere of the house. We had also hoped to buy the couple's tape player, but we lost out on it when they sold it to a man who offered five dollars more than we did.

When Peace Corps Volunteers finished their service, they often held the equivalent of a yard sale. One couple that sold their furniture on a first-come-first-served basis two weeks before they left to start new jobs back in the U.S., accepted down payments to stake a claim on an item. Left unsaid, was that if someone showed up in the interim and paid the full asking price the couple would sell them the piece and return the deposits on various items to the original interested buyer. As a result, several people had their deposit returned to them. One Volunteer lost out on a tape player, a coveted household item, after making a down payment when the next day a man came by and paid the full amount, three dollars more. A Venezuelan woman lost out when she paid a deposit for two beds and promised to return in three days with transportation. When she returned with a truck as planned, she discovered the couple had sold the beds to a man who paid the full amount in cash. She left cursing the Volunteers. The worst occurred when a staff member at AZUPANE gave them 125 bolivars for a stove. When he returned on Saturday, the stove was gone, having been sold for twenty-fifty bolivars more because the new buyer could haul it away the same day. The double-dealing sales technique the Volunteers used became Peace Corps lore. Whatever goodwill they had generated during their time in Venezuela, they lost it on the way out.

Andrea and Luz frequented the bars near the port where they met the crews from cargo ships and oil tankers. A week or two later, they would receive letters from some of the men they met and would ask me to translate the ones written in English. Ian from London wrote about his trip to Colombia and the Caribbean after he left Maracaibo. He thought the heat in Maracaibo was oppressive and missed the drugs available in Colombia. Tom wrote Andrea from Seattle saying he missed her and called the weather in Seattle "crappy." As I translated the letters, Andrea listened stone-faced, which I assumed meant she wasn't interested in either guy. Neither woman ever asked me to translate a return letter into English.

Other bar acquaintances came to the house. Late one night I heard a knock on the front door. When I answered it, a man introduced himself in poor and heavily accented English, "Hello, I am Joseph from Yugoslavia." He asked for a woman named Soraya. I called Andrea and Luz to see if they knew either one. While the women recognized Joseph from the bars they frequented, they had never heard of Soraya. They assured Joseph she was not in the house. With that out of the way, they arranged to meet him at the usual bar near the Urdaneta Bridge the next day. The women invited Juliana and Marta to accompany them to meet

Joseph and other *buenos chicos* (really cool guys) and have some fun. They said no. Maracaibo might have exposed them to new things, but bar hopping and meeting ship's crew didn't seem to be what they had in mind for their weekends. They were here to learn and get certified as teachers before returning to their hometown to take care of their families.

AZUPANE designated the month of May as "Mes de Alegria," the Month of Happiness, which included Mother's Day, a first communion, and the eighth-anniversary party. The month began with a holiday: International Workers' Day. Venezuela, like the rest of the world except for Australia, Canada and the United States, honored the workers of the world on May 1. Venezuelans observed the holiday by doing nothing. In Maracaibo, not even the radio disc jockeys worked. However, the Chinese, Japanese, Middle Eastern and European-owned small businesses were all open. So for dinner, I had chop suey and a strawberry milkshake at the Chinese-owned Golden House.

Mother's Day is a big day in Venezuela. However, when we met to plan activities for the day, the staff wanted to talk about their compensation before anything else. Angry because the Padre expected too much from them without increasing their salary, the staff asked if the rumors were true that they might not be paid by the end of the day because AZUPANE's bank account was depleted again. Ignoring the complaints, the Padre calmed everyone down by promising they would be paid. While the staff was always jittery as pay day approached, wondering if they would get paid, the Padre never missed a pay day during my time at AZUPANE. When we finally got around to discussing Mother's Day, I found myself on the organizing committee. The Padre announced he would make an exception and invite friends, families, and donors to the party, which he scheduled for the Sunday after Mother's Day so as not to interfere with family plans and ensure a good turnout.

Despite the anxiety and late planning that characterized every AZUPANE party and public function, it went off without a flaw. The Maracaibo Municipal Band marched down the driveway to start the party, and a Venezuelan nun directed the La Lago neighborhood high school choir, which the kids loved. The Mass, which the Padre considered to be therapy, ended with the kids sitting through one of the Padre's infamous marathon sermons. I left the Mass early to pour juice and soda into paper cups and put the snacks on paper plates so the visitors, kids and staff could grab refreshments when the service was over. I was shocked at the stampede to the refreshments minutes after the Padre uttered the last word of his sermon. In less time than the band needed to walk down the hundred-foot long driveway, the drinks and people had vanished. The day was a success.

On a cloudy and overcast day, AZUPANE held a first communion, an event that included a bit of mischief. The boys wore coat and ties, and the girls wore dresses. It was the first time I saw the kids dressed up. They marched down the driveway in a procession led by Ramon Eduardo, who had almost drowned on my watch the previous year. The Padre wore a native-style Guajiro cape as he walked to the altar. I stood behind the kids with the rest of the adults. After Mass, the kids ate a breakfast of ham, eggs, bread and coffee in the main building while the staff and guests ate cake and drank soda on the lawn. Off to the side were three men in suits who I had never seen before. Isabel whispered that one was the president of the Bank of Maracaibo, and the women behind the group were presumably their wives. Valeria, the psychologist, attended with her husband, and Sanchez took photos with the Padre's camera. After an hour of small talk, Jose, one of the staff known for his quick temper and practical jokes, started throwing napkins out of boredom. The sister of one of the kids responded by throwing cake in Jose's face, causing him to splatter his soda on the woman standing next to him, which caused her to spill her soda on Jose in turn. Shocked, the staff looked at each other in disbelief, wondering what·had gotten into Jose, who apologized to the woman. The kids ignored the commotion and within the hour everyone had left.

At the end of the month, the Archbishop of Maracaibo Domingo Roa Pére said Mass in commemoration of AZUPANE's eighth anniversary, a less flawless event than Mother's Day. He seemed uncomfortable with the thirty disabled kids sitting in front of him, some paying attention while others moved around and made noises. During Mass, a man I had never seen before stood up and screamed *"La lucha,"* literally translated as "the struggle," a term used more often in a context that is equivalent to meaning, "Right on." No one tried to make him sit down or escort him out of the area. The archbishop, however, looking flustered, rushed through the Mass. Later the staff told me it was the shortest Mass in AZUPANE history.

At AZUPANE, absenteeism because of vacation, various ailments, or pregnancy was high. One staff member attended prenuptial classes in the afternoon for a week. A few positions were vacant because of resignations over the last few months. AZUPANE was in a "crisis," the preferred word of choice whenever a situation worse than a simple problem needed to be solved. The various challenges and issues opened my eyes more than ever to the complexities of managing people.

In a surprise move, the Padre demoted my boss, the coordinator of Expression. Management had been pestering her for months to be more proactive and show more leadership. They wanted new and more dynamic activities. She never took the hint, or maybe she just ignored them, forcing the Padre to transfer her to Remuneration, the section responsible for offering refreshments during breaks and where the older kids made crafts to be sold to the public. The demotion was like taking a teacher out of the classroom and assigning her to lunchroom duty. To the surprise of many, instead of resigning from embarrassment, she welcomed the transfer, something management did not expect. In her place, Juliana, one of the student teachers living in the house, and I together assumed the position of acting coordinator in Expression, supervising some of the most disabled children at AZUPANE, which turned out to be a challenging time.

One day when I was working alone with fourteen high-energy kids, Paco, who was usually well-behaved, uncharacteristically chose to act up. He bullied others, ate their snacks, and dominated each activity even more than he normally did. He was the youngest of three children, had a vivid imagination and was quite a ham as a pantomime, loving to act out cowboys, kung fu fighters, Batman, Superman and other action heroes, all favorite characters on Venezuelan television. When we had theater sessions, and the kids portrayed different scenarios, he always performed the best and once even received a round of applause after finishing one of his routines. When Paco met my parents, he flashed them a big smile.

Far from camera-shy, Paco loved having his picture taken. With little urging, he would pose and smile. A photographer's dream, always active, he knew how to act in front of a lens. I guess the sixteen pictures I shot of him on one beach outing proved he was photogenic. Like most kids, he could be mischievous, too, like the time he used a hose as a gas pump and filled Jeff's motorcycle fuel tank with water. Once, he climbed over the fence and went for a walk in the rain. Staff found him, unharmed, a few blocks away. They thought he deserved to be punished for wandering off, so they took away his lunch. I didn't see the connection between jumping the fence, not giving him lunch and shouting at him. It seemed a waste of time if not inappropriate. I never saw yelling at the kids as a way of achieving much.

On this particular day, he pushed one of the girls to the ground and then started punching Giovanni, an epileptic. Time for order, I grabbed him by the arm and pulled him aside. Juliana and I gathered everyone on the basketball court where they settled down and waited their turn to shoot the ball at the seven-foot basket. Paco, who had the propensity to steal the ball at every opportunity, uncharacteristically waited his turn. The slow, overweight and immobile twins, unable to play, sat on the sidelines jabbing each other. Jose Gregorio, who my mother had said, "had 'that look' in his eye," was an active kid, running off with the ball at every opportunity, creating havoc. The three Diaz siblings, all of whom suffered from epilepsy and were in danger of falling with each step they took, stood on the court waiting their turn. I kept a particularly close eye on them in case one fell. Luzmeri, one of the trio, was shy and seldom got into squabbles, though I had seen her pull the others' hair. Mayela, a pleasant, relaxed, independent little girl, wanted nothing to do with basketball and other games, so she wandered off on her own. Humberto, the oldest in the group, liked playing the role of the boss. He gave orders and kept the equipment for himself, thinking supervisors behaved that way, which often resulted in the younger ones crying. Despite his idiosyncrasies and views of supervision, he could also be remarkably cooperative in a game though I still had to remind him he should pass the ball more and take fewer shots, advice he usually ignored.

Late in the game, the tiny and fragile Diaz girls, fed up with Fernando hogging the ball, and unconcerned that he weighed three times more than they did combined, tried pushing him away and almost took the ball from him. I chuckled at their effort. Seeing Edgar standing off under the basket by himself, I invited him to play. After about twenty minutes, two of the kids grew bored and wandered off. They hoisted a plastic table on their shoulders and carted it around the court like a trophy. When I saw they were enjoying themselves, I left them alone.

It didn't take much for break time to become a chaotic situation. Today, the Diaz girls, Fernando, and Paco chose to cooperate and assist the other kids with their snacks and beverages. All was quiet until Paco seized Maria DeJesus' sandwich for himself, throwing open the door for others to take each other's food and drink. The kids lined up to sip Roberto Jose's milk through a straw. Being blind, he could not see what others were doing, so I grabbed the milk off the table and handed it to him. One of the kids gulped down Edgar's chocolate milk. At one level, a disaster was unfolding though everyone seemed to enjoy it. I didn't hear any complaints and no one seemed to be crying, so I let the chaos continue. I even participated—Lourdes and I ate the twins' cookies. After the break, Paco and Ivan snuck off to the bathroom and had a water fight, using the sink. When I found them, their clothes were soaking wet.

I got along well with the kids and hated disciplining them. For example, if it was time for art class and they would rather fiddle with a musical instrument, I would let them do it. They tended to listen and follow my instructions, sometimes looking at me as the fun guy instead of a boss, or a disciplinarian as many of them perceived the other staff to be.

Once, I devised a story about a shark attacking a boat while the kids were fishing. I guess the movie *Jaws* affected me more than I realized. I included an airplane rescuing them, and afterward, the rescued boaters dined on fish and beer. Although the plotline was absurd, they loved it. Trying to keep their interest, I made each of them into a character in the story, and soon they were cooking, selling refreshments or fishing. When Fernando entered the room, I made him the captain of the vessel. He patted his chest and smiled. The others stood and clapped and yelled with excitement over what might happen next. I had to tell them to sit down so the kids in the back could see. A few minutes later my mind went blank, having run out of ideas, and so the fantasy ended, disappointing everyone. We finished the exhausting but enjoyable day with a few songs.

The type and level of bedlam varied. Once, they destroyed the light fixtures by sitting on them and bending them out of shape. Despite their mobility issues, several were in constant motion, and sometimes we lost track of one or two. One boy made his way to the administration building on the other side of the premises and one girl, who was quite charming and gentle and who liked to engage in conversation even though she was unable to utter a single word, bit one of the other girls. Another of the girls was the opposite, getting angry if you gave her too much attention. One afternoon we taught parts of the body, clothing, and colors. We also sang a few songs, and the kids practiced saying each other's names, as they typically never called each other by name because they had trouble enunciating the sounds.

One Monday morning, we tried to engage the kids in talking about the previous weekend's outing. A few minutes into the activity Paco interrupted and pointed to the story of *Snow White* on the table in the corner indicating he wanted to hear that instead. I said we would first finish discussing the weekend. Paco walked away, having no interest in reminiscing about the beach. When Lourdes followed him, I went to see what they were up to. I found them playing with the dollhouse and told them we were starting *Snow White*, but they didn't care. Another time, I left the room in the middle of the fairy tale to investigate the scuffling outside. I found Paco with a chunk of wood in his hand and Edgar with a brick, both ready to pounce on one of the chickens AZUPANE kept for eggs. The chicken, sensing danger, ran as any chicken could, and the two boys chased after it. The gardener, hearing the bird squawking, came running over to save it. Before either he or I could get there, Edgar threw the brick and Paco the wood, both missing the bird by a mile. The gardener scooped the bird up and put it back in the coop. The kids returned to the activities room.

One rare occurrence happened during break time when twenty-one-year-old Fernando burst into tears when he witnessed one of the boys kissing Monica, who he considered his girlfriend. Elsewhere, the situation might have called for empathy, but not in Venezuela, where the most macho men among the staff teased him relentlessly over the kiss and his tears. The teasing, however, didn't bother him. Fernando took it like a man, glowing from all the attention. By the end of the break, he was smiling, back in his usual cheerful mood.

Overall, though, all was not well. Sanchez changed the schedule again and introduced a longer day. Now we would work from 8-12 and 3-7 Monday through Friday, instead of 8-11 and 3-6. He reasoned that the extra hour in the morning and afternoon could be used for staff meetings, which, in his words "would benefit AZUPANE." The new program angered the Venezuelans, as the workday would end at the same time their night classes at the high schools and university began. No one thought the shorter lunch was worth complaining about. Surprised by the strong reaction, Sanchez postponed the plan's start. Still, he pressured Jeff into signing a paper that said he agreed with the plan, thinking that if he agreed to it, the other staff would go along. Most signed too, saying they did it to keep their job. He did not ask me to sign because I didn't receive a salary. In the end, though, the proposed radical change never went into effect.

Last week, the new drivers were arriving thirty to ninety minutes late to pick up the kids. Worse, one day they left one child behind, stranded, forcing some staff to stay after hours and wait for a van to arrive. So after a week of poor van service, I stayed home from work one afternoon as a protest.

It turned out to be the perfect day to express my frustration by staging a one-person walkout. Sanchez was at the gate minding the kids while the staff attended a training course. He did not expect Jeff would arrive late, or that I would not come to work at all, so he was alone, helping the kids out of the vans. The next day we met to discuss the situation. He thought I was out of order. "It is your duty and responsibility as an assistant to look after the kids. Individual actions like your protest accomplish nothing. Only mass protests are useful." I didn't argue, although I found his take on protests curious. My Spanish was not at a level where I could make a strong argument that I had done the right thing. Sounding very pedantic, he asked if I had told him the drivers had been arriving late. I had not. He said he heard of the latest episode a few hours ago and was unaware of other days like it. Then he cracked a few jokes to break the tension. I smiled despite not getting the humor. The talk ended when I reminded him that the vans had arrived a half an hour late the previous Friday and added, "What next, another one arriving late tomorrow?" He shook his head, and I got up and walked out.

I went over the conversation for days. Did he really think that one-person protests were ineffective? Sanchez, a few years older than me, grew up in Uruguay in the 1960s when protests against the military dictatorship were frequent. I didn't know his political leanings, but he had left Uruguay for Venezuela and better job opportunities, a kind of one-man protest.

The role of Peace Corps Volunteers at AZUPANE evolved slowly. It was a mistake to call us "volunteers," putting us at the same level as the local volunteers who had little, if any responsibility beyond showing up when they said they would. Instead, management should have treated us like full-time employees. At first, being new to

AZUPANE and to the field of special education, I found the arrangement acceptable. Eventually I would conclude that AZUPANE should have treated us as employees, even if we were temporary and couldn't be viewed as interfering with the careers and longer-term commitments of the Venezuelan staff. Comparatively, in San Carlos and elsewhere we were coaches and trainers with IND in a thirty-year-old sports program that suffered from poor management, inadequate infrastructure, and ambivalence about accepting Peace Corps assistance. While I had few ideas of what a Peace Corps Volunteer should be, working as a "volunteer" was not one of them. With only a few months remaining until the end of my service, I had become the equivalent of a full-time worker with the same responsibilities as a Venezuelan employee. I worked a forty-hour workweek, earned comp time and had weekends off, none of which appeared in Peace Corps' manuals or recruiting brochures. I was even incorporated into the guard schedule, a promotion of sorts, and given a group of kids to watch to make sure they arrived and left as planned. As a result, Sanchez invited me to a weeklong series of meetings where some of my ideas were adopted, and I was appointed co-chairman of the new music program, although I would leave Venezuela before it started. Whatever the working conditions, the Peace Corps gave me an excellent opportunity.

What new ideas could motivate the staff and create a better atmosphere? A week of meetings during lunch was scheduled to find out. As acting coordinator of Expression, Sanchez invited me to attend along with seven other staff. On the first day, we congregated in the Padre's office for an announcement. We didn't gather in the Padre's office for just any reason so something must be up other than welcoming us to week-long meetings.

I had been in the Padre's office only twice before, and both times I was struck by its sparseness. It consisted of his desk, a table with a few books and some plants. We all stood, waiting, except for Sanchez, who sat on the floor, legs crossed, giving the impression we were about to endure a profound, life-changing experience. The Padre entered the room, as usual not wearing his Roman collar but wearing his open-collared short-sleeved white shirt; he never dressed as a priest. Wasting no time, he got right to the point and said he had fired the former coordinator of Expression, who he had demoted and moved to the Remuneration area two weeks earlier. He also dismissed the head of Recreation, sacking both because of their negativity. The Padre had grown weary of listening to their criticism and of them rejecting his every suggestion, including the idea that they should add more activities to their sections. Recreation was little more than a swimming program. Why not have athletics and basketball, he wondered. Ever since the first Pan American Games for the Deaf were held in Maracaibo a few months before, which included a strong emphasis on track and field, he wanted similar activities at AZUPANE. He did not want to hear "*Imposible,* (Impossible*)*" or "*No podemos (*No, we can't), words and phrases he considered a little crazy and self-defeating for employees to say to the boss and CEO. He claimed he had no other choice, adding that he also planned to fire Mirla when she returned to work after being out with a bad back and "not feeling well" for a month—during which time staff had spotted her in bars and shopping centers around Maracaibo.

We were in a state of shock at these developments. The Padre never fired anyone, though plenty of staff quit. Nevertheless, he felt the need to tell the staff they should not assume their jobs were in jeopardy. His reassurances weren't enough because later in the day, rumors circulated that he would dismiss a fourth person. However, that proved to be false. No one quarreled with the firings—the Padre gave them severance based on the Venezuelan labor laws—even if they exacerbated the staffing problem; there was too much negativity. The Padre wanted creative people who reflected on their actions rather than just reacting and behaving like logisticians.

As usual, the Padre had a plan to fill the growing number of vacancies, a problem compounded by the shallow pool of applicants. Partnering with the University of Zulia, he would hire students in medicine, nursing, and psychology as volunteers. For example, athletes from the school sports teams could work in Recreation for a specified period in such projects as training in track and field events. The same approach would also replace Jeff and me when we left. After an hour of listening to the Padre on personnel issues, we moved to a larger room in the corner of the former Exxon Oil mansion to talk about the future of AZUPANE.

The meeting began with a discussion of the music program. I first heard about music therapy for persons with disabilities, a new field in the 1970s, on my first day at AZUPANE when the Padre announced he planned to hire a teacher for it. He never did, but over the following fifteen months, the idea of incorporating such a program into the activities would resurface once in a while for no apparent reason. Now, more than a year later, the program once again seemed important enough to be the first agenda item for our week of meetings. Calling on the meager knowledge I had of the subject, including the observation that the most severely disabled kids at AZUPANE reacted positively to hearing music, I led the discussion and challenged the group to describe their understanding of music therapy with some basic questions. Would we teach music or listen to it? Would singing become part of the program? Did we want to invest in instruments or did we only want performers to entertain the kids? Or would it be a combination? Although everyone agreed such a component would be a great addition to AZUPANE, there was no consensus on what it should be or how to do it.

The firing of the two staff members for being critical of proposed new ideas made us all put aside any inclination to say something negative. We needed ideas and solutions not reasons to do nothing. At the end of the discussion, Sanchez appointed me and the Padre's niece, who had taken a music therapy course at the University of Zulia to design a plan. While selecting a person who had studied how music could help children develop made sense, he chose me because I had ideas, mostly random thoughts that came into my head, and I seemed interested. He asked the group to approve us as the two people who would start the program. No one objected. Why would they? Half-seriously, and hoping they would get the hint that I had no qualifications for the task, I said I had no grasp of Venezuelan music and my knowledge of songs was limited to "Manos a la Obra," a popular song about the nationalization of the oil industry. Driving home the point, I said I knew even less in English. My poor singing talents were part of my DNA. Kendellen lore has it that neither my seven siblings nor I can carry a tune or even sing "Happy Birthday" well. A few chuckled, but it changed no one's mind. Not a single person cared about my singing or not knowing the words to any songs. What mattered to them was that somebody else was responsible for starting the program, not them.

The next session concerned a puppet program, an activity the Padre had proposed months ago. While everyone agreed adding such a program was a good idea, debating its importance and priority took some time. The discussion focused less on the subject matter and more on which staff would take the puppet training course, then develop and coordinate the program. As usual, the discussion ended with no resolution, and Sanchez declared that whoever he named coordinator would make all the decisions on staff, content, and scheduling.

The second day of meetings began with two hours of debate over the best use of the fifteen-minute breaks each morning and afternoon. Maruja, the woman in-charge of *Guarapito*, the activity that encompassed skills training and managing the kiosk that sold refreshments to the staff during the breaks, opened the session with a description of her project. Sanchez complimented her on the brief and concise oral report, even though it raised more questions than answers regarding what to do.

The chaos of break time, partly the result of having so many kids under twelve years old, was the underlying issue. We all remembered the day when a group of kids ran around grabbing snacks and drinks from the others while we stood stunned at what we saw. Although such disorder didn't occur every day, it was frequent enough that we agreed some type of organized activity was needed to prevent it. I took the contrary view and reasoned spontaneity should be a major feature of the short respites from the day's regimented activities. I argued we should allow the kids do as they pleased. Breaks without structure would give them more opportunities to mingle. The staff shot down the idea as ridiculous, because it would promote turmoil, not limit it. And besides, the break would then no longer be a rest for the staff. After an hour, order won the debate. But it still was not clear what to do to enforce that order.

The most intriguing idea was a restaurant simulation in which the older kids would act as waiters and take orders for refreshments. While the idea got everybody's attention, the group deemed it too labor-intensive. Plus, it would defeat the purpose of a having a break which everyone considered their rest time. They were receptive to teaching the kids over eighteen about using money and making change and teaching the younger ones the proper way to wait in line, mingle in large groups and order food without simulating a restaurant, just not during the break. Another suggestion had the ten kids, between eighteen and twenty-two, teaching the younger ones to bake, cook, and make cookies and then selling them along with soft drinks and mango and orange juice, and using the revenue to pay the kids for their labor. They could use the money for their bus and taxi fares, as the ten older kids went to and from AZUPANE on their own. Maruja, the coordinator who had a better strategic grip on her section than any of the other five heads of sections, pointed out that some of the boys had already told her they would not make cookies. Some of the more experienced staff expressed doubts whether all ten could assume such a responsibility consistently — plus, thinking that a developmentally disabled twelve-year-old could bake seemed like a fantasy. Maruja added that whatever we decided, the kids expected to receive something in return for their work and would be offended if they did not. Orlando summed it up when he said, "Logically speaking there could not be more answers than questions unless we were talking about several solutions to a problem, and if we were considering more than one, we still could only select one." We contemplated that reasoning for a moment not exactly sure of the meaning and not thinking it necessary to ask since what he said made some sense, before Sanchez said he would consider all the ideas and report back to us at the next meeting.

We broke for lunch. The day before, the secretary had made sandwiches for us as we didn't have time to buy something to eat. Since kindergarten, when we did "the "Wisconsin thing" and made butter in class, which tasted awful, I have always checked to see if sandwiches had fresh butter on them. Now, twenty years later in Venezuela, I faced the possibility of eating butter. So I politely asked if there was any on the sandwiches she made. Negative. Relieved, I enjoyed lunch. Today, concerned about seeing a plate of butter on the table, I inquired if she had buttered the sandwiches. "Yes, of course," she said, "because yesterday, you asked if they were buttered." Amused at her interesting interpretation of my question, I scraped it off the bread when no one was paying attention and ate the sandwich.

The first topic of the afternoon was Remuneration, the section where the kids made crafts in the hopes of selling them. AZUPANE, always uncertain of meeting its fundraising targets and needing money to buy supplies, established Remuneration on the assumption that it would be self-sufficient, pay for itself, and be sustainable. Simply put, it needed enough revenue from its sales to buy more materials and pay the kids something for their work. The Board approved the project because it freed AZUPANE from subsidizing it through the operational budget. Maruja, whose Italian husband considered Benito Mussolini a hero, said the kids understood that if they sold the crafts they made, part of the funds would be used for more supplies, so they could continue to make more. They were less clear about the consequences if the products didn't sell.

The parents were critical in reaching an agreement. They had previously expressed their opinions on the purpose and objectives of Remuneration. Some parents preferred buying supplies themselves and keeping the basket or small weaving their child made. Others could not afford the supplies and expected the tuition they paid to cover all costs. Most favored AZUPANE paying for everything and didn't care if the kids were paid for their work. One mother showed little interest in the minutiae and economics of the program and instead, complained it was demeaning for her child to sweep the workshop floor.

We could not ignore the parents' wishes. Maybe a better option would be to provide subsidies in the low hundreds of dollars to ease the financial pressures. Under this scenario, the kids would take home what they made without worrying about the business-side of the activity. If that happened, it might show the parents their child was benefiting from AZUPANE and put their child in a positive light, someone who had abilities. The discussion did not result in any decisions, leaving Maruja to develop a business plan.

Valeria, the psychologist who fled Chile after Pinochet ousted Salvador Allende in the September 1973 coup, observed the level of participation in the discussion was disappointing, and she pointed out neither Orlando nor I had contributed much. Orlando replied it was his responsibility to take notes for the session so he could provide a summary at the end of it, saying he couldn't participate and take notes at the same time. My excuse, which I kept to myself, was that I didn't know enough about Remuneration to say anything useful or sensible. Why speak just to be on record as "participating," if I had nothing more to say than agreeing with what has already been said.

Still, it was after this session that I became aware that when I did speak up, people listened, though maybe they were sitting up and raising their heads so they could hear my Spanish, sorting out the errors and my accent to make sense of what I was saying. When I offered my ideas on *Guarapito,* others used them—"Mike said"—and Orlando included my comments in his summary of the discussion.

We devoted the rest of the week to concerns involving the beach excursions. Ad hoc planning, comp time off, kitchen duty and the ten dollar fee each family paid to send their child on a three-day outing were the primary issues. Since I'd arrived over a year ago, the most frequent complaint about the excursions was last-minute planning, which inevitably disrupted other activities, ruined weekend plans, jeopardized attendance requirements at night school classes, and interfered with family responsibilities. The staff wanted better organization and more than three days notice to plan. Agreeing to a three-month schedule with dates, or approximate ones, so each section could plan their activities was the easy part. I didn't understand why it took so long to address this one interconnected concern. This was an issue fifteen months ago when I arrived.

A much more complicated issue was compensation time or comp time. A straightforward question described the problem: how many days should staff take off after a beach excursion? On average, beach duty meant forty-eight to-seventy-two hours without additional pay. Although AZUPANE had no written policy on the matter, staff typically took one or two days off the following week. Sanchez agreed with the practice, which I deemed generous, a position few others subscribed to. Instead, the majority wanted two days off for each day at the beach because they considered themselves to be working even when sleeping. That seemed excessive to me as well as impractical. If the policy was adopted and the campouts continued, AZUPANE would rarely have everyone working at once. You can't operate a school id a third of the teachers were never there. However, those advocating for six days' rest after a three-day/two-night outing thought that if it disrupted regular programs, then so be it. They argued there would be no disruption of activities if the six days of comp time were taken over several weeks rather than all at once following the excursion. But if three days of working had worn me out, I would not wait weeks to rest. It seemed illogical to be at the beach, return fatigued, and take days off later. Others with more work experience than me looked at it as a principle, and not up for negotiation just because it caused some inconvenience. After everyone had voiced their views, we turned to Sanchez for the final word. What would he say? After considering the proposal for less than a minute, he said the policy of one comp day for each day at the beach would remain.

With comp time settled, we moved to the next burning issue of sharing the workload in the kitchen, a busy place at the beach given the need for three meals a day plus two snacks as well as cleaning up afterward. When at the beach, I noticed that in the morning, after swimming, in the middle of the afternoon, after dinner or whenever I walked into the kitchen, one of the women was always there cleaning or preparing the next meal. The problem was, the meals were complicated and not all staff members could cook and most of the men didn't think cleaning up was their responsibility. Venezuelans did not barbecue hamburgers or roast hot dogs. Instead, meals at the beach consisted of beef, rice, noodles, and fried bananas, the same as at home. Despite a clear understanding of the problem, the discussion evolved into more of a gripe session from the women. While everyone understood that the culinary skills among the staff varied, shopping, washing dishes, and cleaning up after each meal should be shared among everyone. The men were divided about the arrangement; most could not imagine themselves stepping into the kitchen for any reason other than to eat, while others could at least envision helping with clearing the tables, washing dishes and sweeping the floor.

I changed the subject when I pointed out that the campouts were different when kids under twelve were there as they required various levels of assistance in walking, eating, and getting dressed. Their presence made sharing kitchen responsibilities more challenging than with the older kids, who needed no supervision. My observation didn't generate any comments. After a week of intense discussions, interest in continuing was fading and burnout had set in. Sanchez acknowledged my point but postponed discussion on it. However, everyone agreed all staff would be assigned a time slot to help out in the kitchen during the next beach excursion.

The last controversial issue to take up before we adjourned was the cost to the families for sending their child to the beach for three days, which primarily went towards covering the food expenses. Everyone agreed with the principle of having to contribute something to the outings, but no one was comfortable with the kids who could benefit most from the excursions having to stay home because their parents would not or could not pay the twenty bolivar ($5) charge. The Padre concurred with the staff that no child should be excluded from taking part in a program because their parents could not afford it; refusing to pay was another matter. Best business practices taught the Padre he should not offer an activity for free. The AZUPANE Board already based tuition rates on each family's financial situation. However, being both a moral and fiscal quandary for him he wanted time to think it over.

The last issue regarding camping involved complaints from the parents about their kids coming back from the beach so exhausted they just wanted to sleep. The parents wondered what made them so tired. Even though the AZUPANE beach house was less than two hours from Maracaibo, few families dropped by during the outings to see what the camp-outs entailed. The staff, however, didn't think the parents should be concerned at all. It was a red herring. Was it so unusual for eight-twelve-year-olds to be tired after three days at the beach? Even the staff returned tired, after all. Maybe all that was necessary was to have fewer activities. The discussion was just beginning when someone pointed to their watch and announced it was one o'clock—time for lunch, a sacred break in the day. Being both Friday and lunchtime the workweek and the meetings were over. Further discussion on how to respond to this peculiar complaint would have to wait.

Sanchez proposed extending the meetings into the following week, but the Venezuelans shouted it down. It appeared everyone had had enough of the prickly and inconclusive debates. If the eleven until two time slot was out of the question, the alternatives were unclear. My suggestion that we meet on Saturdays went over like a lead balloon. Saturday was for leisure and household chores not work. One person insisted she would never give up a Saturday to go to a work-related meeting. Negda said she could not endure one more day leaving home at seven in the morning and not returning until eleven at night after her classes. Frank suggested activities be suspended for a full day or an afternoon, allowing time to wrap up the discussions and any loose ends. However, that would mean all the staff would attend, which nobody wanted. The intimacy of five days of intense debate had bonded the eight of us. After hearing a few other failed suggestions on when to continue, Sanchez complained about the negativity in the room. "We can't do this; we can't do that; I don't want to hear it," he parroted, reminding us again of the role the lack of constructive input had played in the dismissal of two staff members earlier in the week. Just thinking about more meetings during the three-hour lunch break was too much. We adjourned with no resolution.

With the meetings over, we returned to work. It had been a month since the Padre transferred the head of Expression, now fired, to Remuneration, leaving Juliana and I in-charge of the section. I was sure I could run it as the permanent supervisor; this was the change I needed as a motivation to stay. However, not being Venezuelan, and knowing

AZUPANE could succeed only if Venezuelans filled all the top positions; my chances were slim at best. Still, for now, because no one had applied, I thought I should be considered for the job.

I liked working at AZUPANE, but getting involved with compensation, the work schedule, and other labor issues, did not appeal to me. The week of meetings had drained me, even though I enjoyed it in most respects. The indecisiveness was annoying, but most of the discussions were thought-provoking. For one, as the unofficial acting coordinator of Expression, the debates put me in a position to make more solid contributions. If I became the head of a section, I could use the platform to express and implement my ideas and focus activities more on the individual than the group. I would give the kids more freedom to explore and do as they pleased. If I wanted the job, which AZUPANE was not advertising, I would have to decide in the next two weeks and inform Sanchez of my interest. Still, seeing the various tensions and competing interests made me wonder if it was better for me to leave in a few months when Peace Corps closed. But I didn't want to go too soon, only to regret it later and second-guess myself forever.

The lease on the house, which expired at the end of August, just three months away, would also influence my decision. Extending it appeared unlikely. Recently, we had all articulated a desire to move on. The two women from AZUPANE were leaving in a few weeks, and Jeff planned to depart when his current three-month visa expired. With two fewer tenants in the house, covering the rent in July and August looked problematic. While I tossed around the pros and cons of staying in Venezuela after Peace Corps, Sanchez, without warning, promoted Negda to the coordinator of Expression, a job she didn't want. He told her she could not refuse it. Now it was evident, I would not be a coordinator.

The puppet program, though, offered a new opportunity, as AZUPANE was recruiting a puppeteer. I had become the most likely person to coordinate the activity with the other sections because during the meetings my enthusiasm and questions trumped my lack of experience, just as it had when Sanchez appointed me to the two-person team to develop a plan for music therapy. My lack of knowledge of puppetry didn't appear to matter. But I delayed committing to the training or running the program until I decided whether I would stay in Venezuela.

The course would begin in August, my last month with the Peace Corps. I couldn't wait much longer. Procrastinating was over. Worse, the Padre was leaving for Europe. As an employee of AZUPANE, I should tell him my plans or at least discuss them before he left. I could always change my mind.

Finally, I told the Padre I was leaving in what seemed like an anti-climactic act. A hard person to find, I caught him as he was walking out of his office carrying a Guajira Indian *tapiz*, a popular tourist purchase.

"Are you busy?" I asked.

"I'm always busy," he said, sounding tired.

Nevertheless, I went ahead and told him in as few words as possible I was leaving in two months.

"At the end of July?" he asked.

"Yes, I'm leaving the Peace Corps and Venezuela."

"Okay."

He didn't ask any questions or try to talk me out of it, giving the impression he thought I might change my mind. A few weeks later, he received confirmation from the Peace Corps. He read the letter to the staff, who for the first time heard that I was leaving, as I had told no one.

On a lazy Sunday morning in mid-June, I was in a hammock on the second-floor porch above the kitchen with Venezuelan music playing softly in the background thinking of my future. In the most recent letters from my father, he asked what I planned to do and when I expected to be home. He hoped I would find a job and settle down and suggested I consider special education, a field in need of more instructors at the time. However, I had no plan.

Sixteen

Phasing Out

Juliana and Marta were leaving AZUPANE and going home in a few weeks, meaning that we would again have to look for new tenants, which has never been a pleasant experience. I remember their efforts at cooking, which were much appreciated and welcome, but lacking in quality. Mayonnaise coated the salads, the soup was too oily, and the spaghetti sauce made from ketchup was unforgettable. And yet we would miss their Saturday night and Sunday noon dinners, even the oily soup.

Once, while I was putting away the groceries, Juliana came into the kitchen, curious to see what I had bought. When she spotted six duck eggs, she asked about them, never having seen one. Not being much of a cook, I considered fried or scrambled eggs a gratifying meal. The next day, I fried three for lunch. The two women watched in amazement as if I was concocting a gourmet Italian dish. I buttered the frying pan and cracked open each egg one at a time. After a few minutes, three splendid-looking sunny-side-up duck eggs were ready to eat.

I always prepared simple meals: eggs for breakfast on weekends (otherwise skipped); baloney sandwiches for lunch; rice, onions, and soup for dinner. Meat was not a regular part of my diet. On some nights, I made a bologna, cheese, and onion sandwich with mustard on white bread. For an occasional change, I went out for pizza or Chinese or splurged at CADA or Tropiburger, a new fast-food hamburger joint. Foods I discovered and enjoyed in Venezuela included mango sherbet, *tequeños*, a snack made of fried dough wrapped around white cheese, and black beans and fried bananas. *Batidos*, a smooth mixture of ice, milk, sugar, and papaya whirled in a blender and served in a twelve-ounce plastic cup, was by far my personal favorite in Venezuela, with the best versions sold by street vendors in Maracaibo.

Tropiburger was the first fast-food hamburger outlet in Venezuela. On their opening night in Maracaibo, I ordered the *guapo*, which means "handsome" or "good-looking" in Spanish and intentionally rhymed with "Whopper," as the new restaurant wanted to convey that message about its most expensive item. What struck me about the eatery was not the food but that it took two people to make a hamburger: one to cook it and the other to place it on a bun, pour ketchup and mustard on it, and throw on a couple of pickles before wrapping it and handing it to the customer.

In contrast, cashing my monthly check from the Peace Corps involved four people. First, a person at the bank would watch me sign the back of the check, and then someone else would stamp it with the day's date while a third employee filled out a receipt before the fourth and final person handed me the cash. On a good day, it took twenty minutes to complete the transaction. At Tropiburger, however, two people could make a *guapo* in half the time.

Since it opened in Maracaibo in 1976, Tropiburger has expanded to other countries in Latin America. Today, a website includes forums where discussions about the great days of the El Guapo Double Cheeseburger occur and debates are held regarding where to find the best hamburger and the differences between El Guapo and a Big Mac. One fan, unfamiliar with the burger restaurant's history, expressed surprise at the number of posts recalling the popularity of Tropiburger in the 1970s and 1980s, which gave him hope that the one he opened at Maiquetia outside Caracas would be successful.

At work, I was scheduled for a three-day beach excursion with fourteen kids, three staff members, three student nurses, and two older kids as assistants. Isabel, a 30-year-old Colombian who had been working at AZUPANE for three years, was supposed to come over to the house so that we could plan the beach activities and the menu. That night, after taking an exam in her night class, where she was studying for her high school diploma, she returned to her car and found it trapped between two others, making her arrive late for our meeting in an irritable mood. She found the owners only after all the instructors left, only to discover that one of the cars blocking her belonged to her teacher.

Despite the rough start, we had a fun three hours. Over dinner, Isabel told me about her strange talk with Sanchez about the purpose of bonfires at the beach. He did not see the relationship between a campfire, land, and water, and she did not understand why that was important. Making a fire and singing, which she told him were typical camping activities, had nothing to do with swimming or anything else. Didn't everyone know camping included a bonfire to wrap up the day? Was he playing devil's advocate, and she misunderstood him? Or was he looking for an existential connection between earth, water, and fire? Whatever the answer, the tale added to Sanchez's mystique of being distant and an intellectual snob. Plus, no one had forgotten the larger dispute with him over the number of compensation days earned for each campout, an issue Isabel disagreed with him about, as she, like most of the staff, considered three days off after a beach outing to be insufficient.

By the end of the night, we had made up a menu and an activity schedule, neither of which we liked very much. For one, we planned too many activities for the outing. The kids would go home exhausted, and the parents would grumble again about their children coming back from the beach so tired, wondering why all they wanted to do was sleep.

The menu presented a problem, too. Weeks earlier, we had agreed that kitchen duty would be mandatory for everyone, but if cooking responsibilities were included, we had to keep the meals simple. Few of the staff knew how to prepare the typical Venezuelan dinner, including all but one of the men. With the meals we selected, a combination of rice, meat, fried bananas, spaghetti, and eggs, we inadvertently chose the same few people to cook. Should we expect each person to prepare a meal they could not make? I guess the default meal plan was embedded in our heads. We developed a weekend at the beach that all but assured the staff responsible for cooking would later complain they did not receive the promised help. If we believed these scenarios and subplots were true, why did we choose such an array of meals? We didn't have the answers.

Instead, we laughed, realizing what we had done. We only wanted a plan Sanchez couldn't refuse, but in creating one, we looked as if we were sucking up to him. Sanchez didn't care who worked in the kitchen; his interest was in the activities. He wanted the kids to be active and not sit and play games or sing. He had become a harsh critic of the time staff spent sitting. Once, he became so irritated when he saw Isabel and me on the floor working with the kids that he kicked us out of the room and told us to spend the day outside. Sanchez wanted everyone to be active and busy at all times, as long as each activity was linked, such as with earth, water, and the bonfire. So we followed the boss's orders and emphasized activities that demanded physical exertion.

I packed light for the trip, bringing just a toothbrush, dental floss, shorts, a swimming suit, an old t-shirt, a camera, and a hammock. The morning we left began with a thunderstorm that flooded the streets, a common occurrence in Maracaibo. I caught a taxi, a miracle considering the weather, but the car broke down after only a few blocks, forcing me to walk the remaining two miles to AZUPANE.

Eleven kids went to the beach. Three did not go because their families remained suspicious as to what caused their children to return from the beach so exhausted. We got off to an inauspicious start when soon after arriving, some of the kids tried to run away. I chased after them and, a few minutes later, found them wandering among the palm trees, playing hide and seek. Down at the water, we caught frogs. I put six in a can; the kids checked on them every few hours over the next three days. By the third day, they had grown tired of the routine and opted for mischief. So several of them pulled the frogs out of the can and shoved them down the front of the others' swimsuits, which made me laugh. Before we left for Maracaibo, I threw the frogs back into the lake.

Other aspects of the weekend did not go as well. We were without water for most of the three days because the early morning storm on the first day knocked out the electricity, and the mosquitoes were worse than ever. Plus, my back stiffened after two nights in a hammock, and I got sunburn for about the tenth time in two years. On the return ride to Maracaibo, with the kids sleeping and the staff looking exhausted, I wondered how I had once spent five days at the beach with twenty people under one roof. I took my petty complaints about mosquitoes, sunburn, and sleeping in a hammock as signs I had been in Venezuela long enough.

While at the beach without radios or a telephone, we were shut off from the rest of the world. Upon returning to Maracaibo, I learned the American ambassador in Lebanon had been assassinated by the Popular Front for the Liberation of Palestine and the national controller, considered one of the most honest people in the Venezuelan government, had resigned after accusing the Pérez administration, though not the president himself, of corruption. Venezuelans were unhappy not because they lost a competent person of integrity working in government, but because it embarrassed the Democratic Action Party.

With both Jeff and me at the beach, the four women were alone at the house for the first time. Although we assumed all would be okay, we were curious to see how the five days had gone for them. When we got home, we realized the answer was "not well." They had not been speaking to each other for a month, a development we hadn't noticed. They each tried explaining to us why they disliked each other, but we understood none of it. Since they planned to leave at the end of the month, I hoped they could refrain from making the next few weeks miserable.

We considered the house as a kind of group home where we all got along and shared meals as one happy family. However, this ideal was only true in the initial months. Now, the Venezuelans living with us did not care if the house was cheery and friendly. They thought of themselves as nothing more than tenants paying rent for a place to sleep and cook. The idea of sharing food expenses was not part of the deal. To them, Jeff and I were the landlords who would sort out problems or fix the plumbing and electricity when needed.

With two empty rooms, we posted a cardboard sign on the fence in the front of the house saying we had rooms available. Our two inquiries came from married couples, and we accepted both of them, our first perfect strangers, out of desperation. Eddie, the husband in one couple, traveled for work, and when he was around, he refused to speak to me because he found my Spanish incomprehensible. I didn't think my Spanish was so crappy that talking to someone was torture. Still, I limited my interactions with him to business: "Where's the rent money, the rent is due next week," or "The rent was due on the tenth"—not the best way to start a conversation. If he had an issue or if he wanted to ask a question, he preferred going through Andrea. However, his wife was more sociable, though prone to breaking dishes. She broke all the glasses in the kitchen in the initial weeks after they moved in, leaving us with old jelly jars as our only options for drinking containers.

One of the few times Eddie was around was a few days before the lease expired on the first of September. While sitting around chatting and enjoying the lazy, unemployed life, knowing we would go our separate ways in a few days, never to see each other again, Eddie walked out of the bathroom shirtless, wearing a pair of shorts, and chewing on a cigar. He went to the kitchen and grabbed a beer from the refrigerator, never acknowledged anyone in the room, planted himself in the rocking chair, and read the horse racing results from the previous day. I found myself caught between missing the good old first months in the house and glad I was leaving.

The husband in the other couple was not around much either. He sold life insurance and traveled a lot. His wife frequently complained he never called her, despite promising to do so. They were a quiet couple who didn't plan on using the kitchen, so it seemed they would be a minimal hassle. But when the husband was away on business, she slept with the lights on so she could get up in time for work—even though the sun rose at six o'clock and she didn't leave for work until nine o'clock. But the light bothered the next-door neighbors. When I told her they complained they couldn't sleep with the light in her room shining on their house, she promised to turn it off, but she never did.

An unexpected event provided a much-needed digression from work, thinking about the future, and dealing with new tenants. In what Venezuelans considered to be one of the biggest scandals in their history, the newly crowned Miss Venezuela, eighteen-year-old Elluz Peraza from Guárico, resigned from her title thirty-six hours into her reign to marry a bank clerk. I remember Peraza causing an outrageous national outcry for giving up the title of Miss Venezuela, unleashing a torrent of unprecedented rumor-mongering and disgrace that provided some lighthearted relief from the grind at AZUPANE. Venezuelans take their beauty pageants seriously and resigning from the Miss Venezuela title was beyond comprehension. The tabloids went crazy.

Her so-called boyfriend purportedly proposed to her a few days before the pageant while sharing chocolate ice cream during a twenty-minute date. The tabloids speculated she was pregnant, which she denied, though she was not helped by her father, who kept the rumors in the news when he cited Penal Code 70, a law allowing men to marry their mistresses. The story, however, was false; she was not expecting a baby. Journalists, pundits, and most of the public said she was naïve, dumb, and a loser. Peraza's father expressed disappointment that his daughter gave up the crown to wed a man who earned a mere 1,200 bolivars a month, or $280, slightly more than a Peace Corps Volunteer.

In contrast, her successor, Judith Castillo from Margarita Island, appeared to be intelligent and smart, the kind of person Venezuelans wanted to represent them.

As it turned out, Elluz Peraza was smarter than people thought; while the eighteen-year-old Miss Guárico may have seemed dense, if not stupid, she went on to have a successful career as an actress in Latin American soap operas, as well as a writer, producer, and film director for a global Evangelical ministry. She divorced the bank clerk in 1980 and married three more times, the last to Jorge Martínez, an Argentine actor eighteen years her senior, in Florida, where she has lived since 2000. In 2007, on her 50th birthday, the entertainment magazine *Fame* gave her a lifetime achievement award. In 2009, Peraza told a Venezuelan journalist she was enjoying life, living in a house with a garden and, in a small way, living the American dream. She expressed no regrets about giving up the Miss Venezuela title in 1976. In 2015, as Peraza approached 60, she had not appeared in a telenovela for years, and the new generation of soap opera fans hardly knew her. It was like today's millennials not knowing Jane Fonda when she was thirty, but only as a 75-year-old in movies they don't see.

In mid-1976, Paul McCartney and Wings were touring the U.S. "Silly Love Songs" by Wings was the number-one hit song. The presidential campaign was well underway. Jimmy Carter and Governor Jerry Brown of California were the frontrunners for the Democratic nomination. Ted Kennedy had dropped out a few weeks earlier. The headline in the *Miami Herald*, available in Maracaibo, was "Daley and Wallace Support Carter," the same George Wallace who blocked African Americans from attending the University of Alabama, and the same Richard Daley whose Chicago police pummeled demonstrators at the Democratic National Convention. On the Republican side, Ronald Reagan was challenging President Gerald Ford for the nomination. It was also the year of the American Bicentennial.

Venezuela was our friend in 1976, and joined in the bicentennial celebrations by issuing a commemorative stamp of George Washington and holding a ceremony in Caracas on his birthday.

They sent a sculpture, titled *Delta Solar*, by Alejandro Otero, one of the country's leading artists, to the National Air and Space Museum in

Washington, DC. Today, the stainless steel public art piece is still on exhibit in front of the museum. Venezuela also sent a statue of eighteenth-century patriot Francisco Miranda, who fought in the American Revolutionary War, to Philadelphia, where it sits across from the Fels Planetarium and the Franklin Institute. Venezuela also honored the two hundredth anniversary of America's independence by inviting Sarah Caldwell, the first woman conductor at the Metropolitan Opera in New York, to give a concert in Caracas, and the American consul in Maracaibo wrote an article on the history of the U.S. in the Americas for a local newspaper.

Delta Solar sculpture in front of the Air and Space Museum in Washington, DC.
(Photo by Mike Kendellen)

I celebrated the Fourth of July with a breakfast of pancakes and a glass of water. From across the street, on the same field where we introduced Frisbee and American football to the neighborhood, I could hear shouts of a baseball game. All I needed was apple pie and my Independence Day celebration would have been complete.

The next day, July 5, was Independence Day in Venezuela. Air Force planes flew over the city, and neighbors set off fireworks throughout the day. On the Plaza Bolívar, the local officials congratulated each other with backslaps over the great success of democracy in Venezuela, all to commemorate the day in 1811 when

Venezuela declared it was separating from Spain to become an independent nation.

Now that my departure was final, I needed to get serious about planning for the trip, starting with figuring out the amount of money I had. Since I was not going directly home, I would receive the equivalent of a plane ticket home in cash while forfeiting the forty-two pounds of excess baggage the airlines allowed Peace Corps Volunteers. In Caracas, I would also receive about $700, one-third of what had accumulated in my readjustment allowance, which Volunteers earned $75 for each month of service. Add savings of around $2,000, and I was set with $2,700 in cash and traveler's checks (and no credit card) to take a trip in South America for an undetermined length of time.

I would travel alone.

I planned to begin in Colombia and head south to Ecuador by bus. I intended to stay in cheap hotels, hike the Inca Trail in Peru, join a cattle run in Patagonia, and hang out on the beach in Chile. Since the coup in Argentina, going there seemed dicey. For now, those were my only real ideas. Money and enjoying the travel would influence my decision on when to call it quits and go home. Although I was looking forward to the adventure, I knew that after thirty-one months in Venezuela, my eagerness to return to the U.S. might trump my desire to see South America.

Mark, who had recently completed his Peace Corps service, stopped in Maracaibo on his way to Colombia. On the way, he visited a Volunteer who was staying in Venezuela as a track and field coach for $250 a month and no benefits, allowing him to be with his twice-divorced Venezuelan girlfriend. Soon after Mark arrived, he and Andrea struck up a relationship, but keeping to his plan, he left for Colombia after a week only to return two weeks later to be with Andrea, giving us another tenant.

Andrea invited her twenty-year-old sister, Mila, to move in because Andrea thought she would be better off staying at the house than with her mother. Andrea set a seven o'clock curfew for her sister. If she came back after that, Andrea would slap her in the face as punishment. Mila, not fazed by the warning, ignored it and usually returned late, then argued with Andrea about it. I don't know if they ever got physical, but they yelled a lot. After two weeks, Andrea kicked her out and sent her home to live with their mother.

One night at 11:30, the doorbell rang. When I answered it, a man introduced himself as Nick, a sailor in the Greek Navy, and asked for Andrea. He came to tell her how sad he felt over Lila, another of Andrea's sisters, who had turned down his marriage proposal. A year earlier, Lila had met him at a bar near the docks in Maracaibo and stayed in contact with him while she attended flight attendant school in Caracas, partly because he sent her one hundred dollars a month for her tuition. He was now back, and wanted to marry her to avoid going to fight in the war between Greece and Turkey over Cyprus. If he were married, he could get an exemption and resign from the navy.

When his ship docked in Costa Rica the week before, he took a few days off and flew to Caracas, planning to propose to Lila. But she wouldn't see him. The Greek, heartbroken, took a bus to Maracaibo to tell Andrea his story. When he finished, Andrea, showing no sympathy and not offering to intervene, thanked him and said goodbye. After he had left, she explained the situation. Lila's current beau was a German, married with children, who had also proposed to her. She was thinking it over.

Andrea herself once had a German boyfriend she had met at a bar near the dock. She told Mark that if Rudy ever returned and asked her to marry him, she would turn him down, like Lila turned down the Greek. This version of events differed from what Andrea told me weeks earlier. Then, she said, she would gladly marry Rudy despite having spent only six hours with him. She banished those dreams and sidelined Rudy when Mark, the American, arrived.

One evening, Mark and Andrea went to the movie *CIA Secret Story (Faccia di Spia)*. When they returned after the show, Andrea was sobbing. As she went to the kitchen, Mark said that scenes in the movie, either in the form of suspect actual footage or reenactments, depicted horrible acts by CIA agents: murder, chopping off hands, and in one, the alleged agent put a hot needle into the penis of a suspected Communist to get information from him. Zev Toledano, the author of *The Worldwide Celluloid Massacre: An Encyclopedia of Extreme, Surreal and Bizarre Movies*, and the only person known to have reviewed the 1975 Italian film, described it as "A pseudo-documentary splicing together stock footage of various political events throughout the world and fake acting. The movie jumps from one violent or clandestine event to another in Cuba,

Bolivia, Italy, Vietnam, and Chile, the common thread being some kind of American CIA and business involvement. In between, video shows people shot and tortured in nasty ways." He concluded it was nothing more than propaganda and stated that watching it was itself a form of torture.

Andrea, who knew other Americans, had a different take. "She believes Jeff, Tory, you, and me are spies, and the CIA tortures people," Mark told me in the kitchen near midnight as Andrea cried in her room.

Mark didn't know what to do. "I have no idea if our relationship is over. Yes, she believes we are in the CIA, but she doesn't think we are responsible for what the movie portrayed. To her, we are spies in the same way she is a typesetter at a newspaper. It's just a job, something you get paid to do."

"How can people believe this bullshit?" I demanded. "So, even though the CIA, our supposed employer, tortures and commits murder, we Peace Corps Volunteers are innocent, and as human beings, are still worth knowing and befriending?" I asked rhetorically, knowing the whole premise was ridiculous.

"Apparently so," Mark said, shrugging. "Maybe she'll be over it in the morning."

He did not sleep well, dreaming of the film and Andrea's reaction to it. The next morning, Andrea greeted us with a smile and a jovial *"buenos dias"* as she made herself a coffee. She did not bring up the movie, and no one dared raise the subject. Mark and Andrea spent the day looking for an apartment they could share. We never spoke of the movie again.

Needing a job if he planned to stay in Maracaibo, Mark signed a six-month contract starting in September that paid six hundred bolivars ($140) a month for teaching English twelve hours a week. He figured it gave him a few more months to see if his relationship with Andrea was serious or not. If it didn't work out, he would face the facts and leave.

Unexpectedly, Mark's former girlfriend, Maria, traveled twenty hours by bus from eastern Venezuela to see him. Not knowing his new living arrangements, she went to the post office to get his address and telephone number. The postal worker refused to give her the information, but when she started to cry and said she knew no one else in Maracaibo and had no place to go, the clerk gave her our number. When she called, Mark agreed to meet her, but not at the house. The last thing he wanted was for Andrea and Maria to meet. If they did, sparks would fly.

He also knew it was impossible to get back together with Maria because her mother hated his guts. "She would be here with a shotgun looking for me if we got back together," he had said. From the start of their relationship, she had tolerated Mark, convinced he would eventually leave her daughter for another woman. After they met for lunch, Maria left Maracaibo.

It had been months since the media reported on the strange case of the William Niehous kidnapping, a story I followed in the local newspapers. From Maracaibo, the kidnapping looked like an incident from another world. Venezuela appeared calm and safe at the time. Caracas never requested Volunteers to be more vigilant after Niehous, the CEO of Owens-Illinois, was kidnapped. I had never heard of the company. Why would anyone kidnap an executive from a glass company based in Toledo, Ohio?

During training, the Peace Corps told us Communists made up a significant part of the student body at the university, as if that fact alone, if valid, explained Venezuelan politics and current events—though in retrospect, the Cold War was still going on in the 1970s and Communists were considered the primary enemy of U.S. interests. Leftist parties accused Niehous of working for the CIA. In early August, police arrested sixteen people, including two congressmen, for their role in the crime, even though the Venezuelan constitution granted immunity to members of congress. Analysts believed Venezuela was on the verge of a crisis after arresting them, a blatant abuse of power that could bring down the government.

An equally serious development was that a suspect had died from his injuries after the police severely beat him. The head of the Socialist Party criticized the police for the brutality and torture, which they said was standard operating procedure for them. The government promised they would prosecute those responsible.

Media reports made clear the kidnapping embarrassed the government, making the security services look incompetent. The opposition parties wondered why they had not found Niehous. What was taking them so long? He was kidnapped five months earlier. Few Venezuelans found credible the government position that the police or the intelligence services did not know where Neihous was. I suspected that with no leads and the government looking incompetent, if the police or the army found the kidnappers, they would be shot dead on the spot, even if they offered no resistance.

News articles speculated on the man's whereabouts. Rumors placed him in Maico, a town in Colombia north of Maracaibo. Or maybe he was in the Andes Mountains, on the east coast of Venezuela, or in a national park near Caracas. *El Panorama,* the major newspaper in Maracaibo, recommended that if anyone spotted Niehous they should call the police. Some opponents of the Pérez administration believed the man had secretly returned to the United States even though Mrs. Niehous was still demanding answers from the government. Other rumors circulated that his kidnappers had killed him. Anonymous calls to authorities said the body could be found in such-and-such a place, but the reports never checked out. Others believed he was buried beneath Avenida Francisco Miranda in Caracas, similar to the speculation that Jimmy Hoffa, the former Teamster leader, was entombed in cement under a parking lot in Michigan or New Jersey. Whatever the theory of the week might have been when I left Venezuela in September 1976, the police did not know if Niehous was dead or alive.

One afternoon while reading the paper, I heard firecrackers. Because it wasn't a holiday, the sounds were unusual. I got up to see what the commotion was. By the time I reached the front gate, two men were firing guns while jumping over the wall of the field across the street. Neighbors rushed out of their homes and filled the sidewalks. After a minute, the shooting ceased, and a third man came running across the open field toward our house while the neighbors shouted at him to hurry to safety. He jumped the wall right in front of me and ran down the street. A policeman followed in pursuit, with the neighbors heckling him. The cop swore at them: *Coño de tu madre!* The brown shirt the policeman was wearing, open to his navel, made him look more like a hoodlum than a local law enforcement officer. I didn't see a holster or a badge, and his gun looked like a toy.

Then two men in blue uniforms appeared. I had paid so little attention to the police in Venezuela that I didn't know if their uniforms indicated they were police or private security guards. They apprehended the suspect, a thin man who looked to be in his forties, but he could have been ten years younger. The police marched him down the street with his hands behind his back until they flagged a passing car. They pushed the man into the back seat and hit him in the head and neck with a gun. The car took off, screeching its tires. At the corner, a bystander threw a rock at the car, falling short. The police didn't notice, and the car sped away. I went back to reading the paper.

My final beach excursion included seventeen kids between eight and twenty-four years of age. It was the first camping trip for me that involved kids over sixteen, a welcome change. The older kids were self-reliant, not requiring supervision, and they could help out, too. Parents again complained their kids returned sick from the beach, so several did not send them. Gardening, rather than earth, wind, and fire, was the theme of the weekend, along with a side trip to the fishing village of El Mojan on Lake Maracaibo where they would paint a few walls of the school. Other activities included gathering wood, watering plants, collecting and cutting open coconuts for a snack, making a bonfire, and celebrating a birthday for one of the girls with cake and soda.

For the first time, we used tents, which most of the kids loved. Ivan in particular loved sleeping in the tent. Unfortunately, on the second night, he filled his pants in bed, forcing a move to a hammock in the house. After he had moved indoors, he filled his pants again. One person who did not like the tents was ten-year-old Mayela. She preferred sleeping in a hammock indoors. I couldn't blame her: the high winds off Lake Maracaibo caused the wings of the tent to flap as if we were in the middle of a hurricane.

On the last night, one of the kids vomited three times, and Adriana couldn't sleep, wandering around the house all night. I strung up Edgar's hammock and slept in my jeans and a jacket, as it was strangely chilly for being on the equator. By Sunday afternoon, the kids had earaches, runny noses, and were homesick. I, too, felt lousy. Everyone was ready to go home after five days. My shoulders were peeling from too much sun, and Isabel wanted me to help her with her English, as she had a test the next day at 8 a.m. In the morning, as we were packing to return to Maracaibo, Julio Cesar wet his pants and Isabel quickly changed him into khaki shorts and knee-high socks, making him look like a rich kid. When we dropped him off at home, his mother let out a cry: "Julio, what were you doing?" I took two much-needed comp days before returning to work.

Dinner at the beach with AZUPANE
(Photo by Mike Kendellen)

When I returned, the Padre asked me to write an article for the August issue of the AZUPANE magazine about my experience working there. I wrote it in Spanish the same week Thomas Jefferson was on the cover of the special bicentennial issue of *TIME*. Forty years later, it seems corny at best.

Peace Corps is a United States government volunteer service established by the U.S. Congress at the behest of President John F. Kennedy in 1961. Volunteers serve in seventy countries, including thirteen in Latin America and the Caribbean. It serves only in those countries where the host national government requests the group's services. Peace Corps started in Venezuela in 1962 with programs in agriculture, health, education, community development, and sports and recreation. The Ministries of Education, Agriculture, and Public Works and the National Institute of Sports (IND) have been host agencies. Together with the Peace Corps, these government agencies determine where Volunteers may be of help to the Venezuelan people.

After two months of language training in Los Teques, I arrived in San Carlos on April 1, 1974. I was there for ten months as a baseball coach. My host agency was IND. My overall experience was positive but not satisfying. Learning about myself and life in the Llanos overwhelmed the mundaneness of being a coach in the midst of poverty and illiteracy. I have been a great fan of baseball all my life, though it had no significance beyond the outfield. It's just a game.

So I asked for a change, with an emphasis on social work and something more intellectually stimulating. My program director told me about AZUPANE. After a two-day visit in December 1974, I decided I would finish my service here. When I made the decision, I didn't know anything about it or its philosophy. I had no previous experience in special education. From my visit, Maracaibo looked more appealing than San Carlos. I needed something different from what San Carlos had to offer. I wasn't sure if AZUPANE had what I wanted, but after seventeen months, I have realized I have been lucky to have been associated with it.

As Americans celebrate the country's two hundredth birthday, I pondered what Thomas Jefferson wrote in the Declaration of Independence in 1776. He said it was the right of every individual to have the freedom to pursue happiness. AZUPANE is a vehicle where the developmentally disabled can pursue happiness. It is not dogma, nor does it guarantee success; it does, though, provide an opportunity. AZUPANE is about responsibility where individuals determine their success.

I always received great personal satisfaction from a simple "hello" from any of the kids, a hug from another, playing ball with another, or just from talking to them. They have needs, and I think I have helped achieved a few of theirs. When you think about it, our needs are the same. All people are looking for understanding, friendship, and love. Sometimes they are hard to find because man is a complicated being. I believe that after seventeen months, I have reached an understanding that I could be a vehicle of happiness for them.

It is also critical to the success of AZUPANE that each worker knows where he or she is going in life. It is not necessary to have achieved happiness to show the way, but it is essential to be on the path. If you are on the way to happiness, why not take a few of the kids along with you? Make a conscious effort to share your knowledge with them. Happiness is not a handout; it is pursued and achieved.

Peace Corps will leave Venezuela shortly after fourteen years. I will also leave soon to travel, maybe as far as Chile over an indefinite period. Upon my return to the United States, I will either write, start graduate school, or try to start my own business. Whatever I do, it will be for the pursuit happiness. I will always remember the people associated with AZUPANE. I have many pleasant memories of generosity, understanding, and friendship. In return for the goodwill and generosity I received from all the friends, families, and staff, my home will always be open to you.

My last day at AZUPANE was in late July. The few staff not on vacation threw a small party, a *despidida*, for me, as well as for Jeff and Sister Theresa, who were also leaving. As a going-away gift, the Padre presented each of us with a handmade *tapiz*, a tapestry made by the inhabitants of the Guajira peninsula, north of Maracaibo. Now it was time to get ready to leave.

Seventeen

The Road Home

In mid-August, I went to Caracas to "terminate," the Peace Corps' odd term for the process of ending service. I handed a stool sample to the nurse, urinated in another cup, and went to the dentist, all of which showed that, except for a few amoebas, I was healthy. I also returned the typewriter I had borrowed more than a year before.

By this time, the Peace Corps had moved to the embassy to save money. The Marine guard checked my ID card before letting me enter. I was directed to the cafeteria, where I ordered a hamburger. Afterward, I went to the Peace Corps office to say goodbye to the remaining Venezuelan staff and Neil Volkmann, the program officer. I shook hands with Peter Stevens, the director, and then left to catch a taxi to the bus station to return to Maracaibo. Looking back on the thirty-one months I was in Venezuela, Peace Corps had treated me well, tolerating my indecisiveness, getting me out of San Carlos and the sports world, and arranging a change of sites. Despite a few ups and downs along the way, it was amazing and fun overall.

I spent my last two weeks in Venezuela packing, selling some household items, discarding the rest, and sending home personal papers, souvenirs, photographs, various memos, newsletters, and training materials, and the journals I would later use to write this book.

Initially, I planned to discard all 330 letters I received, until I re-read them and changed my mind. Realizing they represented the period

I was in the Peace Corps, I packed them with my other belongings. I also packed newspaper clippings and the *Newsweek* and *TIME* editions about Nixon's resignation, which I figured would be collector's items one day. As it turned out, I was wrong about their long-term financial value. In 2015, sellers of both magazines on the Internet were asking for less than $20.

The only book I brought to Venezuela was *The Theory of Literature*, a gift from a friend that I never read and wound up leaving behind, though I still shipped forty-five other books home. A popular hobby in the U.S. in the mid-1970s was collecting beer cans, so I brought home four different Venezuelan empty cans. Years later, I threw them away—maybe too soon. While writing this book, I found Zulia beer cans for sale on eBay for between $3 and $7.95, with free shipping.

The Peace Corp's "Suggested List of Clothing to Bring" had included a coat and tie for special occasions. Not wanting to dress inappropriately, I brought my eighth-grade graduation jacket but never wore it. Now, with the jacket more than ten years old but still fitting, I tossed it in the garbage. I packed everything into the pea green suitcase my father used while in the Army in World War II, and into a leather bag I had bought in Colombia, and then shipped them as unaccompanied luggage on Pan American Airlines, a service and airline long since discontinued. As part of the paperwork, I had to put a value on the contents. Because I considered the pictures priceless and the letters and other papers irreplaceable, I entered "zero." How would I price them? I mailed them the keys in the event customs wanted to see what was in the bags. I wrote "Peace Corps" on the bags, hoping customs would see the markings and not ask my parents to open them.

I informed the AZUPANE staff that our furniture and appliances were for sale. One wanted the refrigerator for his mother. Others wanted the ping pong/dinner table, my chess set, and table lamp. One of the women bought my mattress, and I threw in a few old sheets for free. I was unable to sell a pair of pants. With two days to go, there were only chairs and kitchen items left. Before Jeff left, he sold his Polaroid camera for twenty dollars. He also sold his motorcycle for $650, as well as his electric shaver, though no one showed interest in my electric toothbrush.

I shipped my belongings, emptied the house, and said goodbye to Tory, Ana, and AZUPANE. Jeff had left a week before and I had a last coffee with Mark and Andrea.

I was ready to leave and looking forward to traveling and getting to Chile, my latest destination. If I had still had enough money, I would continue to Argentina. I was flexible and would go with the flow. I packed light, stuffing two pairs of pants, a sweater, a green and black checkered wool jacket, three pairs of socks, three t-shirts, one shirt with a collar, and a pair of boots into a backpack. For first aid, I had Band-Aids and two-year-old anti-diarrheal medicine from my Peace Corps medical kit, which didn't have an expiration date. I would hide dollars, bolivars, and traveler's checks worth $2,700 on my body in four different places, including a money belt, while carrying both my gray Peace Corps passport and my new blue Bicentennial Passport. I squeezed three books into the backpack: *Zen and the Art of Motorcycle Maintenance* by R. M. Pirsig, *One Hundred Years of Solitude* by Gabriel Garcia Marquez, and *Dune* by Frank Herbert.

Dealing with an embassy, even for American citizens, is not always pleasant, even before the heightened security measures found at embassies today. So I would not use the American embassy in each country as an address to receive mail along the way, a service they once provided. Instead, I planned to send postcards and an occasional letter to keep friends and family informed of my whereabouts. Along the way, I would stay abreast of world events through local newspapers, but figured I would be without news from home for a few months. I ruled out emergencies happening while I was traveling and made no plan in case of one.

On my penultimate evening in Venezuela, Mark, Andrea, and I went to the Chinese diner, but were disappointed they could not serve us beer; a few weeks earlier, President Pérez had decreed that only restaurants could sell beer on Sunday. Government regulations said the family-owned Wily Quink Lunch was a diner, not a restaurant. We ordered dinner and afterward went to a pizza restaurant for a final Zulia, Maracaibo's best beer.

After pizza and beers, I went to CANTV, the Venezuelan telephone company, to call home. I gave the operator the number and sat down to wait. A few minutes later, she said the line at my parents' house was dead. "Impossible, telephone lines in America don't die!" I told her. She tried twice more. Nothing. I asked her to try again.

She refused. "Dead means dead and, no, I will not try again." I gave up and took a taxi back to the house.

The Road Home

The next morning, I woke up with such a stomachache that when Isabel came over in the late afternoon to say goodbye, I could not sit up or get out of bed. I had never felt so sick since being in Venezuela and it was awkward saying goodbye to her while lying down. Whatever ailed me, it was gone the next morning, my last day in Venezuela.

Harry picked me up after breakfast for a day of errands. First, we went to see his lawyer.

On the way, with one hand on the wheel and the other pointing to a woman walking down the street, he screamed, "Look at her. I wouldn't fuck her with your prick," which is my final memory of Harry. When we arrived at the lawyer's house, I stayed in the truck. A Venezuelan woman answered the door. From the truck where I was waiting and already sweating bullets at ten in the morning, I could hear Harry shouting, "I'm no sucker. I am intelligent. You can't screw me." Angry, he turned around and came back to the truck, and we left. I did not ask about his problems or even much about the man himself. Why was he in Venezuela? How did he earn money? Why did he live in a junkyard? Writing about Harry forty years later, I wondered what had happened to him, concluding he had passed away.

We returned to the house and loaded the remaining household items, including old underwear, a bottle opener, and a knife handle with no blades into Harry's truck. Harry, believing his own motto, "Take it all and leave nothing," took the refrigerator, the ping pong table, and everything else nobody wanted.

The American couple who left a few months earlier and sold their furniture and household items on the premise that money talks, might have been right when they sold their belongings to whoever was the first to pay the full amount in cash. Unlike the couple from the American school, I was more trusting, so when potential buyers said they would pay for their desires when they picked it up, I agreed. Jorge, the gardener, was the first to prove me wrong. He said he would buy our refrigerator for his mother, but he had to change his plan because his mother bought a new one a few days before I left. Frank never picked up the ping pong table or paid for the chess set. I had let him take the set with a promise he would pay me later.

Andrea and Mark were not at the house. They were looking for an apartment together, which was proving difficult. If necessary, they

261

planned to move in with Harry, who lived in a trailer in a junkyard on the outskirts of the city. While loading the truck, the traveling insurance agent walked out of his room carrying a pair of bloody slacks.

"Is everything okay?"

"My wife suffered a miscarriage last week but she's fine now."

We did not know she was pregnant.

On the morning of September 2, 1976, I left Maracaibo. From the house, I walked a block to the corner and hailed a taxi to the bus terminal but arrived too late for the 7:30 a.m. bus. I waited three hours for a *por puesto,* or group taxi, to fill with enough passengers to head to San Cristobal. Along the way, we stopped for lunch, and as a farewell meal, I indulged in my last Zulia beer and *arepa*. Six hours later, we were in San Cristobal, thirty-five miles from the Colombian border, where I ran into two Ecuadorian women I knew from Maracaibo who were going to Quito for their sister's wedding. We shared a taxi to the border, where I caught a bus to Pamplona.

Twenty-four hours later, the bus arrived. The town appeared as quiet as it had been two years earlier when I first visited. I imagined that not much would change in the next five or ten years, either. Progress can be slow. Arab, and Italian businesses occupied the streets near the bus station, which was a block off the central plaza, while the cathedral dominated the square. The token "Yanqui Go Home" graffiti, illustrating Columbia's more general criticism of U.S. foreign policy, covered several walls, which contrasted with the favorite subjects of Venezuela's political artists: Nixon, Kissinger, and the CIA.

I asked the teenagers hanging around the plaza where I could find a cheap place to stay. They walked me over to the Hotel Santander, named after the Colombian general who collaborated with Simon Bolívar in the fight for independence from Spain. A windowless room with a private bathroom with cold water for a shower and three wool blankets for warmth cost $2.75 a night.

After a short nap, I went for dinner on the square, where I ordered a tortilla and a bottle of Bavaria beer. The nurse in Caracas had given me antibiotics for the amoebas found in my stool sample, but she never said I couldn't drink alcohol, so I figured one beer wouldn't hurt. After dinner, I walked around the town.

The Road Home

When I woke up the next morning, it was already light. I dressed in a few minutes and went for breakfast only to learn when I got outside and saw the clock on the cathedral bell tower that it was only six o'clock, meaning no restaurants or cafés were open yet. Instead of returning to my hotel, I sat in the plaza and absorbed the tranquility. The only human activity was a man sleeping on a bench and another sweeping the square with a broom. Around seven, I heard metal security doors being lifted at the Hotel Roma, a rooming house with a restaurant opposite the cathedral. I walked over to the empty restaurant and ordered *desayuno,* the set breakfast menu. Fifteen minutes later, the waiter brought me yucca, rice, liver, soup, bread, and hot chocolate, a favorite drink in Columbia's Andes.

After breakfast, I went shopping for two notebooks and a shoulder bag, which cost $3 total. I also bought film for my camera, settling on the Fuji brand from Japan instead of American Kodak or Agfa from West Germany, the brand I had been using in Venezuela. The vendor said Fuji was better because the ASA was 100 instead of 80. A beginner in photography, these numbers meant nothing. I took him at his word and bought the 100 ASA film. As it would turn out, I wasn't in a picture-taking mood, a sign of burnout, and would return home with just two photos from this last trip.

In the afternoon, I was sitting in the plaza decompressing from Venezuela and wondering how far I would travel before I turned around and went home when three young men approached and surprised me by asking me my opinion of Gibson guitars. Though clueless on where the first mass-produced electric solid-body guitar ranked in the pantheon of musical instruments, I knew Les Paul invented it because he lived in Waukesha, Wisconsin, about twenty miles from where I grew up. Despite my limited knowledge of the Gibson guitar, they were excited that an American tourist had heard of it. Next, they were interested in my opinions of musicians.

"What do you think about Jimi Hendrix, Janis Joplin, and Bob Dylan?" they asked, rattling off the names of future Rock 'n Roll Hall of Famers in succession.

Surprised at their selection, I replied, *"Muy bueno, muy bueno"* ("Very good, very good").

"Bob Dylan is a good poet," one of them volunteered.

263

The comment surprised me, since none of his songs had been translated into Spanish, and it was difficult enough for native speakers of English to understand what he was singing about. Before I could respond to the idea of Bob Dylan as a poet, they asked me my opinion of Blue Oyster Cult.

"What's that?" I asked, having no idea what they were talking about.

"They are an American band. Do you know them?"

I didn't, and there was no purpose in pretending. "No, I never heard of them," I said without hesitation.

My ignorance of their favorite band shocked and insulted them, if I read their faces correctly. Did I make them feel stupid? Did they think my response meant Blue Oyster Cult was not popular in America? In my head, I did a rapid inventory of best excuses and settled for, "I've been out of the United States for over two years and am not familiar with all the music now." Apparently satisfied, they invited me to their house to listen to music. On the way, the conversation changed from musicians to asking if I had ever tried heroin. For a moment I considered making up a story, then thought better of it thinking they might not have taken it well if it was too incredible. So I just said I wasn't interested and left it at that.

The house was empty. The thermometer in the room where we listened to music, about as large as a pantry in a mansion, read 62°. It felt colder. Posters of Steve McQueen from the movie *The Great Escape*, Raquel Welch in a bikini, and Latin America's favorite revolutionary, Che Guevara, covered the walls. A Spanish edition of *Reader's Digest* was in the bathroom, a tiny room with a toilet and sink. They put a Blue Oyster Cult tape into a VHS player, which they connected to a Gibson amplifier. The sound shook the walls. It was the only time I knowingly ever listened to Blue Oyster Cult. Their music left no impression. After listening twice to the tape, I left.

The next day I woke up early and took a walk above the city, whose official altitude was 8,500 feet. I had not felt so cold since I left the United States more than two and half years before. Dogs and cows wandered in the surrounding fields. I hiked along a winding road leading to Bogotá as far as the last police checkpoint. Instead of turning around, I walked into the hills, sat down on a rock in the middle of a pasture, and read *One Hundred Years of Solitude* for the second time.

After reading fifty pages, I realized it was one of the best novels I ever read. However, I needed to move. My rear end hurt from sitting on a rock and with cows moving towards me, I got up and walked back to town. I went over to Flipper, the shop where I had squabbled with the owner about the price of an ice cream cone on an earlier trip. This time I ordered a soft drink and read *El Espectador,* a local newspaper.

An article in the paper reported that Bucaramanga, the city where I planned to be the next day, was in the middle of a heat wave and a water shortage. I hoped my hotel room had a fan. One tidbit said a judge felt insulted because all the taxis and rental cars in the city were old and run down. As a magistrate and a man of stature, he believed he was entitled to ride in a better vehicle. The editorial disagreed. It argued that a wealthy public servant like him in a city where the majority of people lived in poverty or on the edge of it should reconsider his desire to be chauffeured around town in a Mercedes-Benz. It might be better, they suggested, if he kept a low profile and found a driver with an old car like a 1955 Plymouth. In other words, the *El Especatador* advised the judge to shut up.

I arrived in Bucaramanga on a Sunday morning and checked into the Hotel Astoria near the bus station, assuming it had been upgraded since an earlier trip two years ago. But it wasn't. It still looked shabby and a room still cost two dollars a night. They gave me one with a bed that was too short for me, even though I was less than six feet tall, and a bathroom without a shower. There was no fan. The thin walls were three feet short of the ceiling. I had to ask for toilet paper.

In the afternoon, I attended a soccer game between the local professional team and Santa Fe, the best team in Colombia. It would be years before the drug lords bought soccer franchises and used them to launder their profits, in what became known as narco-soccer. Santa Fe was one of those teams. The El Dorado drug cartel, allegedly laundered part of its billion dollar profits through the club. Since I had never been to a game before, I didn't know how much time would be spent sitting around, so I brought a newspaper to read. The police patted me down as I entered the stadium and confiscated the paper because they said it posed a security risk. They didn't explain.

I took my seat in the tenth row on the side where the sun was in my face. Most fans wore team caps and carried radios so they could listen to the broadcast of the game. The stands were about 90 percent full, including women and families. A fence topped with barbed wire surrounded the field. Violence at soccer games in Latin America was not uncommon, requiring armed soldiers to guard the players' underground dressing rooms as a precaution. In a live pre-match interview conducted on the playing field, the announcer asked the Argentine goalie for the Bucaramanga team what he thought of the local crowd. He had only one possible response to the loaded question: "The fans are great!" People around me nodded. No fights broke out during the match, which ended in a tie.

I hit the sack early because I planned to take the 7 a.m. bus to Bogotá the next day, but noise from the room next door kept me awake. I was sound asleep until I heard people shouting and something fall and break. After concluding it was just a chair, I went back to sleep. I woke again to the sound of a door opening on the other side. Someone collapsed on a bed while letting out a scream, while the other vomited on the floor. Was he drunk? I dozed off again and woke to one of the men telling a woman to leave immediately. She yelled back, "*Yo no puta*," ("I'm not a whore") and then started crying. The men threatened to call the police. The woman shot back, "Go ahead." I dozed off again until the woman slammed the door as she left the room next door and woke me up. She met the manager in the hallway, who said she should stay because it was late. I looked at my watch. It was 5 a.m. She left anyway.

My next stop was Bogotá, a city I liked. This was my third trip to the capital of Colombia, where I spent a considerable amount of time walking between the Gold Museum and the Planetarium on Seventh Avenue, one of the city's best-known streets. Shoeshine boys, Marlboro cigarette peddlers, beggars, drug dealers, and hawkers selling fake emeralds made up a large part of the street-hustling population. Occasionally, men stopped me on the street and offered to sell me various illegal substances.

For the most part, the hawkers were not aggressive, insistent, or threatening. They would open a conversation by asking where I was from, followed by asking how long I had been in Bogotá. Not caring about my response, they would usually pop the big question: "Do you want something for your head?" When I showed no interest, they left me alone. One street hawker wearing a long leather coat stopped in front of me, blocking my path. He opened his jacket, showing pockets filled with various drugs. I said, "No thanks," and continued walking.

If I planned on traveling indefinitely, I would need a way to ditch the street hustlers before they got to their sales pitch. The perfunctory introductory pleasantries were always about my nationality and country. As a rookie traveler, I answered the question honestly and politely, though I never gave my real hometown or state. Instead, I settled on Chicago, a word with easily pronounceable hard syllables, and a city known through movies as one about gangsters and Al Capone. *Boom. Boom. Boom,* people would say as they pointed their forefingers and pretended to pull the trigger.

After almost three years of answering "Where are you from?" I needed a different response, something that would not generate unwanted conversation about criminals while people were trying to fleece me. It didn't matter which city or state I chose; I was searching for a reply that would stop the conversation. Saying I was from Chicago facilitated more questions, and I wanted the opposite to occur. After considering a few cities and all fifty states, I decided that the next time a street peddler, beggar, or scam artist asked me where I came from, my reply would be, "Connecticut," the state with the most syllables and one few foreigners knew. The four-syllable state, if said rapidly, sounds frightening but serious, giving me confidence that when hustlers and other strangers heard it, they would walk away and leave me alone. I called it the Connecticut Defense.

After two years of travel, I concluded it was as much about routine, planning, and logistics as it was about adventure. I would arrive at each destination and trust a street kid to find me the best and cheapest hotel, which had to be no more than a ten-minute walk from the bus station. After paying him two pesos as a finder's fee, I would check in and go to my room, then spend the first few minutes wondering if they had overcharged me even though a room with a bed and a cold shower cost less than three dollars a night. I would then shower, eat, do some tourism, get a beer, and read a little. When I arrived in towns after a long bus ride, I wanted to take a good crap in my hotel room, only to find the bathrooms usually did not have toilet paper.

After a week, the routine was already tedious; a sign the trip might be short. Now, in my first days of possibly months of buses and cheap hotels, every place already looked the same, another bad sign. As the bus crept through the Andes Mountains, I gazed out the window and ruminated more about life in the United States and seeing family and friends again and less about Ecuador, Peru, and Chile. How had America changed? How had I changed? I knew whatever emotions occurred upon returning, they would wear off soon. Nevertheless, getting back home was becoming more important than seeing South America.

One side of my brain was telling the other side to go home. I needed some American living, to hear a funny joke and have a good laugh, which seemed lacking the last months in Maracaibo. There were no light moments or humor in late rent payments or managing tenants or discussions on comp time. I went to a travel agency and booked a flight to Miami. With my return to the U.S. now definite, I spent the next two days shopping for Christmas gifts, even though it was only September. For my final dinner in Bogotá, I had pizza by candlelight.

While packing in my room, one of the hotel staff brought me *The Temple of the Dawn,* the third novel of the Sea of Fertility tetralogy by Yukio Mishima, a Japanese writer who committed suicide in 1970. An American tourist had left it behind a few months earlier. I accepted one of the great works of the twentieth century, according to the excerpts from reviews on the back cover, and thanked him. I left the book on the bed when I checked out.

On the flight from Bogotá, I revisited Venezuela: AZUPANE, the house, Harry and his truck, street life in Maracaibo. Now I was thinking about my arrival in the U.S., and what the future might bring after being away for more than two and half years.

I arrived at Miami International Airport at three o'clock on a beautiful Saturday afternoon on September 11, 1976, the same day when, twenty-five years later, I would watch the Pentagon burn from my Washington, DC office window in Dupont Circle. The immigration official told me he was bored and wanted something more fascinating than checking passports. It is rare for immigration officials to say more than "welcome home," much less complain to a traveler.

Years later at Dulles International Airport, when returning from a conference on landmines, an immigration official let down his guard, showing he had a heartbeat while asking perfunctory questions such as, "What countries did you visit and what do you do?" He asked if I was carrying any landmines with me. I was pretty certain he was joking, but I wasn't completely sure. You never know about security officials, and people have strange ideas about landmines. Not wanting to be detained or arrested for insulting a U.S. border official, I carefully considered my reply. Before I could answer, he said, "Because if you do, I want to take one of them and put it under my supervisor's desk," pointing to him about fifty feet away. I laughed. So did he. He stamped my passport and said, "Welcome home."

In Miami, the customs officials waved me through when I said I was returning from more than two years in the Peace Corps. The lady behind me was not so lucky when they confiscated a live turtle she had in her checked luggage. After exiting customs, a young woman identified herself as a member of Hare Krishna and asked me for a quarter, which I hesitated to give since, for the past week, I had been warding off beggars. When the woman sensed my reluctance, she said the group cared for the poor, and handed me a booklet called *Back to Godhead*, the same booklet Hare Krishna Man in Colombia waved in my face. I gave her a quarter and continued walking through the airport, past large posters of O.J. Simpson, who was still twenty years away from acquittal for the murder of his ex-wife Nicole Brown and her friend Ron Goldman in "The Trial of the Century." In the poster, he was wearing a three-piece suit, running from the Hertz counter to catch his plane.

I stayed at the airport hotel rather than go into the city, as my flight home was the next morning. I wasn't sure if the check-in procedures at an American hotel were the same as in Venezuela and Colombia, forcing me to ask the same question I had been asking for over two years: "What are your rates?"

The perky clerk quickly answered: "We have two types of rooms: a small one for $18.72 or a larger one for $24."

Having mostly stayed in "rooms" with only a bed, a desk, a chair, a portable closet with two hangers, and no bathroom, toilet paper, or hot water, I needed more information. "What's included in the room?"

The question surprised her. She looked at me as if I were from another planet. I didn't wait for an explanation. I took the cheaper room to save six dollars. It had everything I needed: windows, a comfortable bed with enough covers to keep me warm from the cold air conditioning, a private bath with hot water, and a lamp on a table, a welcome change from the bare light bulb I had grown accustomed to having. However, the toilet leaked. I called the desk. Instead of sending a plumber, they moved me to a larger and more expensive room at no extra cost.

I turned on the television and discovered America. On a Saturday afternoon in September, football, baseball, golf, and tennis consumed most of the channels. Having never seen a professional tennis match, I was intrigued to watch Jimmy Connors play Guillermo Vilas from Argentina and Bjorn Borg of Sweden play Ilie Nastase from Romania in the U.S. Open. On the evening news, I heard Jimmy Carter speak for the first time. He was in Plains, Georgia, his hometown, at a chicken barbecue denying he lacked the experience to be an effective president.

While watching the evening news, I recalled events of the past two and a half years, none of which I saw on television. Nixon had resigned in my first year in Venezuela, and the Vietnam War ended in my second. From Nixon, we begot Jerry Ford and his opponent in the 1976 presidential campaign, Jimmy Carter. Patty Hearst, kidnapped a few months after I arrived in Venezuela, was in jail for bank robbery hoping her famous lawyer, F. Lee Bailey, could get her out on bail. *TIME* magazine reported unemployment stood at eight million and had declared Bruce Springsteen the next rock superstar, putting him on its cover. The World Football League started and went out of business before I watched a game. I tried to imagine the challenges of living in a bad economy. In contrast, the Venezuelan economy was flourishing.

I missed the 1976 Montreal Olympics except for the televised welterweight championship between the East German Jochen Bachfeld and the Venezuelan Pedro Gamarro. Venezuelans believed the judges robbed Gamarro when they scored the fight 3-2 for the German.

I was so engrossed in the news and television I forgot about eating. It was too late to go to a restaurant, so I ordered room service, the first time I'd used a telephone in over a year. I enjoyed the luxury of having my dinner brought to the room, an American meal of a cheeseburger, French fries, and a Coca-Cola. The raw onions tasted better than the onions I had been eating the past thirty-one months. While enjoying my meal, I continued watching television. Team Canada was playing the Soviet Union in the Canada Cup. When I changed channels between periods, the only movie I could find was *The Claw*. The next day I flew home.

Once home, I was unsure how I would explain or describe my

time in Venezuela. I didn't know how it would be perceived or the questions people would ask. How would I close the gap between what I experienced and what others were interested in hearing? Maybe there would be commonality in AZUPANE, particularly with friends who worked in special education, but with everyone else, I wasn't sure what to expect.

I was off base assuming there would be interest in what I had been doing. Most people wanted to know more about the government and Venezuelan customs, traditions, and habits than I could explain. Even today, forty years later, few have asked what I did in Venezuela and most seem amazed to learn Peace Corps was even there; just hearing I had been a Peace Corps Volunteer satisfied them. The details of the job were irrelevant. I kept my answers short by saying I coached baseball and worked with disabled children in as few words as possible.

The coaching part usually drew a look of surprise. Sports fans wondered why Venezuela needed baseball coaches, and few were puzzled as to why Peace Corps Volunteers coached any sport. Although no one asked if I worked for the CIA or some other clandestine government agency, I would have denied it anyway, knowing some wondered what I really did. Most of the time, trying to explain AZUPANE drew silence. In one unexpected conversation, I stunned a neighbor when he inquired about wildlife. Unprepared and having lived in urban settings, wildlife to me meant rats and cockroaches, not birds, reptiles, and animals, so I said, "Rats." Shocked, and maybe insulted at the same time, he returned to mowing the lawn and never asked me more about Venezuela.

Forty years later, while having dinner in suburban Milwaukee with my wife and in-laws, a man at the next table recognized me. He identified himself as old grade-school acquaintance, who I remembered after he gave his name. Covering four decades, he could have asked about my profession, marital status, kids, my whereabouts, or what I was doing at the restaurant. Instead, he asked if I had really joined the Peace Corps. He wasn't curious about the details or the wildlife, or whether I engaged in spying or other nonsense—he just wanted confirmation   I   had   been   a   Peace   Corp   Volunteer.

Epilogue

Of all the events and incidents that occurred while I was in Venezuela, the William Niehous kidnapping was without a doubt the most intriguing. Essentially a political crime story, the abduction did not capture the public's interest at the time nearly as much as nationalizing the oil industry, Miss Venezuela relinquishing her title, or the rise of Johnny Cecotto in world motocross competition. But researching the kidnapping while writing this book gave me insight into a side of Venezuela I knew nothing about. Over the years, interviews, books, memoirs, government records, trials, and the personal papers of a former high-ranking CIA official at the Library of Congress have revealed details of the kidnapping, the subsequent investigation, and the aftermath. They opened the door to a complicated history, foreign policy, and a cast of characters that includes informers, terrorists, Nazi hunters, quacks, politicians, intelligence agencies, and the Cuban exile community. A remarkable number of institutions, companies, and agencies with direct or indirect associations with informants, drug traffickers, terrorists, assassins, Iran-Contra, the Bay of Pigs, plots against Fidel Castro's life, the JFK assassination, and quacks are linked, directly and indirectly, to the Niehous kidnapping investigation.

The Niehous kidnapping, a shock in Venezuela, seems less surprising when put into the context of the 1970s and the Cold War atmosphere, when extremist groups in the Middle East, Europe, and Latin America used hijackings, kidnappings, bombings, and assassinations to bring attention to their causes and political battles. Some incidents are better known than others. One of the most prominent was the massacre of the Israeli Olympic team by the Palestinian Black September group in Munich in 1972. In December 1975, two months before Niehous disappeared, a Greek Marxist urban guerrilla group killed Richard Welsh, the CIA station chief, in front of his house in Athens. In the same month, Carlos the Jackal, a Venezuelan, took seventy OPEC ministers hostage in Vienna. In Argentina, dozens of businessmen, including one from Coca-Cola, were seized. The Mujahadin-E Khalq (MEK), a Marxist-Islamic organization in Iran, assassinated three Rockwell International Corporation employees. In Latin America, anti- Castro exiles in Florida and Venezuela played key roles in attacks against Cuba and tried numerous times to kill Fidel Castro in the decades after the Bay of Pigs debacle.

In this global context, the Argimiro Gabaldón Revolutionary Command (AGRC), a group in Venezuela no one had ever heard of, kidnapped William Niehous, general manager of the Owens-Illinois Glass Company, in February 1976.

Lanz Rodriguez, the mastermind behind the Niehous kidnapping, said he got the idea from reading about the Revolutionary Movement Eighth of October (MR8) seizing the U.S. ambassador to Brazil, Charles Burke Elbrick, in 1969. Although the government released fifteen political prisoners and the group's manifesto exposed the Brazilian military regime for its repression, it was, in many ways, too late: Elbrick was severely beaten and died years later from injuries sustained while in captivity. The kidnappers were caught and after spending some time in prison were sent to Algeria, a haven for dozens of liberation movements at the time, in exchange for the West German ambassador. Their leader, Fernando Gabeira, returned to Brazil eight years later and in 1995 was elected to the Brazilian Congress. In a 2009 interview, he admitted the kidnapping was a mistake.

Seven years later, in February 1976, when President Carlos Andres Pérez was at the peak of his popularity after nationalizing the oil industry, raising the hopes of the Venezuelan people that they might benefit from the billions of dollars in annual revenue, the unknown AGRC attempted to copy the Brazilians. On the night of February 22, 1976, they knocked on the front door of the Niehous residence in Prados del Este in the hills above Caracas. At the time, Donna Niehous was sitting under a hair dryer and Bill Niehous, the American general manager of the Owens-Illinois Glass Company's operations in Venezuela, was in the upstairs bedroom. The maid answered the door, and seven men rushed in, two carrying machine guns. In a few minutes, the kidnappers bound the two women and dragged Bill, groggy from an injection they'd given him, out of the house.

With so many American companies in Venezuela, why Owens-Illinois? Why Bill Niehous? Surely there were bigger fish among the executives in Caracas. Mrs. Niehous believes her husband was seized for the simple reason that they lived in an isolated neighborhood without security; he was an easy target.

The kidnappers quickly proclaimed the Venezuelan government was incompetent and Owens-Illinois represented the unchecked corruption so typical of multi-national companies. They also said Niehous worked for the CIA.

The Venezuelan Communist Party had a different take. They believed the only reasonable explanation for the kidnapping was that the CIA did it. The crime fit the CIA's destabilization plans, they said.

In the first three months, the kidnappers issued demands and expressed a willingness to negotiate a ransom. While the company met the kidnappers' requirements of giving a five hundred bolivar bonus — about 70 percent of my Peace Corps living allowance — to each of the 1,600 Venezuelan employees and distributing 18,000 packages of food in poor Caracas neighborhoods, the government would not consent to the local papers printing the group's platform. Determined to free, Niehous, the company then paid *The New York Times*, the *London Times,* and *Le Monde* to print it, infuriating the Pérez administration, which said it offended the dignity of the country and promoted subversion. In retribution, Venezuela moved to nationalize Owens-Illinois, though it never followed through.

Notes from a conversation at the White House with Brent Scowcroft, Assistant to the President for National Security Affairs, Edwin Dodd, president of Owens-Illinois, Ohio Senator Robert Taft and two members of the National Security Council, indicate the White House was reluctant to get involved, thinking any U.S. government overtures would result in Perez adopting harsher measures than appropriating the company. Stephen Low from the NSC pointed out that if the White House engaged in negotiations or was even perceived to be involved, it would encourage more kidnappings.

With an impasse at hand, a CIA analysis, only released in 2007, concluded the Niehous family was in the middle of a dogfight between the government and the kidnappers, and unless one side softened its position, Niehous could remain in captivity for a long time.

Frustrated, Owens-Illinois hired John "Jake" Longan, an expert on Latin American terrorism and hostage situations from his time as a public safety advisor in Venezuela in the 1960s. For her part, Mrs. Niehous asked Bruce Berckmans Jr. and the Wackenhut Corporation to help find her husband.

Wackenhut, founded in 1954 and based in Coral Gables, Florida, was no ordinary company. They opened their first foreign office in Caracas in 1968 under Venezolana de Seguridad y Vigilancia, C.A., better known as Vesevica. In the 1970s, they provided security at the Kennedy Space Center, the Atomic Energy Commission's nuclear test site in Nevada, and several American embassies; the firm also conducted a wide range of investigations and sting operations. Critics of clandestine U.S. intelligence operations accused the firm many times of being a CIA front organization. *SPY*, a humor magazine noted for its outstanding political reporting that closed down in 1998, published a lengthy piece in 1992 detailing the company's associations with the American intelligence agencies, including several former Langley officials who served as advisors. Among them were Defense Secretary and CIA Deputy Director Frank Carlucci and William J. Casey, who served as legal counsel before later becoming CIA director.

Bruce Berckmans Jr. had a background in intelligence, too. He was forced to resign from the CIA when Philip Agee, in his book, *Inside the Company: CIA Diary* identified him as an operations officer tasked with penetrating the Mexican Communist Party while posing as the Latin American representative for agribusiness development and working undercover as director of Estudios Economicos y Promociones Industriales SA. After being outed and resigning, he took a job with Wackenhut in Coral Gables and remained in the intelligence and security field the rest of his life, often using Roger Merriweather Greever as an alias. William and Donna Niehous had befriended Berckmans when they were in Mexico City on a previous assignment with Owens-Illinois. Donna Niehous told me they did not know he worked for the CIA.

John Longan's expertise was more in security than intelligence. As an advisor in the Office of Public Safety (OPS) in the 1960s, he worked in Venezuela and Guatemala. The United States Aid for International Development (USAID) program trained local law enforcement officers around the world and supplied them with equipment. Many of its top officials had worked for the CIA, including its director, Byron Engle. Critics and analysts considered OPS both a CIA partner and a recruiting ground for the agency. Others denounced it as being nothing more than a means to control the conduct of foreign law enforcement to achieve U.S. political ends.

The fundamental goal of the program was to unify a country's police and military under a central command, overseen by OPS advisors. But wherever the OPS operated, brutality followed. In Guatemala, disappearances and murders became so prevalent in 1966 that the deputy chief of mission, Varon Vaky, warned Washington that if continued, it could result in political instability. A State Department declassified cable verified what the new police units were doing: "Comprised of both military and civilian personnel, the Special Unit has carried out abductions, bombings, street assassinations, and executions of real and alleged communists and occasionally has acted against other vaguely defined enemies of the government."

Congress ended the program in 1974 after its hearings and investigations revealed that trainers were complicit in torture, state terror, and human rights abuses in Brazil, Greece, Iran, South Vietnam, Taiwan, and Uruguay, giving it a black mark among foreign aid programs. In one of the most widely publicized incidents, the Tupamaros, an urban guerrilla group in Montevideo, killed Dan Mitrione, an OPS advisor in Uruguay, in 1970 for allegedly training the local police in riot control techniques that led to student deaths at the University. Costa-Gavras based his 1972 Golden Globe-nominated film *State of Siege*, which was the first movie I saw in Venezuela, on the kidnapping and murder of Mitrione. Declassified State Department records confirm American advisors trained police in torture techniques.

Compared to versions in other countries, the Office of Public Safety in Venezuela is less well-known. In 1962, when the program began, policemen were being killed daily, and university students were behind many of the civil disturbances. A report Longan submitted to Washington in 1966 said he created a task force to combat urban terrorism, principally kidnappings and bombings, which improved coordination among law enforcement agencies. In April 1974, the same month I started coaching baseball in San Carlos, a final evaluation of the OPS program in Venezuela concluded those threats remained, and the politicized and inefficient agencies needed further training. At stake was continued stability and security in the oil industry and American investments, estimated at more than three billion dollars. Even though Venezuela offered to pay the whole $250,000 budget for fiscal year 1975, which represented 80 percent of the USAID program in the country, the U.S. Congress, having already made up its mind, declined, and reiterated that OPS would not continue under any circumstances.

The kidnappers allowed Bill Niehous to write letters to reassure everyone he was alive. He wrote that he was in good health, had not been tortured, ate at least one meal a day, and had newspapers and books to read, including Ernest Hemingway and Arthur Miller. But he didn't understand why his captors had not released him after paid the workers and prepared the food packages as they demanded. The kidnappers told him they couldn't let him go until they received a ransom. He did not know if his captors wanted too much money or if was low-balling the payment during the negotiations. He gave the benefit of the doubt to his employer and blamed his captors for being too greedy. Surely, wasn't taking a hard line in the negotiations because they thought paying a ransom might harm their long-term interests in Venezuela.

In one of his last letters in July 1976, Niehous tried to make sense of his captivity, looking at the pros and cons, or winners and losers. He opined that the government of Venezuela was the only winner. They had gained three businesses in retaliation for the company publishing the AGRC manifesto in *The New York Times*, the *London Times,* and *Le Monde,* and by refusing to negotiate, the government had the kidnappers and their group on the run and threatened to arrest anyone who helped them. Niehous thought his captors had won when met their demands to pay their employees a five hundred bolivar bonus and distribute food packages, but then they fumbled the victory away by asking for a ten million -bolivar ($2.5 million) ransom. The biggest loser was his family, from whom he had been separated for more than 125 days.

The most important government agency in the saga was the Directorate of Intelligence and Prevention Services (*Dirección General Sectorial de los Servicios de Inteligencia y Prevención*, DISIP), Venezuela's intelligence agency—commonly known as the secret police, or as Venezuelans preferred to call it, the political police. Established in 1969 by President Rafael Caldera—the same President Caldera who embraced the expansion of the Peace Corps' Sports and Recreation program—

DISIP investigated matters involving national security and conducted overt and covert operations against groups they considered a danger to the stability of the country.

Longan was in luck when President Pérez put Erasto Fernandez, an old colleague from the police training program in the 1960s, in charge of the Niehous case. Fernandez, once the head of DIGIPOL, the predecessor of DISIP, would weave in and out of the investigation, but was most valuable for his direct line of contact with the president. Longan also established contact with Orlando Garcia and Ricardo Morales, both Cuban exiles working for DISIP. He knew Morales from other unspecified work.

After had met two of the kidnappers' three demands and had paid newspapers in the U.S. and Europe to publish the group's leftist manifesto, all of which Longan advised O-I not to do; there wasn't much reason for Longan to stay in Venezuela. Having accomplished what he was hired to do and frustrated with the company's seemingly less than robust commitment to finding Niehous, at times putting the company's long-term interests in Venezuela ahead of finding their employee, he quit. Mrs. Niehous, also frustrated with the Venezuelan authorities and the embassy, then hired Longan.

After a failed ransom exchange in Caracas in July where DISIP mistakenly seized a German tourist who had wandered onto the drop site by accident, the group arrested several politicians, including Ivan Padilla and David Nieves, a co-director of the new Socialist League, and tortured both. Under duress, Padilla pointed to Jorge Rodriguez, the Youth Socialist League Secretary General, as one of the people involved in the kidnapping. After arresting him, DISIP agents beat him; he died in jail from broken ribs and liver failure.

According to some of the participants in the crime, negotiations between the government and the kidnappers on releasing Niehous broke off after the death of Rodriguez. They had expected to reach a settlement over Niehous, but when Rodriguez died while in DISIP custody, the kidnappers realized the government wasn't interested in negotiating with them. Instead, over the next year, DISIP rounded up or killed four hundred of its members.

Based on information provided through interrogating Rodriguez, Padilla, and Nieves, DISIP thought Niehous was being held in a guerilla mountain camp about a five-hour walk from the road. The army sent its Special Forces to search in the vicinity of San Jose de Guaribe, two hundred and fifty miles south of Caracas in the state of Anzoátegui, now located in the state of Guárico. But the army didn't find him.

Years later, Nieves would say DISIP arrested, tortured, and killed Jorge Rodriguez more for political reasons than for his alleged part in the abduction or to try to find out where Niehous was being held. In fact, according to Nieves, Rodriguez didn't know the whereabouts of Niehous. Plus, he said Niehous's captors never intended to kill him. They only abducted him because they needed a platform to promote their group's agenda and a kidnapping would give them one. Whatever their motivation, they failed miserably in using the crime to advance their interests.

By August, the government had spent two million bolivars looking for Niehous and his captors while losing politically in the eyes of the public. Most Venezuelans I knew were incredulous that the police could not find Niehous. More than a few were convinced the police knew where he was being held captive—but they couldn't explain if that were true, why he hadn't been rescued.

Meanwhile, Longan said the kidnappers had spent two hundred thousand bolivars on keeping Niehous captive and they needed money, but there was no way the government was going to approve a ransom. So in August 1976, President Pérez had little choice but to announce that he hoped they would find Niehous soon and unharmed.

Around mid-1976, the kidnappers issued an undated memorandum titled "Preliminary Answers to (sic) the American Citizen William Niehous," summarizing the findings from the Revolutionary Tribunal they had convened in the jungle. They called it an "irrefutable record of the exploitation, pillage, and corruption of the Venezuelan conscience." They gave Niehous the chance to explain himself and U.S. foreign policy but his argument was so ridiculously simple—"If we don't intervene, the Russians will,"—that his captors said it bordered on stupidity.

They wanted to hear more than that. He could have mentioned American military exploits in Guatemala, the Dominican Republican, Nicaragua, Korea, Vietnam, and Cambodia, they wondered. Niehous, not rising to the moment, could only manage to say, "I don't understand U.S. foreign policy very well." Could he have known so little or did he see the tribunal as so absurd he did not think it was worth his time to take it seriously? He was convinced they weren't going to kill him under any circumstances. It was the Cold War. Our enemies were the Soviet Union and the Eastern bloc, comprising Czechoslovakia, East Germany, Hungary, Poland, and Romania. In January 1976, in the midst of the Chinese Cultural Revolution, Premier Zhou Enlai had died, and Mao Zedong was dying. Our twenty-year engagement in Vietnam, based on the premise that if Vietnam fell to the Communists so would the rest of Southeast Asia, had just ended.

During the interrogation, Niehous admitted that Owens-Illinois had discussed the ongoing Andean Pact negotiations over proposed regulations on manufacturing glass in South America with the Venezuelan government. But they only lobbied for rules that would not harm the company, as any business would do in the United States when a new trade agreement was being negotiated.

More damaging to Niehous were the links the kidnappers made between the American Institute for Free Labor Development (AIFLD) and the CIA. More than sixty corporations had joined the venture, including Owens-Illinois. Its aim was to support unions around the world and persuade them to embrace private-sector growth. Funding from the CIA through USAID assisted that goal.

The kidnappers said Niehous represented his company at AIFLD regional meetings. When he denied it, they told him the operatives they sent to the gatherings reported back that they had seen him at such assemblies. There are no known public records to substantiate the claims. Even if Niehous did not attend such meetings, the kidnappers had other support for their case connecting labor unions to the CIA. In 1967, Victor Reuther, the head of the United Auto Workers (UAW) Education Department and its primary representative on the international level, and the older brother of Walter Reuther, the president of the UAW told trade union leaders that the AFL-CIO served as a front for the State Department and the CIA, alluding to the AFL-CIO role in weakening unions before the 1964 coup in Brazil. The first AIFLD director in Venezuela, Serafino Romualdi, was the principal CIA agent for labor affairs in Latin America and helped drive out the Communist Party and other leftists from the Confederation of Venezuelan Workers

(CTV), according to Philip Agee in his book, *Inside the Company: CIA Diary.*

Before the 1973 coup, AIFLD programs in Chile were coordinated with the U.S. embassy, where Harry Schlaudeman, the envoy to Venezuela at the time of the Niehous kidnapping, was the deputy ambassador. With Owens-Illinois, a member of AIFLD, and Harry Shlaudeman at the embassy in Santiago from 1969–73, when Niehous was in Spain, the kidnappers, striving to connect the dots, assumed and Niehous were up to no good in Venezuela. With Schlaudeman as the ambassador in Caracas, they presumed he must be plotting with on a plan to disrupt Venezuelan democracy, considering he was in Chile and the Dominican Republic where the U.S. played a role on creating political instability. Even Peter Stevens, the Peace Corps director in Venezuela, wondered what kind of situations might arise with Schlaudeman as the ambassador.

However, hard evidence was lacking. Beginning with the Church and Pike Committee hearings in 1975, Congress, the CIA, and the State Department have released records confirming U.S. government involvement in destabilizing Chile but nowhere in the thousands of pages of documents are Owens-Illinois or Niehous found, making the relationship questionable. The history of O-I, available on the company's website, first mentions Chile in 1977. Donna Niehous told me her husband had never been to Chile.

Did Niehous work for the CIA? In March 1978, Bruce Berckmans asked Mrs. Niehous if her husband was a spy. She said no and then, somewhat unsure of how to say it, added, "Knowing him as I do, I suspect that…well, maybe he wouldn't have told me, but I think he would. But he never told me. I don't know but I think he would have told me. You [Berckmans] could probably tell better than I could whether I would, in fact, know it." In the margin of the interview transcript found in the Library of Congress among the papers of David Atlee Phillips, a twenty-five-year veteran of the agency, during which he spent all but two years on Latin American operations, he cryptically wrote "yes," to Mrs. Niehous's last comment. But what did Phillips mean? Was he saying Berckmans was well-qualified to determine if Bill Niehous was a spy? Or did "yes" mean that Phillips, deeply involved in clandestine operations in Latin America, was confirming Niehous worked for the CIA?

Epilogue

We'll probably never know. When I asked Mrs. Niehous in October 2015 if her husband was a CIA operative, she said no. But, as history has taught us, that doesn't mean he wasn't doing some work for the CIA.

Although Niehous's kidnappers couldn't prove Owens-Illinois was a CIA front, the company's real crime, according to Lanz Rodriguez, the leader of the Argimiro Gabaldón Revolutionary Command, was corruption and exploiting its employees by paying them low wages while earning millions of dollars in profits, a common complaint regarding most corporations, both then and now.

In August 1976, Berckmans recommended the White House appoint a special envoy and seek advice from the president of Venezuela on how should continue if they wanted to move forward in finding Niehous. Embassy cables released by Wikileaks that are a part of the "Kissinger Papers" collection show U.S. officials had been in contact with the police, the Ministry of Interior, and DISIP, the Venezuelan intelligence agency, seeking updates on the government's investigation. The standard communication channels were open and functioned at a satisfactory level, according to the embassy. The Ford Administration rejected the idea of a special envoy.

When Venezuela created DISIP, the CIA recommended anti-Castro Cuban exiles for some of the top posts. One of them was Ricardo "The Monkey" Morales Navarrete. He first started in law enforcement working in airport security in Havana under Castro. In 1960, he fled to Florida, where he joined Operation 40, a CIA-sponsored program made up of Cuban exiles that was intended to oust Castro. When he got in trouble with the law in 1968, he became a government informant, and for the next fourteen years, provided evidence to the FBI, the CIA, the DEA, the IRS, the Miami and Dade County police, and the state and federal prosecutors' offices on a range of criminal and terrorist activities. John Longan, Bruce Berckmans, Owens-Illinois and the U.S. embassy apparently did not know this about Morales, and if the CIA was aware, they told no one working on the kidnapping case.

In October 1976, Morales supplied the explosives that Cuban exiles, based in Venezuela, used to blow up a Cuban airliner in an incident that killed seventy-three passengers, including Cuba's national fencing team and five North Korean diplomats. But Morales was not arrested. Instead, he was the informer who told the FBI that Orlando

282

Epilogue

Bosch and Luis Posada Carriles, both major figures in the anti-Castro Cuban exile community with ties to the CIA, and whom the FBI considered terrorists, were the masterminds behind the bombing. The Venezuelan police arrested and jailed them— but not Morales, as he was too valuable as an informant to arrest. Morales had not only named Bosch and Posada, both imprisoned while they awaited charges, but also several DISIP agents as having a role in this international act of terrorism. The information was too much for Venezuela, so they declared Morales *persona non grata,* forcing him out of the country.

Bosch, who did his internship in pediatrics at the University of Toledo in Ohio in the 1950s, was a schoolmate of Castro's in Havana. After the revolution, Castro appointed him governor of Las Villas province, where he had commanded rebel forces against Batista. But he quickly soured on Castro and fled to the U.S., where he joined the CIA-sponsored Operation 40, which led him to a life of crime and terrorism. The Department of Justice linked him to a network of associations that carried out acts of sabotage in the United States, Puerto Rico, Panama, and Cuba from 1961 through 1968. As if that wasn't enough, the Cuban government said he played a role in seventy-eight terrorist attacks against it in Spain, England, Japan, Mexico, Poland, and other countries. Bosch was also implicated in the murder of Orlando Letelier, the former minister of Defense, Foreign Affairs and Interior under Allende in Chile, in Washington, DC in September 1976.

Luis Posada has a similar history. Like Morales and Bosch, Posada was a CIA asset, including being hired by Erasto Fernandez as head of security for DIGITOL, the Venezuelan intelligence before it was renamed DISIP. Later, he became head of counter-intelligence with DISIP. After he and Bosch were arrested for planning the Cuban airliner bombing, they spent years as prison cellmates in Venezuela.

The CIA trained him for the Bay of Pigs operation; he befriended Mafia dons and, like Bosch and other Cuban exiles, makes the list of suspects implicated in the conspiracy to kill President Kennedy. Peter Kornbluh of the National Security Archive has called Posada, "One of the most dangerous terrorists in recent history" and the "godfather of Cuban exile violence." Cuban government officials call him "the Osama bin Laden of Latin America." In Miami, where he has lived since 2007, the Cuban diaspora considers him a hero.

With DISIP occupied with investigating both the airline bombing and the murder of former defense minister in Chile under President Allende, Orlando Letelier, the, in Washington, D.C. in September 1976, there was nothing but silence from DISIP on the Niehous kidnapping.

From October 1976 to mid-1978, the only news about Niehous was that he was dead. John Longan, now working for Donna Niehous, theorized he had died of a heart attack and was buried near Barcelona, east of Caracas, but it was not clear if Longan believed any of it. Mrs. Niehous, not sure what to think, wrote in her diary that Bill Coleman, the O-I vice president in-charge of the investigation, had a "zillion theories" on the conflict, all of them convoluted relationships between leftist groups and politicians. She held out hope her husband was still alive. O-I, wanting proof before believing the rumors, sent someone to the burial site to photograph the gravestone. The photographer returned with pictures showing a single flat stone with the engraving "Jose Garcia," the Spanish equivalent of "Joe Smith," chiseled on it, next to three other graves. It was supposedly evidence Niehous was dead. No one believed it.

In the meantime, DISIP had arrested Lanz Rodriguez, the mastermind of the kidnapping, in February 1977, a year after Niehous disappeared. A military court sentenced him to eight years in prison on the charge of rebelling against the army. Still, Niehous was not released and his whereabouts remained unknown.

With no leads and total silence from both the kidnappers and the Venezuelan government, quacks, mercenaries, and scam artists looking for a payday called O-I and Donna Niehous saying they could find her husband and get him released for $10,000 to $50,000. So many cranks were calling Mrs. Niehous that the FBI installed a recorder on her phone. Among the callers was a guy who claimed he'd met her in Egypt two thousand years ago.

Another was James Heller, whom the Justice Department indicted for engaging in extortion through interstate commerce when he demanded $50,000 over the course of five telephone calls to Owens-Illinois in October 1976. Heller claimed he knew where the kidnappers were holding Niehous in Venezuela and could obtain his release because he knew a few of the terrorists. The FBI traced his calls to a phone booth in New York City and arrested him in the midst of his fifth try to get O-I to hire him. After his arrest, he quickly admitted he had made it all up and knew nothing about Niehous, the kidnappers, or Venezuela. After the judge refused to dismiss the case, he pleaded no contest but appealed on the grounds he was wrongly charged. Seven months later, the court reversed the ruling when it concluded the prosecutors had overreached and had incorrectly charged him with extortion. The appeals court found no criminal intent. They said Heller just wanted a job that would pay him $50,000.

It was time for John Longan and Bill Coleman to put their own plan into action. In March 1977, Longan contacted Ricardo Morales in Florida to see if he was interested in helping to find Niehous. Neither man knew Morales had been implicated in the airline bombing, or that he had moved to the U.S. because DISIP had declared him *persona non grata* after he informed the FBI about who was involved in the Cuban airliner bombing. That Latin diplomatic phrase means, "You are no longer welcome in our country" and is essentially an order to leave immediately.

Morales agreed to help, but he wanted to make himself clear: "I don't give a damn about Bill Niehous. I don't care if he is dead or alive. But I will help you. I have my own motives. But I will only deal with you—you, Jake Longan. You are not to discuss this with Donna Niehous."

He went on to say that if another letter appeared saying Niehous was alive, he would quit. He would only help confirm that Niehous was dead and where he was buried. He said, "If he's alive, I won't touch it."

Not worried about the bluster, they hired him. Two months later, Longan and Coleman met Morales in Atlanta, hoping he would have news. But he had nothing to report, though he agreed to continue on the case if Mrs. Niehous withdrew her offer of a $500,000 reward for finding her husband. She quickly agreed, and Morales pursued his investigation. Shortly after the meeting, Coleman told the State Department that Niehous could be alive—apparently on the basis that Morales had given them a ray of hope by saying he was not dead, even though five months earlier, the Venezuelan media had reported Niehous's death, a story the U.S. embassy diplomatically called "an exaggeration," paraphrasing Mark Twain's famous quote, "Reports of my death have been greatly exaggerated." However, at their next meeting in July, Morales said that Niehous had, in fact, died, though he provided no evidence.

Epilogue

Then there was Erich Erdstein, the Nazi hunter. It's not clear whether O-I contacted him or if he contacted the company. Erdstein was a Jewish refugee who had fled Vienna for Argentina before Hitler annexed Austria in the late 1930s; he became a law enforcement agent in Brazil dealing with drug traffickers, and in his spare time, looked for former Nazis believed to be hiding in South America. Bill Coleman thought he could perhaps find Niehous.

Erdstein was best known for claiming in 1968 that he had tracked Josef Mengele, the German SS officer and notorious Auschwitz physician, to Paraguay and killed him in a gunfight. A contemporary account of the incident in the *Indiana Jewish Post*, reprinted from *The Jerusalem Post*, described Erdstein as a charlatan who regularly promised both survivors of the Holocaust and the government of West Germany that he was on the trail of former Nazis, but never apprehended any. However, in early 1978, after his book *Inside the Fourth Reich* was published and the movie version of the best-selling novel *The Boys from Brazil* starring Gregory Peck and Laurence Olivier, a dramatized science fiction story of Nazi hunters, was creating buzz over its pending release, Owens-Illinois agreed to pay him $10,000 to find Bill Niehous.

A few days later, Erdstein flew to Caracas. When he returned after a week, he reported Niehous had died and was buried in eastern Venezuela. For $8,000, he would provide proof. Longan interviewed him regarding his trip and concluded he was lying about going anywhere outside Caracas, much less finding Niehous's gravesite. Longan dismissed him and considered the whole episode a waste of time and money."

On April 15, 1978, the nefarious Ricardo Morales reappeared. Miami police had arrested him with $1.5 million worth of marijuana and a DISIP ID card in his wallet. The *Miami News* described him as a "high-ranking officer in the Venezuelan secret police," though at the time of his arrest, he was *persona non grata* in Venezuela for informing U.S. law enforcement on the role Orlando Bosch, Luis Posada, and the Venezuelan government played in the bombing of the Cuban airliner, which was causing headaches for Venezuela.

Bruce Berckmans, still at Wackenhut, saw an opportunity when he read about the arrest, remembering Morales had earlier told Owens-Illinois and John Longan that Niehous was dead. He sent Morales a letter through his lawyer on May 24, 1978, asking for an interview, apparently not privy to what Owens-Illinois told the State Department months prior. Five days earlier, the Venezuelan newspaper *El Nacional* published a letter from Mrs. Niehous telling her husband she was working to get him released. Berckmans never saw it.

The letter to Morales began, "I believe you, and I have some mutual friends who could vouch for my integrity." Among them was John Longan, but considering their years of association with clandestine operations in Latin America, they probably had several other mutual acquaintances. Morales agreed to an interview at the Dade County jail, but when they met, he declined to say what he told William Coleman a year earlier other than to repeat that Niehous was not alive.

Berckmans did not believe him, reasoning the kidnappers had everything to lose and nothing to gain by killing Niehous. Also, utilizing his years of experience in clandestine and security operations, he rationalized that in such cases, the captors would produce a body, so when they didn't more than a year after the Venezuelan media reported the story, he concluded Morales was lying.

Unhappy with the interview, and not knowing Morales was a longtime FBI, DEA, and CIA informant, or that Venezuela had banished him from the country, Berckmans tried to meet him again. He wrote Janet Reno, the Dade County state's attorney, and later the attorney general of the United States under the Clinton Administration, asking if she would offer Morales a plea bargain for a lesser drug charge, hoping it might motivate him to provide enough information about Niehous to solve the international kidnapping case. Reno refused. A short while later, the court dropped all the charges against Morales because the police had used an illegal wiretap. After his release, he disappeared.

Four years later, in 1982, he was back in the news. Morales was the main government witness in a multimillion-dollar cocaine smuggling operation involving the military leaders of Bolivia, fifty right-wing anti-Castro Cubans, including Frank Castro (no relation to Fidel), who played a role in the Cuban airline bombing and in Orlando Letelier's assassination in Washington, DC, and who was setting up a venture in Central America as part of Iran-Contra. However, the judge dismissed the charges, in what was called the Tick-Tock drug trial, against all forty-eight suspects because he did not consider Morales a credible witness. The FBI suggested Morales enter the Witness Protection Program because he had ratted on too many dangerous people, but he declined the offer.

A few months later, in December 1982 in a Key Biscayne, Florida bar, witnesses said Morales reached for his gun after a man he was drinking with called him a *maricon,* Spanish slang for a gay person. When he saw Morales pulling a gun out of his ankle holster, the man got up, took a few steps, and shot Morales in the back of the head, critically injuring him. Morales died in the hospital the next day. The police called it a justifiable homicide. It was big news all over Florida because Morales had become a public figure as a government witness in the Tick-Tock trial. His attorney, John Komorowski, believed Cubans, the Cuban exile community, drug dealers, or the CIA had killed him. The speculation was not unreasonable. He had snitched twice on Orlando Bosch and once each on Luis Posada and Frank Castro, three of the most notorious Cuban exiles engaged in terrorism and espionage.

News stories after his murder called Morales many things, none of them good. The *Washington Post* described him as "a spy, counterspy, mercenary, confessed murderer, bomber, informer, dope dealer, and operator extraordinary." His obituary labeled him as an anti-Castro terrorist, a mercenary, and a police informant. Orlando Bosch, a partner in terrorism and the person imprisoned twice based on evidence from Morales, called him "a drunk, a lost soul, and a snitch." A judge in a case where Morales had been an informant and witness described him as "a man known to the police as someone who sells himself to the highest bidder...a man highly suspect in the law enforcement community." A few years later, the Miami detective investigating the case said Morales was likely killed over what he knew about the bombing of the Cuban airliner in 1976. George Kiszynski, an FBI agent who had interviewed him, said Morales was decadent and devious. Although none of the obituaries or news stories about Morales mentioned the Niehous kidnapping, his name appeared in CIA and FBI memos as well as several documents in David Atlee Phillips's papers in the Library of Congress

While he may have been all of those things, why did he tell Owens-Illinois that William Niehous was dead? Was he trying to get back on good terms with DISIP? Was it a ploy to help DISIP end the case and allow the government of Venezuela to move on to the upcoming elections and deal with the economy, which was in trouble because of the drop in oil prices, putting national development plans in jeopardy?

By 1979, the kidnapping began to cause political problems for the newly elected government of Luis Herrera Campin, who had succeeded Pérez in March 1979. He wanted a clean slate before moving forward with controversial economic policies to continue ambitious national development plans. He would see an opening soon. But first, in May, the kidnappers sent Jack Anderson a photo of Niehous and a ransom demand of $7 million, indicating Niehous was alive—but again, the kidnappers failed to respond after Anderson replied he was ready to act as an intermediary. Then, on June 19, 1979, the embassy informed Washington through a cable classified as "secret" and only released in March 2014, that Niehous might be released in Europe but that the State Department should not follow up with the government of Venezuela, implying the government was not the source or that the person in the government who leaked the information to the embassy had done so with the agreement that they could not ask the government. Donna Niehous and John Longan were also notified.

Around the same time, the Venezuelan government was engaged in an unrelated standoff with armed members of the Socialist League at the Central University of Venezuela. President Campin saw an opportunity to end the three-year-old case. As a way to end the standoff and the Niehous saga, he demanded the student members of the Socialist League tell him the whereabouts of Niehous. The trapped students complied.

Eleven days later, on June 30, 1979, the police found Niehous while two Venezuelan police officers and two local farmers were conducting routine searches for cattle rustlers in Bolívar state. They apparently stumbled upon Niehous in a rancher's hut, along with two men who were guarding him. A short Radio Caracas Televisión (RCT) video of the rescue on YouTube shows a chaotic scene. The police shot and killed the two men watching over Niehous, just as I predicted would happen.

In retelling what happened that day, Niehous said shooting the two guards made no sense because they were not resisting arrest or putting up a fight. They never threatened him. In interviews, he recalled moving frequently during his three-year captivity, living in the jungle and using plastic sheeting for shelter. He argued politics with his masked captors, learned to play dominoes, taught his captors to play poker, listened to the radio, and read local newspapers they brought him to pass the time. He recounted:

From the first day of the kidnapping until the last, they said that I would never be shot, I would never be killed. They would always release me alive. Why? I don't know, except they said they were not assassins. They were not murderers. They were strictly political in their approach. What does that mean outside of the fact that they extolled communism? They extolled a Marxist-Leninist theory. I don't know more than that. I was treated, under the circumstances, satisfactorily. I was not tortured. I was not mistreated. I was not threatened with death.

The one thing they would not let him do was send letters to his wife.

The next day, the army escorted Niehous to Caracas, where they put him on a plane to Toledo, Ohio, never to return to Venezuela. Donna Niehous told me that when her husband would tell the story of his "rescue" to friends, he described it as a comedic farce comparable to an episode in a Keystone Kops movie, and similar to what the RCT video portrays.

Few people accept as true the story that the police found Niehous in the home state of Lanz Rodriguez, the mastermind of the crime, by coincidence. David Nieves believes the kidnappers and the government worked to find a way out of the situation without saying whether the information regarding where Niehous was being held was given during the showdown at the Central University of Venezuela between the Socialist League and the police. Thirty years later, Nieves, now a retired diplomat, described the kidnapping as a "political horror show" and said it was the low point in the history of the Left in Venezuela, stating that exposing corruption was the aim of the abduction and it failed miserably.

The three-and-a-half-year ordeal ended from fatigue and with no winners, only losers. In 1980, a military court convicted four DISIP officers of prisoner mistreatment and involuntary manslaughter for their role in Rodriguez's death and sentenced them to eleven years and six months in prison.

While Americans may have forgotten the kidnapping, if they even knew about it in the first place, Venezuelans are periodically reminded of the incident. One such time was when Niehous died in 2013. While his obituaries in the U.S. focused on the suffering he experienced in captivity and how he had moved on from the saga, in

Venezuela, Niehous's survival was secondary to examinations of the rationale behind the kidnapping, the politics and corruption and the death of Jorge Rodriguez while in the custody of DISIP. The kidnappers have never apologized.

The saga concludes with conceivably the most compelling figure of all, David Atlee Phillips.

I discovered Phillips when I Googled "William Niehous kidnapping." On the second page of results, a link to "David Atlee Phillips papers 1920-1989" at the Library of Congress in Washington, DC appeared. Curious, I clicked on it, and found there were six boxes of his personal papers in the library, including a manuscript on the kidnapping. I had never heard of Phillips, but over several months of searching the internet and visiting the library to see what his collection contained, I learned quite a bit.

Phillips was a 25-year veteran of the Central Intelligence Agency, first recruited in 1950 in Chile where he was publishing a newspaper. He retired in May 1975 as chief of Latin American and Caribbean operations for the CIA's Operations Directorate; some observers also call the position "the director of Western Hemisphere clandestine operations." After starting out in Chile, where he recruited local informants, Phillips's career took him to Guatemala; Lebanon; Cuba, both before and during Castro's time; Washington during the Bay of Pigs; Mexico, where he allegedly crossed paths with Lee Harvey Oswald; Miami, where he was part of JM WAVE, the CIA anti-Castro operation; Brazil; the Dominican Republic; and Venezuela, where he was station chief. As head of Latin American and Caribbean operations in Washington, he directed the agency's covert activities in Chile during the rise and fall of President Salvador Allende.

For organizing a disinformation campaign in Guatemala in 1954 that was fundamental to ousting President Jacobo Arbenz, he was awarded with the Career Intelligence Medal, the CIA's equivalent of the Medal of Honor. In the late 1950s, he posed as a businessman in Cuba, and later enlisted Cuban exiles for the Bay of Pigs invasion, including Ricardo Morales. In *The Night Watch,* Phillips's autobiography published in 1977, he defended clandestine operations on moral grounds, which at the time usually meant stopping a country from becoming communist and from confiscating American companies.

291

Phillips was deeply immersed in anti-Castro activities. He wept after the Bay of Pigs failed, when he learned some of the Cubans he had recruited were killed or captured. He ran anti-Castro operations out of the U.S. embassy in Mexico City in the early 1960s, which included overseeing the surveillance of Lee Harvey Oswald. Win Scott, the CIA station chief in Mexico at the time, said Phillips was the best covert action officer he had ever met. Phillips then worked at JM WAVE, the codename for the covert 1960s CIA program based in a remote corner of the University of Miami campus that is now the Miami Zoo whose purpose was to topple Castro. Bosch, Morales, and Posada were also involved with JM WAVE.

Phillips claimed in *The Night Watch* that during his tenure as CIA station chief in Venezuela from 1972–73 that no covert operations were conducted, even though Caracas had always served as a base for planning anti-Castro activities. Perhaps it wasn't, and maybe we'll never know, but why would Langley assign one of its most experienced officers in Latin America to Venezuela if nothing serious was going on? Phillips was acquainted with many of the Cuban exiles through his other assignments and was plausibly the perfect person to be station chief in Caracas.

However, he didn't stay long. After a year, he went to Washington to become the head of the Western Hemisphere Division of the Clandestine Services until May 1975, when he retired in the midst of a national uproar over CIA covert operations. What secret operations occurred in the two years when he headed the division is uncertain, other than the CIA-supported coup in Chile. In retirement, following the revelations from the Pike and Church Committee hearings in 1975–76 on U.S. intelligence activities, Phillips formed the Association of Former Intelligence Officers (AFIO) to educate Congress and the public on the value of government information-gathering and covert operations. He made speeches around the world, did television interviews, engaged in debates with adversaries, and wrote his CIA-approved autobiography. Phillips also wrote four other books in retirement. The sixth would have been on the kidnapping in Venezuela, but he never finished it.

According to the brief description of his papers in the Library of Congress, Bill and Donna Niehous "commissioned" Phillips to write the official story of the kidnapping. Donna Niehous, however, told me they did not commission anyone to write a book; she does not remember meeting Phillips in Washington, DC either, though Phillips repeated that assertion on three different occasions. Nonetheless, among Phillips's papers there is a draft of a manuscript titled *The Niehous Ordeal: An American Family Survives a Terrorist Kidnapping*. Mrs. Niehous also told me she did not know there were papers and documents on her husband's abduction in the Library of Congress.

Using sappy and awkward prose, Phillips characterized the three-year nightmare as a "poignant love story and an inspirational saga of survival," an attempt at showing how the kidnapping brought William and Donna Niehous closer together.

He summarized the ordeal almost like a novel, describing it as

...events dwarfed by the magnitude of the quiet courage mustered by one man and one woman against fearsome odds. The initial perception of Bill and Donna is deceptively that of a typical American couple thrust into adversity. As the story unfolds, however, we realize that they were not typical, but rather extraordinary people who were, from the outset of their ordeal, captains of their fate.

The numerous handwritten notes and corrections in the margins indicate that Phillips was far from finished and that he planned to continue his research, including calling on former President Carlos Andres Pérez for an interview, a not unreasonable plan since Phillips was acquainted with him from when Pérez was the minister of Interior in 1962–63.

Around the time he began researching the Niehous kidnapping, news stories appeared claiming Phillips had a part in the assassination of Orlando Letelier, the Chilean diplomat killed by a car bomb in Washington, DC in September 1976. He spent much of the remainder of his life bogged down in a lawsuit disputing the claim. In the book *Death in Washington*, writers Donald Freed and Fred Simon Landis asserted that Phillips played a role in Letelier's death. He sued them and their publisher, Lawrence C. Hill, for malicious libel, seeking $90 million in damages. The authors retracted their allegations against him and settled out of court for an undisclosed sum.

In another legal case, Phillips sued *The Observer* in London over two articles they published in 1980 based on excerpts from *Conspiracy*, a nonfiction book by Anthony Summers that linked him to the assassination through an alleged meeting with Lee Harvey Oswald in

Dallas in August 1963 and through being identified by anti-Castro Cuban exiles as "Maurice Bishop," the CIA contact in the murder. *The Observer* and Phillips settled in 1987; the conditions included an apology from the paper and a statement saying Phillips was not involved in the assassination. The paper also paid him the relatively small sum of £10,000, approximately $2,500. Phillips died in July 1988 and is buried in Arlington National Cemetery, along with many other CIA operatives and spies. In April 2017, Antonio Veciana, a Cuban refugee who headed assassination attempts against Castro and worked for the CIA, claims in his memoir, *Trained to Kill: The Inside Story of CIA Plots against Castro, Kennedy, and Che* that "Maurice Bishop," was David Atlee Phillips.

After his release, Niehous worked at the Owens-Illinois corporate headquarters in Toledo, Ohio, which has since moved a little over one hundred miles southeast to Perrysville. The kidnapping served as a wake-up call to international companies that their executives were vulnerable to political instability. Soon after, the security and protection business became a growth industry.

Niehous himself was a case study in survival while in captivity. At a forum on security and management, he recommended five ways hostages should behave: (1) be human; (2) communicate; (3) set individual goals; (4) eat and exercise; and (5) have faith. He amazed his wife, friends, and acquaintances with how he put the ordeal behind him. In an interview after he died, Donna Niehous said, "He came back the same man he had always been, as far as I could tell. He was never bitter; never let the experience define him."

Several people linked to the kidnapping were later appointed to government positions in Caracas. In 1998, Venezuelan President Hugo Chávez made Lanz Rodriguez his vice minister of higher education. Rodriguez then created controversy when he promoted the idea that all students should work in sugar fields and that Venezuelans should improve their diets by replacing sodas and hamburgers with sugarcane juice and *cachapas*, Venezuelan-style pancakes. In recent years, he has written over three hundred articles, including: "17 Direct Questions about Imperial Strategy and Para-militarism," "Transition and Productive Development," "Obama and the Death Cartel," "Obama's Strategy," and "Outsourcing Intelligence / Obama Strategic Precedents," all available on *Aporrea,* a website devoted to political and social developments in Venezuela.

Chavez also appointed Ivan Padilla as a vice minister, though Venezuelans on the left had not forgiven him for handing over Jorge Rodriguez to DISIP in 1976. David Nieves served in several diplomatic posts. Jorge Rodriguez Jr., just eleven years old when DISIP agents tortured his father while trying to solve the Niehous kidnapping, served as vice president in the Chavez administration from 2007–08. As of August 2017, he was the mayor of Liberator Municipality in Caracas and a staunch supporter of President Nicolás Maduro.

After Carlos Andres Pérez completed his term as president of Venezuela in 1979, he sought to become an international statesman. He supported South-South cooperation, an ideal holding that underdeveloped countries should help each other, and he actively participated in the Socialist International, where he served as vice president for three consecutive terms under the presidency of Willy Brandt from West Germany. He promoted talks to end the wars in Central America in the 1980s. President George H. W. Bush called Pérez one of the hemisphere's great democratic leaders.

But he got into trouble after he was elected president of Venezuela again in 1988. In 1992, he survived a coup attempt by Hugo Chavez, but was impeached a year later for diverting $17 million of public money to a secret fund that he said had gone to Violeta Chamorro's presidential campaign in Nicaragua, including sending a team of police experts to provide security when she ran against the Sandinistas and won. Nevertheless, the Supreme Court removed him from office. In 1998, when Chavez was elected president, Pérez, fearing arrest, fled to the Dominican Republic before going to Miami in 2000; he died there in December 2010.

Even in death he created controversy. After a nine-month legal battle between his estranged wife and his longtime mistress over where he should be buried, his body was returned to Venezuela for internment at the Guairita Cemetery in suburban Caracas, where six other former presidents are buried.

Today, Venezuela is a different country than the one I lived in as a Peace Corps Volunteer from 1974–76, when it was full of promise and hope. Since then, the country has survived oil price shocks, recessions and recoveries, and coup attempts. Since 2017, the country has been in an economic freefall, with triple-digit inflation; long lines for food, medicine, and other essentials; and shortages of electricity and toilet paper.

Economists have attributed the various shortages to price controls and excessive government regulation, though the 50 percent drop in the price of oil since 2014, disrupting the government's budget, has also played a significant role. In December 2016, oil was priced just over $50 a barrel, compared to $102 two years earlier. Besides declining revenues, oil production had also dropped by one million bpd since 1993, to 2.4 million, the same level as in 1976, when Venezuela nationalized the foreign oil companies.

In April 2016, in the midst of a drought and an economic crisis, President Nicolás Maduro reduced the work week for public employees to two days—or, as a few observers put it, introduced the five-day weekend—ostensibly to save electricity. The drought was so bad that after it rained in Guri, Electricity Minister Luis Motta Dominguez took to Twitter and told the country, "Comrades, today it rained long and hard over the Guri, Glory to God. We will overcome!" President Maduro requested that women stop using hair dryers. "I think a woman looks better when she runs her fingers through her hair and lets it dry naturally," he told the country.

President Maduro, on the other hand, has blamed the economic collapse on Saudi Arabia's refusal to cut oil production, natural gas in the United States, Wall Street speculation, and hoarding by Venezuela's own "parasitic bourgeoisie," the same group Hugo Chavez criticized in 2006 for drinking too much whisky and engaging in orgies. In November 2016, Maduro blamed the economic mess on an unsubstantiated cyberattack and an "economic war" led by the opposition with assistance from "imperialist forces" in Washington, coordinated by the CIA. A survey by pollster Alfredo Keller however, found only 1 percent of the Venezuelan people believed the U.S. was at fault; over three-quarters blamed Maduro. When shoppers at a Caracas supermarket screamed at an election official Maduro called it a hate crime.

The economic situation has forced women to choose sterilization over raising children. The *Washington Post* reported that PLAFAM, the biggest family planning clinic in the country, estimated that 25 percent more Venezuelan women were being sterilized, with the financial crisis being given as one of the main reasons for the increase. The shortages and the cost of contraceptive methods like condoms also turned women to sterilization, even though the procedure can cost as much as $1,500.

Epilogue

In February 2016, the Observatory of Venezuelan Violence declared Venezuela the most dangerous country in the world, with a murder rate of 91 murders per 100,000 people, compared to the global average of six per 100,000, and held Caracas as the most dangerous city. Local human rights groups believe the murder rate is actually much higher than the government figures. The Mexico-based Citizens Council for Public Security and Criminal Justice pegs the Venezuelan rate at 80 homicides per 100,000, putting it in second place behind El Salvador, while also saying the data from Venezuela was unreliable and difficult to collect.

Kidnapping is a problem, too. Major league baseball players with multi-million dollar contracts make them kidnapping targets. As a result, many Venezuelan professionals playing in the U.S. no longer return home in the off-season and some have become American citizens. Most murders and kidnappings remain unsolved. Rafael Narváez, a criminal defense and human rights lawyer, has described Venezuela as a "zoo of delinquency."

The economic and political chaos has also affected baseball, the country's national sport. In the 1990s, twenty-three Major League teams had training academies in Venezuela. In March 2017, there were only four. The Seattle Mariners closed their academy when they couldn't find enough food to prepare three meals a day for their players. The summer league shut down when Major League teams stopped sending their top prospects to play and the winter league has been reduced to four teams. Venezuela was scheduled to host the 2018 Caribbean Series tournament, but the Caribbean Professional Baseball Confederation moved it to Mexico amidst the street protests.

Strangely, Venezuela has become a global and regional leader in both obesity and cosmetic surgeries. In 2013, the country was second in the world to Germany in penis enlargement surgery, according to the International Society of Aesthetic Plastic Surgery (ISAPS). The World Health Organization followed with a report that 68 percent of Venezuelans over age twenty were overweight in 2014, more than in any country in South America and nearly equal to the 69 percent in the United States. However, in 2017 surveys found that Venezuelans had lost, on average, twenty pounds per person due to the shortage of food. In the midst of food shortages and rising unemployment, Venezuelans found enough money to lead the Americas in breast implants and the removal of excess fat and skin, known as tummy tucks, and they were second in face lifts, liposuction, buttock augmentation, and nose surgery.

Desperate to try anything to counter food shortages and inadequate medical supplies, and to boost his popularity, President Maduro launched a radio show dedicated to salsa and the country's culture in November 2016, hoping it would "multiply happiness."

As is often the case, poor economic conditions breed hopelessness that can lead to people fleeing the country for a better life. In the 2016 U.S. presidential campaign, illegal immigration was a major topic, focusing on illegal immigrants entering the U.S. from Mexico. By the end of 2016, an estimated 150,000 Venezuelans had fled the country. *The Guardian* reported an estimated 30,000 Venezuelans were in the Brazilian state of Roraima looking for food, jobs, and medical care; a situation that threatened to overwhelm hospitals, law enforcement, and social services. Asylum applications filed by Venezuelans in the U.S. jumped 168 percent in fiscal 2016 compared with the same time period a year earlier, according to a Pew Research Center analysis of U.S. Citizenship and Immigration Services data. From October 2015 to June 2016, Venezuelans were among the top nations of origin for asylum applicants to the U.S., exceeded only be China and Mexico. As of April 2016, about 225,000 Venezuelan-born immigrants were living in the U.S.; the majority are now American citizens. About half live in Florida, with many residing in Doral, a suburb of Miami.

Over a two-week period during the U.S. presidential campaign in September 2016, former Miss Venezuela and Miss Universe Alicia Machado and Republican nominee Donald J. Trump engaged in a war of words on Twitter, television, and Instagram. Machado became the center of attention when Democratic nominee Hillary Rodham Clinton chastised Trump during a presidential debate for mocking Machado for gaining weight after she won the Miss Universe competition in 1996. At the time, Trump had owned the Miss Universe pageant and was known to hang out backstage with the young contestants. During the debate, Clinton repeated some of the remarks Trump had made about women over the decades, including calling Machado "Miss Housekeeping" because she was Latina and "Miss Piggy" for her weight. Machado, now an American citizen, went on to make campaign appearances for Clinton.

As for me, nine months after I returned from Venezuela, in June

Epilogue

1977, I rejoined the Peace Corps as an English teacher and went to Morocco, where I stayed for three and a half years. After that, I went on to a career in post-war humanitarian and development assistance, working in Asia, Central Asia, Europe, the Caucasus and Washington, DC.

Appendix 1

Books I Read in Venezuela

1974:

Listen Yankee, C. Wright Mills
Childhood's End, Arthur C. Clarke
Journey to Ixtlan, Carlos Casteneda
Catch-22, Joseph Heller
Beyond Success or Failure: Ways to Self-Reliance and Maturity, Willard and Marguerite Beecher
The Anarchists, edited by Irving Horowitz
Candide, Voltaire
Satyricon, Petronius
Latin American Politics, edited by Robert D. Tomasek
Bury My Heart at Wounded Knee, Dee Brown
An American Dream, Norman Mailer
The Kingdom and the Power, Gay Talese
Dangling Man, Saul Bellow
Power of Attorney, Louis Auchincloss
Stern, Bruce Jay Friedman
A Mother's Kisses, Bruce Jay Friedman
Steambath, Bruce Jay Friedman
The Painted Bird, Jerzy Kosinski
The Odessa File, Frederick Forsyth
Billiards at Half-Past Nine, Heinrich Boll
One Hand Clapping, Anthony Burgess
The Gang that Couldn't Shoot Straight, Jimmy Breslin
The World of Jimmy Breslin, Jimmy Breslin
Principato, Tom McHale
The Dick, Bruce Jay Friedman
What Makes Sammy Run, Budd Schulberg
The Proud Tower, Barbara Tuchman
The Left Hand of Darkness, Ursula K. LeGuin
Fahrenheit 451, Ray Bradbury
Death for the Ladies, Norman Mailer
...And Every Day You Take Another Bite, Larry Merchant
Barabbas, Par Lagerkvist
A Clockwork Orange, Anthony Burgess
Haircut and Other Stories, Ring Lardner

1975:

The Pump House Gang, Tom Wolfe
The Memoirs of an Erotic Bookseller, Armand Coppens
The Bell Jar, Sylvia Plath
The Boys on the Bus, Timothy Crouse
The Electric Kool-Aid Acid Test, Tom Wolfe
All the President's Men, Bob Woodward and Carl Bernstein
When All the Laughter Died in Sorrow, Lance Rentzel
The Colonizer and the Colonized, Albert Memmi
Goodbye Columbus, Philip Roth
Rendezvous with Rama, Arthur C. Clarke
The Loved One, Evelyn Waugh
Advertisements for Myself, Norman Mailer
Mailer, Richard Poirier
Celebration of Awareness, Ivan Illich
The Wreckage of Agathon, John Gardner
Nickel Mountain, John Gardner
Our Gang, Philip Roth
The Great American Novel, Philip Roth
Enderby, Anthony Burgess
Buried Alive, Myra Friedman
The Teachings of Don Juan, Carlos Casteneda
The Implosion Conspiracy, Louis Nizer
The Summer Game, Roger Angell
World Without End, Amen, Jimmy Breslin
A Separate Reality, Carlos Casteneda
Steps, Jerzy Kosinski
Being There, Jerzy Kosinski
Herman Kahnsciousness: The Megaton Ideas of the One-Man Think Tank, Jerome Agel
Fear of Flying, Erica Jong
The Centaur, John Updike
Fire in the Lake, Frances Fitzgerald
How To Be Your Own Best Friend with Two Psychoanalysts, Mildred Newman and Bernard Berkowitz
Go Ask Alice, Anonymous
Ladies and Gentlemen, Lenny Bruce, Albert Goldman
The Terminal Man, Michael Crichton
20,000 Leagues Under the Sea, Jules Verne
Games People Play, Eric Berne
Jaws, Peter Benchley

Cosell, Howard Cosell
Catcher in the Rye, J.D. Salinger
Nine Stories, J.D. Salinger
North Dallas Forty, Peter Gent
Beneath the Wheel, Herman Hesse
Demian, Herman Hesse
Siddartha, Herman Hesse
One Hundred Years of Solitude, Gabriel Garcia Marquez
The Heroin Trail, Newsday
Steppenwolf, Herman Hesse
Baseball the Beautiful: Decoding the Diamond, Marvin Cohen
Chariots of the Gods, Erich Von Daniken
Sometimes a Great Notion, Ken Kesey
Narcissus and Goldmund, Herman Hesse *Death in the Afternoon,* Ernest Hemingway
Or I'll Dress You in the Mourning, Larry Collins and Dominique Lapierre
Franny and Zooey, J.D. Salinger
Papillon, Henri Charriere
Banco, Henri Charriere
The Politics of Experience, R.D. Laing
Exploring Madness (Experience, Theory and Research), James Fadiman
Word Play (What Happens When People Talk), Peter Farb
Body Language, Julius Fast
The Divided Self, R.D. Laing

1976:

Contemporary Latin American Short Stories, edited by Pat McNees Mancini
Gullible Travels, etc., Ring Lardner
The Invisible Government, David Wise and Thomas Ross
One Hundred Dollar Misunderstanding, Robert Gover
Inside the Company: CIA Diary, Philip Agee
Night Games, Mai Zetterling
Zen and the Art of Motorcycle Maintenance, Robert Pirsig
Chocolate Days and Popsicle Weeks, Edward Hannibal
The Green House, Mario Vargas Llosa
The President, Miguel Angel Asturias
Love Story, Erich Segal
The Conquest of the Incas, John Hemming
Alive, Piers Paul Read

Enough Room for Joy, Bill Clarke
Peter Camenzind, Herman Hesse
I Never Promised You a Rose Garden, Joanne Greenberg
Here Goes Kitten, Robert Gover
J.C. Saves, Robert Gover
The Devil Tree, Jerzy Kosinski
The Lives of Children: The Story of the First Street School, George Dennison
Flowers for Algernon, Daniel Keyes
Honor Thy Father, Gay Talese
The Godfather, Mario Puzo
Then She Was Good, Philip Roth
Deliverance, James Dickey
Gertrude, Herman Hesse
Letting Go, Philip Roth
Helter Skelter, Vincent Bugliosi
KGB, John Barron
The Harrad Experiment, Robert D. Rimmer

Appendix 2

Movies I Saw in Venezuela

1974:

State of Siege, directed by Costa Gavras
The Dirty Dozen, Jim Brown, Lee Marvin, Clint Walker
High Plains Drifter, Clint Eastwood
Ben and Charley, Lee Van Cleef, Lo Lieh
How to Murder Your Wife, Jack Lemmon
Bandits in Rome, John Cassavettes
To Live and Let Die, James Colburn
The Man Who Shot Liberty Valance, John Wayne, Jimmy Stewart
They Call Me Trinity, Terrence Hill, Bud Spencer
A Funny Thing Happened on the Way to the Forum, Zero Mostel
Trick Baby, Kiel Martin, Mel Stewart
Hellfighters, John Wayne
To Live and Let Die, Sean Connery
Pete 'n' Tillie, Carol Burnett, Walter Matthau
Paper Moon, Ryan O'Neal
8 on a Lam, Bob Hope
Romeo and Juliet, directed by Franco Zeffirelli
Battle of the Bulge, Charles Bronson, Robert Ryan
Last of Sheila, Richard Benjamin, James Colburn, Dyan Cannon
A Passion for Danger, Burt Reynolds
The Last Ten Days of Hitler, Alec Guinness
Blume in Love, George Segal
Dillinger, Robert Gates
They Call Me Amen, Alfio Caltabiano, Luc Merenda
The Discreet Charm of the Bourgeoisie, directed by Luis Bunuel
Pope Joan, Liv Ullman
The Stonekiller, Charles Bronson
The Last American Hero, Jeff Bridges
Hit Man, Bernie Casey
The Man Who Loved Cat Dancing, Burt Reynolds, Sarah Niles
Magnum Force, Clint Eastwood
To Kill a Clown, Alan Alda
40 Carats, Liv Ullman, Gene Kelley
Papillon, Steve McQueen, Dustin Hoffman
Slaughter's Rip-Off, Jim Brown, Ed McMahon
Standing in the Rain, Charles Bronson

Joanna, Donald Sutherland, Genevieve Waite
The Night Evelyn Came Out of the Grave, directed by Emilio Miraglia (Italy)
M.A.S.H., Donald Sutherland, Elliot Gould, Sally Kellerman
The Heartbreak Kid, Cybil Shepherd, Jeanne Berlin, Eddie Albert
A Touch of Class, Glenda Jackson, George Segal
The Boys Are Back, Terrence Hill, Bud Spencer
Theater of Blood, Vincent Price, Diana Rigg
The Steagle, Richard Benjamin, Cloris Leachman, Chill Wills
Oklahoma Crude, George C. Scott, Faye Dunaway
Weekend with the Babysitter, George E. Carey, Susan Romen
Westworld, Yul Brynner, Richard Benjamin, James Brolin
Doctors Prefer Them Nude, Argentina
The Little Cigars Mob, Angel Thompkins
The Three Musketeers, Michael York, Richard Chamberlain, Raquel Welch
Cleopatra Jones, Bernie Casey
*The Last Great War (*documentary*),* Italy
Black Caesar, Fred Williamson
The Boys of the Games, Les Charlots (France)
The Green Berets, John Wayne
The Mackintosh Man, Paul Newman, Dominique Sanda
The Cross and the Switchblade, Pat Boone
The Five-Man Army, Peter Graves, Bud Spencer, Jim Daley
Seven-Up, Roy Schneider
The Saltzburg Connection, Barry Newman, Ann Karina
A Pain in the Ass, Directed by Edouard Molinaro (France)
From Beyond the Grave, David Warner
100 Rifles, Jim Brown, Burt Reynolds, Raquel Welch
If Don Juan Was a Woman, Brigitte Bardot, Roger Vadim
The Mad Adventures of Rabbi Jacob, Louis de Funes, Claude Giraud (France)
Fear Is the Key, Barry Newman
A Day for Night, Jacklyn Bisset, directed by Francois Truffaut
The Last Lion, Jack Hawkins
Walking Tall, Joe Don Baker
The Day of the Dolphin, George C. Scott
Pat Garret and Billy the Kid, Kris Kristofferson, Bob Dylan, James Colburn
Kid Blue, Dennis Hopper, Warren Oates, Ben Johnson, Peter Boyle
And Hope to Die, Robert Ryan

1975:

The Odessa File, Jon Voight
Black Belt Jones, Jim Kesley
My Names Is Nobody, Henry Fonda, Terrence Hill
Uptown Saturday Night, Bill Cosby, Sydney Poitier, Harry Belafonte
Together They Are Dynamite, Terrence Hill, Bud Spencer
Man on a Swing, Joel Grey, Cliff Robertson
That's Entertainment, Fred Astaire, Bing Crosby
The Return of the Dragon, Bruce Lee
Crazy Larry Dirty Mary, Peter Fonda, Susan George
Chinatown, Jack Nicholson, Faye Dunaway
Airport 1975, Karen Black, Charlton Heston, Kareem Abdul Jabbar
The Phallax View, Warren Beatty
Narazin, Directed by Luis Bunuel
Amacord, Directed by Federico Fellini
California Split, Elliot Gould, George Segal
Maracaibo Petroleum Company (documentary), Venezuela
Bring Me the Head of Alfredo Garcia, Warren Oates
Godfather Part II, Al Pacino, Diane Keaton
Panic in Needle Park, Al Pacino, Kitty Winn
The Towering Inferno, Paul Newman, Steve McQueen, Faye Dunaway
Earthquake, Charlton Heston, George Kennedy, Genevieve Bujold
French Connection II, Gene Hackman
Latin American Film Festival (Argentina, Bolivia, Brazil, Chile, Cuba, Venezuela)
El Fantasma de la Libertad, directed by Luis Buñuel
The Passenger, Jack Nicholson, Maria Schneider
Harakiri, directed by Masaki Kobayashu (Japan)
Huckleberry Finn, Jim Winfield, Jerry East
Belle d'Jour, Luis Bunuel
Tommy, Ken Russell
Citizen Kane, Orson Wells
A Man Called Horse, Richard Harris

1976:

Jaws, Roy Schneider
The Patagonia Rebellion, (documentary), Argentina
Juan Vicente Gomez, V (documentary), Venezuela
The Trial of Billy Jack, Tom McLaughlin, Dolores Taylor
Lenny, Dustin Hoffman, Valerie Perrin

Alice Doesn't Live Here Anymore, Ellen Burstyn, Kris Kristofferson
Midnight Cowboy, Dustin Hoffman, Jon Voight
One Flew Over the Cuckoo's Nest, Jack Nicholson (saw three times)
Dog Day Afternoon, Al Pacino
Jeremiah Johnson, Robert Redford
8½, Directed by Federico Fellini
The Wind and the Lion, Sean Connery
The Mother, directed by Vsevolod Pudovkin (Soviet Union)
Breezy,   Kay Lenz, William Holden
A Clockwork Orange,   directed by Stanley Kubrick
Shampoo, Warren Beatty, Julie Christie, Goldie Hawn
The Hindenburg, George C. Scott
Special Section, directed by Gosta Gavras
The Sunshine Boys, Walter Matthau, George Burns
Sherlock Holmes's Smarter Brother, Gene Wilder, Marty Feldman
The Graduate, Dustin   Hoffman,   Katherine   Ross,   Ann   Bancroft

NOTES

The National Archives and Records Administration in College Park, Maryland comprise 800 boxes on the Peace Corps, primarily files from administrative staff based in Washington, DC. Some are online but most require a trip to College Park to access them. The records are incomplete, strong on the 1960s, weak on the 1970s when Peace Corps was part of ACTION, and overall very weak on Venezuela. Nevertheless, the records were enjoyable to read, even when they did not pertain to Venezuela.

The voice of Volunteers is not part of the Archives. The Volunteer experience in various forms are scattered around the Presidential libraries of Kennedy, Johnson, Nixon, Ford and Carter, a few universities, and wherever former Volunteers store their stuff.

Wikileaks, the multi-national media organization often associated with publishing classified and unclassified political documents, released 1.7 million documents covering the 1970s, they named the "Kissinger Papers." Among the papers are American embassy cables discussing pending Peace Corps budget cuts in Venezuela and a dozen other countries, when Congress was looking for ways to reduce the Federal budget during the economic downturn after the 1973 oil embargo.

Google helped me find hundreds of articles, reports, blogs, abstracts, and books on the events, incidents, and places described in this book. The personal papers of David Atlee Phillips at the Library of Congress in Washington, DC were an important source on the Niehous kidnapping as were newspaper articles when he was released in June 1979.

1. Being There

Author's journal.

2. Training

"The McAllister Was City's First High-Rise Hotel," *Miami Herald*, 3 December 1987.

From cable sent by the U.S. embassy in Caracas to the State Department, with excerpts from "Volunteers of Peace," an editorial in *La Republica*, 18 November 1961; retrieved from the National Archives and Records Administration, College Park, Maryland, April 2016.

Letter from Sargent Shriver to Dr. Jose Antonio Mayobre, Venezuelan ambassador to the United States, 20 February 1962.

"Mexico," 100 Years," The Rockefeller Foundation, http://rockefeller100.org

Letter from Don Alder, the Peace Corps director in Venezuela, informing new Volunteers about working in Venezuela, October 1973.

Elizabeth Cobbs Hoffman, *All You Need Is Love: The Peace Corps and the Spirit of the 1960s*, Harvard University Press, 1998.

Cachivache: A Guide for Incoming Volunteers, Peace Corps Venezuela publication.

Peace Corps newsletters and memos in 1974, author's collection.

"Tip-Off Leads Venezuela Cops to Toilet Paper Stash," *Breitbart News*, 13 May 2013, and *Agence France-Presse, 31 May 2013.*

"Confianza" by Jeff Barber, *Associate Peace Corps director,* undated.

David Wise and Thomas B. Ross, *The Invisible Government*, Chapter 19, "Purity in the Peace Corps," 1964.

Memo from Lyman Kirkpatrick, inspector general, to the director of Central Intelligence, 26 April 1961, Subject: Agenda for Senior Staff Meeting, 1 May 1961, obtained by author through the Freedom of Information Act, 2 March 2016.

"Deputies Meeting," CIA, 31 May 1961, obtained by author through the Freedom of Information Act, 2 March 2016.

Memo from Stanley Sporkin, CIA general counsel to William Casey, director of the CIA, 18 July 1983, obtained by author through the Freedom of Information Act, 2 March 2016.

Correspondence between Loret Ruppe, Peace Corps director, and William Casey, CIA director, October/November 1983, obtained by author through the Freedom of Information Act, 2 March 2016.

Notes

Denton R. Vaughan, Peace Corps Volunteer Chile 1965–1967, "A Peace Corps Volunteer's Disillusionment," *The Washington Post,* 26 September 1974.

Tim Padgett, "Why Venezuela's Chávez Dug Up Bolívar's Bones," *TIME,* 17 July 2010.

Rory Carroll, "Hugo Chávez's Twitter Habit Proves a Popular Success," *The Guardian,* 10 August 2010.

"Venezuela Hero Simon Bolívar 'Death Tests' Inconclusive," *British Broadcasting Corporation (BBC),* 26 July 2011.

"Luis Aparicio," Baseball Hall of Fame, http://baseballhall.org

Leonte Landino, "Luis Aparicio," Society for American Baseball Research, http://sabr.org/bioproj/person/87c077f1

Norman Gill, "Oil and Democracy in Venezuela Part II: The Marginal Man," http://www.normangall.com/venezuela_art2.htm

Tom Phillips and Virginia Lopez, "Hugo Chávez Claims Simon Bolívar Was Murdered Not Backed by Science," *The Guardian,* 26 July 2011.

Joseph J. Ellis, "Book Review: *Bolívar: American Liberator* by Marie Arana," *The Washington Post,* 5 April 2013.

"The Streak," www.superseventies.com/sw_streak.html

3. Play Ball!

F. Depons, *Travels in Parts of South America During the Years 1801, 1802, 1803, and 1804.*

Bonnie Hamre, "Llaneros—Cowboys of Colombia and Venezuela: First cowboys of the Americas," http://gosouthamerica.about.com/od/venartandculture/a/llaneros.htm

Milton H. Jamail, *Venezuelan Bust, Baseball Boom*, Bison Books, 2008.

Leonte Landino, "Luis Aparicio," Society for American Baseball Research, http://sabr.org

Caribbean Baseball, Major League Baseball, http://mlb.mlb.com/milb/stats

Tom McNichol, "I Am Not a Kook: Richard Nixon's Bizarre Visit to the Lincoln Memorial," *The Atlantic,* 14 November 2011.

Karen Schwarz, *What You Can Do for Your Country: An Oral History of the Peace Corps,* William Morrow & Co, 1991.

John Coyne, "RPCVs Sit-In at the Peace Corps," 11 April 2011, http://peacecorpsworldwide.org

Volunteer, vol. VI, May-June 1970, http://peacecorpsonline.org/historyofthepeacecorps

Dave Sheinin, "The Dodgers Are Ready to Give Yasiel Puig Another Opportunity—For Now," *The Washington Post*, 20 February 2017.

Simon Romero, "A Culture of Naming that Even a Law May Not Tame," *The New York Times*, 5 September 2007.

"Venezuela Seeks to Crack Down on Odd Baby Names," *Fox News*, 1 September 2007.

4. What Do I Do Now?

The Peacemaker, the monthly newsletter in Venezuela in 1974, author's collection.

Noam S. Cohen, "Lawrence Speiser, 68, a Civil Liberties Lawyer," *The New York Times*, 1 September 1991.

"Visit of EEO Action Investigator," cable from State Department to U.S. embassy in Caracas, 13 November 1974, retrieved from Wikileaks, "The Kissinger Papers."

Peter Stevens (director, Peace Corps Venezuela), "Living Allowance Committee Results," Memorandum No. 33, 19 June 1974, author's collection.

Richard M. Nixon, *Six Crisis*, Doubleday & Company, 1962.

"Moments in U.S. Diplomatic History," http://adst.org/2013/05/the-day-venezuelans-attacked-nixon

"Vice President Nixon Is Attacked," *History.com*

Evan Ward, "IBEC and the Transformation of Consumer Culture in Latin America," 2004.

Notes

Shane Hamilton, "From Bodega to Supermercado: Nelson A. Rockefeller's Agro-Industrial Counterrevolution in Venezuela, 1947-1969," University of Georgia, Yale Agrarian Studies Workshop, 4 November 2011, available at http://www.yale.edu/agrarianstudies/colloqpapers/09hamilton.pdf

Megan Morrissey, *The Architecture of Urban Inequality: Foreign Influence and Urban Planning in Ciudad Guayana, Venezuela*, chapter 2, p. 49, Georgetown University, 2008.

Cory Fischer-Hoffman, "Maduro Creates Council to 'Revolutionize' Food Production in Venezuela," *VenezuelaAnalysis,* 8 September 2014.

Frances Martel, "Amputations Skyrocket in Venezuela Due to Lack of Medical Equipment," *Breitbart*, 27 May 2014.

Fabiola Sanchez, "Horse Poisoning Alarms Venezuela Racing," *Associated Press*, 9 October 2014.

"This Week in Baseball History: Ten Cent Beer Night;" http:/coffeyvillewhirlwind.wordpress.com/2006/06/06/this-week-in-baseball-history-ten-cent-beer-night

Paul Jackson, "The Night Beer and Violence Bubbled over in Cleveland," *ESPN*, 4 June 2008.

5. Colombia

Robert W. Drexler, deputy chief of mission, Bogota (1975-1978); interviewed by Charles Stuart Kennedy, 1996, Association for Diplomatic Studies and Training Foreign Affairs Oral History Project, http://www.loc.gov/item/mfdipbib001207

James Mollison, "Rise and Fall of the Cocaine King," *The Guardian*, 28 September 2007.

"Hit Movie Revives Rumors of Peace Corps Workers' Link to Cocaine," edited by Curt Wagner and Molly Marinik, *Chicago Tribune*, 12 November 2004.

"Colombia PCVs Damaged by Juan Gabriel Vasquez Novel, *The Sound of Things*," email from Dennis Grubb (Colombia 1961-62) posted on the "John Coyne Babbles" website on the history of Peace Corps, http://peacecorpsworldwide.org/babbles/2014/06/08/colombia-pcvs

Lina Britt, "A Traffickers' Paradise: The 'War on Drugs' and the New Cold War in Colombia," *Contemporánea, Historia y problemas del siglo XX | Volumen 1, Año 1, 2010*, ISSN: 1688-7638.

Josh Clinton and Carrie Roush, "Poll: Persistent Partisan Divide Over 'Birther' Question," *NBC News*, 11 August 2016.

Alanah Eriksen, "One in Seven Believe U.S. Government Staged the 9/11 Attacks in Conspiracy," *The Daily Mail*, 29 August 2011.

6. The Peace Corps Cuts Back

Mid-Service Conference Report, IND III (Sports and Recreation), (527-73-01) Caracas, 18-22 March 1974; and Records of the Office of Planning, Evaluation, and Research, Mid-Service Conference Reports 1971-1975, National Archives and Record Administration.

"Exploding Baseball Bat in Chile Kills 1, Hurts American," *United Press International*, 18 November 1990.

"FY 1976 Peace Corps Program," cable from ACTION to 21 embassies and the State Department, 26 October 1974. Public Library of U.S. Diplomacy, cables from 4 April 1974 to 5 November 1974 on Peace Corps budget submission FY1976, retrieved from Wikileaks, "The Kissinger Papers."

Peace Corps Annual Operations Report Fiscal Year 1975, available at http://files.peacecorps.gov/manuals/cbj/1975.pdf

Mid-Service Conference Report, Municipal Management III, Caracas, 1-2 December 1971 Records of the Office of Planning, Evaluation, and Research, Mid-Service Conference Reports 1971-1975.

7. A New Job

"Peace Corps: Bring the World Home," http://www.peacecorps.gov/resources/returned/thirdgoal

Ian Skeet, *OPEC: Twenty-Five Years of Prices and Politics*, London: Cambridge University Press, 1988.

Catherine K. Harbour and Pallab K. Maulik, "History of Intellectual Disability," Department of Mental Health, Johns Hopkins School of Public Health, http://cirrie.buffalo.edu/encyclopedia/en/article/143

Edwin Black, "The Horrifying American Roots of Nazi Eugenics," *History News Network*, September 2003, http://historynewsnetwork.org/article/1796

Paul A. Lombardo, *Three Generations, No Imbeciles: Eugenics, the Supreme Court, and Buck v. Bell,* Johns Hopkins University Press, 31 August 2010.

Adam Cohen, *Imbeciles: The Supreme Court, American Eugenics, and the Sterilization of Carrie Buck,* Penguin Press, 1 March 2016.

David Oshinsky, "Imbeciles' and 'Illiberal Reformers," *The New York Times*, 14 March 2016.

Russell Sparkes, "The Enemy of Eugenics," *Second Spring*, http://www.secondspring.co.uk/articles/sparkes.htm

H. H. Goddard, *The Kallikak Family: A Study in the Heredity of Feeble Mindedness*, New York: MacMillan, 1913.

R.J. Karp, Q.H. Quazi, K.A Moller, W.A. Angelo, J.M. & Davis, J.M., "Fetal Alcohol Syndrome at the Turn of the Century: An Unexpected Explanation of the Kallikak Family," *Archives of Pediatrics and Adolescent Medicine, 149*(1), 1995, pp. 45-48, http://jamanetwork.com/journals/jamapediatrics/article-abstract/517429

Samuel Kirk, "Educating Exceptional Children," 1962, Oxford, England: Houghton Mifflin, abstract available at http://psycnet.apa.org/psycinfo/1963-01948-000

8. Maracaibo

Nellie Bly, *Ten Days in a Mad-House,* New York: Ian L. Munro, 1887.

"Eugenics in the United States," Wikipedia.

"Segregation or Community Integration: Ensuring the Civil Rights of People with Developmental Disabilities in Illinois," *Equip for Equality*, 2004, http://www.ndrn.org/images/Documents/Issues/Community_integration/NDRN_Report_on_Olmstead_enforcement_in_Illinois.pdf

"Rosemary Kennedy, JFK's Sister, Dies at 86," *Associated Press*, 8 January 2005.
President's Panel on Mental Retardation, http://mn.gov/mnddc/parallels/five/5c/5c_html/ht1.html

"Community Mental Health Act of 1963," The National Council for Behavioral Health,
https://www.thenationalcouncil.org/about/national-mental-health-association/overview/community-mental-health-act

Notes

Matt Ford, "America's Largest Mental Hospital Is a Jail," *The Atlantic*, 8 June 2015.

Michael B. Friedman, "Keeping the Promise of Community Mental Health," *The Journal News*, 8 August 2003, http://www.michaelbfriedman.com/mbf/images/stories/mental_health_policy/Ne w_Freedom_Commission/President's_Commission_2003.pdf

Ford, "America's Largest Mental Hospital Is a Jail."

Wyatt v. Stickney Civ. A. No. 3195-N. 325 F.Supp. 781 (1971), http://www.leagle.com/decision/19711106325FSupp781_1948.xml/WYATT%2 0v.%20STICKNEY

"History of United Nations and Persons with Disabilities—A Human Rights Approach: the 1970s," *United Nations*, http://www.un.org/disabilities/default.asp?id=130

"A Brief History of the Disability Rights Movement," *Anti-Defamation League*, 2005, http://archive.adl.org/education/curriculum_connections/fall_2005/fall_2005_les son5_history.html

Rehabilitation Act of 1973; Public Law 111-256 111th Congress, 5 October 2010 - [S. 2781], http://www.gpo.gov/fdsys/pkg/PLAW-111publ256/html/PLAW-111publ256.htm

"Convention on the Rights of Persons with Disabilities," *United Nations Treaty Collection*, https://treaties.un.org/Pages/ViewDetails.aspx?src=TREATY&mtdsg_no=iv-15&chapter=4&lang=en

Steven Groves, "The U.S. Doesn't Need the U.N.'s Disability Treaty," *U.S. News and World Report*, 20 January 2014.

Rose Marie Sosa, *Mental Retardation in the Republic of Venezuela*, University of Texas, Masters of Arts Thesis, August 1974, p. 30.

"AVEPANE," http://avepane.org/

Russell Goldman, "Hugo Chavez, Venezuelan President, Dead at 58," *ABC News*, 5 March 2013.

Robin Rymarczuk, "Autism and LSD-25: Freeing the Most Imprisoned Minds?" *The Faults of Ewowid*, v 1.1, 30 June 2014,

Notes

https://www.erowid.org/chemicals/lsd/lsd_article4.shtml

J. Sigafoos, V.A. Green, C. Edrisinha, and G.E. Lancioni, "Flashback to the 1960s: LSD in the Treatment of Autism," *Journal of Developmental Neurorehabilitation*, abstract, Jan-Mar 2007, 10(1):75-81, https://www.erowid.org/chemicals/lsd/lsd_article4.shtml

American Theilard Association, http://teilharddechardin.org/index.php/biography

"Pierre Teilhard de Chardin Facts," http://biography.yourdictionary.com/pierre-teilhard-de-chardin.

David Gibson, "U.S. Nuns Haunted by Dead Jesuit: The Ghost of Pierre Teilhard de Chardin," *The Washington Post*, 22 May 2014.

Andrew Todd and Franco La Cecla, "Ivan Illich," *The Guardian*, 8 December 2002.

Ivan Illich, "To Hell with Good Intentions," http://www.swaraj.org/illich_hell.htm

Chase Madar, "The People's Priest," *The American Conservative*, 1 February 2010.

"Peace Corps July Training Group," cable from U.S. embassy in Caracas to ACTION Peace Corps, Washington, 23 May 1975; and "Peace Corps Financing," cable from U.S. embassy to ACTION Peace Corps, Washington, 2 June 1975, retrieved from Wikileaks, "The Kissinger Papers."

Peace Corps Annual Operations Report Fiscal Year 1975, http://files.peacecorps.gov/manuals/cbj/1975.pdf

Interview with Harry W. Schlaudeman, U.S. ambassador to Venezuela, Caracas (1975-1976), conducted by William E. Knight, 24 May 1993, The Association for Diplomatic Studies and Training Foreign Affairs Oral History Project, http://www.adst.org/OH%20TOCs/Shlaudeman,%20Harry.toc.pdf

Seymour Hersh, "Huge C.I.A. Operation Reported in U.S. Against Antiwar Forces, Other Dissidents in Nixon Years," *The New York Times,* 22 December 1974.

Philip Agee, *Inside the Company: CIA Diary*, New York: Penguin Books, 1975.

"Inside the Company: CIA Diary Reviews," *Facts on File World News Digest*, 25 January 1975, http://bailey83221.livejournal.com/98872.html#C

Notes

"Agee Book," 10 December 1974, cable from State Department to U.S. embassy in Lima, retrieved from Wikileaks.

A review of *Inside the Company: CIA Diary* by Philip Agee, no author cited, CIA, Historical Document, released 2 July 1996, https://www.cia.gov/library/center-for-the-study-of-intelligence/kent-csi/vol19no2/html/v19i2a06p_0001.htm

David Atlee Phillips, *The Night Watch*, New York: Atheneum, 1977.

Jesse Walker, "Agee's Revenge," *Reason.com*, July 14, 2005.

"Former CIA Agent Agee Dies in Cuba at Age 72," *Associated Press*, 9 January 2008, http://www.nbcnews.com/id/22571961/#.VQxgX-HpwnI

"Timeline of U.S. Involvement in Vietnam Conflict," http://mahargpress.com/wounded/additional-material/timeline-of-vietnamconflict

Richard Nixon, "Executive Order 11497 - Amending the Selective Service Regulations to Prescribe Random Selection," 26 November 1969, http://www.presidency.ucsb.edu/ws/?pid=106002

Elizabeth Cobbs Hoffman, *All You Need Is Love: The Peace Corps and the Spirit of the 1960s*, Cambridge, MA: Harvard University Press, 1998.

"1969 Draft Lottery," http://www.landscaper.net/draft.htm

Hataipreuk Rkasnuam and Jeanne Batalova, "Vietnamese Immigrants in the United States," *Migration Policy Institute*, 25 August 2014, http://www.migrationpolicy.org/article/vietnamese-immigrants-united-states

"Vietnamese Population in the United States," *VietTV*, http://vietv.com/10-vietnamese-population-united-states.html

"Seizing Arab Oil: Henry Kissinger, 1975," posted by Dan Christensen (*Cubanews*) – 29 December 2004, http://www.aboutmytalk.com/t176133/s&.html

Andrew Scott Cooper, *The Oil Kings: How the U.S., Iran, and Saudi Arabia Changed the Balance of Power in the Middle East* (reprint edition*)*, New York: Simon & Schuster, 2012.

U.S., Congress, Committee on International Relations, Special Subcommittee on

Investigations, *Oil Fields as Military Objectives: A Feasibility Study*, report prepared by the Congressional Research Service, 94th Cong., 1st sess., 21 August 1975, (Washington, D.C.: US Government Printing Office, 1975), Parts I and II, pp. 1-39,
https://www.mtholyoke.edu/acad/intrel/Petroleum/fields.htm

"Venezuela Battles Obesity Amid Dearth of Good Food," *Daily Mail*, 26 August 2014.

9. The Grind

Philip Roos and Brian M. McCann, "Major Trends in Mental Retardation," *International Journal of Mental Health*, Spring 1977.

10. Let's Get to Work

Miguel Tinker Salas, *The Enduring Legacy: Oil, Culture and Society in Venezuela*, Durham, NC: Duke University Press, 2009, p. 205-206.

"The Asphalt Lake in Venezuela," *The New York Times*, 17 February 1901.

Anibal Martinez, *Chronology of Venezuelan Oil*, Purnell and Sons LTD, February 1969.

Daniel Yergin, *The Prize: The Epic Quest for Oil, Money and Power*, New York: Simon and Schuster, 1990.

"Venezuela: A Century of Caudillos," http://www.country-data.com/cgi-bin/query/r-14516.html

"Oil Concessions: Sovereignty Concessions, History of Petroleos de Venezuela, S.A. (PVDSA)," *Petroleos de Venezuela, S.A.,* www.pdvsa.com

"Guanoco: Lago de Asfalto de Guanoco,"
http://www.orienteweb.com/Sitios/PariaLagoGuanoco.html

B.S. McBeth, *Juan Vicente Gomez and the Oil Companies in Venezuela, 1908-1935*, London: Cambridge University Press, 1983.

"More of the World's Oddball Airports," *Love2Fly*,
http://love2fly.iberia.com/2014/06/more-of-the-worlds-oddball-airports

David S. Painter, "Oil and the American Century," *The Journal of American History*, 2012.

Notes

Peter Van Doren, "A Brief History of Energy Regulations," February 2009, www.downsizinggovernment.gov

"Historical Oil Prices 1861-2009," http://chartsbin.com/view/oau

"President Pérez Hails Venezuela's Petroleum Nationalization," cable ee11652 from U.S. embassy in Caracas to the State Department, 2 January 1976, retrieved from Wikileaks, "The Kissinger Papers."

Interview with Harry W. Schlaudeman, U.S. ambassador to Venezuela, Caracas (1975-1976), The Association for Diplomatic Studies and Training Foreign Affairs Oral History Project.

"Oil Nationalization—Status Report After One Month," cable from U.S. embassy in Caracas to State Department, 29 January 1976, retrieved from Wikileaks, "The Kissinger Papers."

Interview with Robert B. Morley, economic officer, Caracas (1976-1979), conducted by William E. Knight, 1993, The Association for Diplomatic Studies and Training Foreign Affairs Oral History Project, http://www.adst.org/OH%20TOCs/Morley,%20Robert%20B.toc.pdf

"Countries that Give the Most in Foreign Aid Statistics," *Statistic Brain Research Institute,* http://www.statisticbrain.com/countries-that-give-the-most-in-foreign-aid-statistics

Library of Congress, "Venezuela: A Country Study," edited by Richard A. Haggerty, December 1990.

"Venezuela: Defense Spending," http://www.globalsecurity.org/military/world/venezuela/budget.htm

"Many Venezuelans Pessimistic about Venezuela's Future Prospects," cable from U.S. embassy in Caracas to the State Department, 31 December 1975, retrieved from Wikileaks, "The Kissinger Papers."

11. My Parents Come to Visit

"Ford Maverick (Americas)," Wikipedia.

Serge F. Kovaleski, "Shantytowns Hit Hardest by Venezuelan Floods / Shacks, people on steep slopes just swept away," *The Washington Post*, 21 December 1999.

"¿Por qué están destruidos el Macuto Sheraton y el Meliá Caribe?" (Why are the

Macuto Sheraton and Meliá Caribe Hotels in Ruins?), *ElPitazoTV*, https://www.youtube.com/watch?v=ut7PgUMNu-A

"Mérida Cable Car," Wikipedia; Nick Chu, "Teleférico de Merida Reconstruction," 2012.

"En lo Más Alto," *FITVen2013*, https://www.youtube.com/watch?v=dpoHQKgldX8

12. Back to Normal

"Color TV—Venezuela," cable from U.S. embassy to State Department, 17 October 1975, retrieved from Wikileaks, "The Kissinger Papers."

"En Gaceta estado de excepción en tres municipios fronterizos de Zulia," (State of emergency declared in three municipalities in Zulia), *El Mundo*, 8 September 2015.

Glenn Sunshine, "José Gregorio Hernández (1864-1919)," *Christian Worldview Journal*, 12 January 2015.

"Statue of the Virgin Mary," *Lonely Planet.*

William Neuman, "As Catholic Church Seeks Proof, Venezuela Sees a Saint," *The New York Times*, 29 September 2014.

13. Holiday Time

Author's journal.

14. Crime, Camping, and a Coup

James D. Henderson, *Colombia's Narcotics Nightmare: How the Drug Trade Destroyed Peace,* Jefferson, NC: McFarland, 2015.

Cable from U.S. embassy in Buenos Aires to State Department, February 1976, retrieved from National Security Archive, http://nsarchive.gwu.edu

Robin Yapp, "Former Argentine Dictator Jorge Videla Sentenced to Life in Prison," *The Telegraph*, 22 December 2010.

Nickolas Caistor, "General Jorge Rafael Videla: Dictator Who Brought Terror to Argentina in the 'Dirty War'," *The Independent*, 17 May 2013.

Notes

Luciana Bertoia "Brazil, Argentina Agree to Share Plan Condor Details," *Buenos Aires Herald*, 30 January 2014.

Francisco Goldman, "Children of the Dirty War," *The New Yorker*, 19 March 2012.

"Operation Condor: National Security Archive Presents Trove of Declassified Documentation in Historic Trial in Argentina," *National Security Archive*, 6 May 2015, http://nsarchive.gwu.edu

J. Patrice McSherry, "Operation Condor: Deciphering the U.S. Role, Crimes of War," *GlobalPolicy.org* July 2001, https://www.globalpolicy.org/component/content/article/168/28173.html

"FY 1976 Peace Corps Program," cable from U.S. embassy to Secretary of State, November 1974, confidential, declassified 30 June 2005, retrieved from Wikileaks, "The Kissinger Papers."

John Chromy, "Why the Peace Corps Left India," 21 January 2013, http://ganga633.squarespace.com/stories-to-share

Stanley Meisler, "Peace Corps Host Countries," http://www.stanleymeisler.com/peacecorps/host-countries.html

Report by Bruce Berckmans Jr., "The Niehous Kidnapping in Venezuela – Summary of the Case and Request for White House Guidance," 18 August 1976, Containers 2-3, David Atlee Phillips Papers, Manuscript Division, Library of Congress, Washington, DC.

"Briefing Memorandum: Kidnapping of American Businessman in Venezuela-Update," unclassified, 29 February 1976; and "Niehous Kidnapping: Reaction from the Far Left," unclassified, 3 March 1976, retrieved from Wikileaks, "The Kissinger Papers."

Amy Stillman, "Chávez Is Failing Women," *New Statesman*, 27 August 2009.

15. Change

Author's journal.

16. Phasing Out

321

"TropiBurger | El local de TropiBurger en el Paraiso," *Cuando Era Cham.com: A Look at the Past,* 2009-2015.http://www.cuandoerachamo.com/tropi-burger-el-local-de-tropi-burger-en-el-paraiso
#Guapo
"#Guapo Doble #Margarita #Maiquetía #FelizLunes," 18 July 2016, https://twitter.com/eltropiburger/status/755037673383919616

"American Ambassadors Killed (1968 - 1976)," CIA and State Department files, http://talkingpointsmemo.com/dc/the-seven-u-s-ambassadors-killed-in-the-line-of-duty-photos

Jose Orozco, "Carlos Andres Pérez, President of Venezuela in 1970s Oil Boom, Dies at 88," *The New York Times*, 26 December 2010.

Elluz Peraza, "In Love with a Man 18 Years Her Junior?" *Informe21,* 27 September 2009, http://informe21.com:8080/arte-espectaculos/elluz-peraza-enamorada-hombre-18-anos-menor-ella

"Hace 28 años Elluz Peraza renunció y Judith Castillo fue la reina" (28 years ago Elluz Peraza renounces her title to Judith Castillo), *Belleza Venezolana*, 2004, www.bellezavenezolana.net/news/2004/Mayo/20040521.htm

"Gift of Venezuelan Sculpture to the U.S." Cable no. 1976CARACA01055_b, unclassified, 29 January 1976, retrieved from Wikileaks, "The Kissinger Papers."

Zev Toledano, "The Worldwide Celluloid Massacre: An Encyclopedia of Extreme, Surreal, and Bizarre Movies," *The Last Exit*, http://thelastexit.net/cinema/shock.html#Faccia%20di%20Spia

17. The Road Home

Adam Bernstein, "Les Paul, 94: 'Wizard of Waukesha' Invented Guitars that Changed Popular Music," *The Washington Post,* 14 August 14, 2009.

Epilogue

"Remembering CIA's Heroes: Richard S. Welch," Central Intelligence Agency (CIA), www.cia.gov

"U.S. Terrorism Report: MEK and Jundallah," *United States Institute for Peace*, 23 August 2011.

"Weekly Situation Report on International Terrorism," Central Intelligence

Notes

Agency, 18 January 1977, released 22 January 2014, www.cia.gov

David Atlee Phillips, *The Night Watch, 25 Years Inside the CIA.*

Chris Sibilla, "Four Days in September—The Kidnapping of the U.S. Ambassador to Brazil," *Moments in Diplomatic History*, Association for Diplomatic Studies and Training, http://adst.org/2013/01/four-days-in-september-kidnapping-of-ambassador-to-brazil

"Revolutionary Movement of October 8 (MR-8)," *Terrorist Organization Profiles*, University of Maryland,
http://www.start.umd.edu/tops/terrorist_organization_profile.asp?id=4119

John Corry, "Portrait of a Terrorist," *The New York Times*, 20 May 1986.

"Analysis of Niehous Kidnapping" Cable 1976CARACA03844_b, from U.S. embassy to State Department, 3 April 1976.

George Ciccariello-Maher, *We Created Chávez: A People's History of the Venezuelan Revolution*, Durham, NC: Duke University Press, 17 April 2013.

"Weekly Situation Report on International Terrorism," Central Intelligence Agency, 6 April 1976, released 11 May 2007.

"The Wackenhut Corp.," *Encyclopedia.com*,
http://www.encyclopedia.com/topic/The_Wackenhut_Corp.aspx

John Connelly, "Inside the Shadow CIA," *Spy Magazine*, September 1992.

Jennifer Bayotjan, "George Wackenhut, 85, Dies; Founded Elite Security Firm," *The New York Times*, 8 January 2005.

Nicholas Spangler, "Spy Game," 21 May 2004,
https://nicholasspangler.wordpress.com/2009/03/20/spy-game

U.S. Department of State, Director of Intelligence and Research, from Thomas Hughes to the Secretary, Subject: "Guatemala – Counter-insurgency running wild?" 23 October 1967;
http://nsarchive.gwu.edu/NSAEBB/NSAEBB32/vol2.html

Adolph Saenz, Plaintiff-appellant, v. Playboy Enterprises, Inc. and Roger Morris, Defendants-appellees, 841 F.2d 1309 (7th Cir. 1988); Argued Oct. 2, 1987. Decided Feb. 26, 1988,
http://law.justia.com/cases/federal/appellate-courts/F2/841/1309/421080

Encyclopedia of U.S. Military Interventions in Latin America, edited by Alan

Notes

McPherson, ABC-CLIO, 8 July 2013.

"Daniel Mitrione," http://spartacus-educational.com/JFKmitrione.htm

What the U.S. Files Reveal," The National Security Archive, http://nsarchive.gwu.edu/NSAEBB/NSAEBB32

The Public Safety Story: An Informal Recollection of Events and Individuals Leading to the Formation of the A.I.D. Office of Public Safety, compiled and written by Reg Davis and Harry James, Santee, CA: 2001, http://pdf.usaid.gov/pdf_docs/pcaab135.pdf

Stanley W. Guth and Bryan L. Quick, "Termination Phase-Out Study, Public Safety Project Venezuela," Agency for International Development Office of Public Safety, Washington, DC, April 1974.

Report from John Longan to Byron Engel, director of Office of Public Safety, on his mission to Guatemala from 27 November to 7 December 1965, 4 January 1966.

"Information on USAID Development Assistance to Venezuela," Cable R011814Z, from U.S. embassy to State Department, April 1975.

Bruce Berckmans Jr.'s interview with John Longan, Dallas, Texas, May 30, 1978, Containers 2-3, David Atlee Phillips Papers, Manuscript Division, Library of Congress, Washington, DC.

David Nieves: "El secuestro de Niehous fue un horror político, la peor acción militar de la izquierda," *Noticias24 Radio,* 18, October 2013, http://www.noticias24.com/venezuela/noticia/200984/en-vivo-el-exconsul-david-nieves-conversa-sobre-la-actualidad-politica-nacional

David Nieves, "Jorge Rodríguez (padre) no tenía ni la menor idea de donde estaba Niehous" (Jorge Rodríguez (father) had no idea where Niehous was,) *La Iguana*, 25 July 2016, https://www.aporrea.org/ddhh/n294367.html

"Weekly Situation Report on International Terrorism," Central Intelligence Agency, 10 August 1976, released 23 July 2009.

Peter Gribbin, "Brazil and CIA," *CounterSpy*, April-May 1979, pp. 4-23.
Memo from the kidnappers on a tribunal they conducted regarding Owens-Illinois and William Niehous. No date or location are mentioned, but likely took place in 1976, David Atlee Phillips Papers, Library of Congress.

Charles Walker, "Victor Reuther's Revelations about U.S. Labor and the CIA," *Socialist Viewpoint*, April 2003,

Notes

http://www.socialistviewpoint.org/apr_03/apr_03_36.html

Harry Kelber, "AFL-CIO's Dark Past (4): U.S. Labor Reps. Conspired to Overthrow Elected Governments in Latin America," *The Labor Educator*, 29 November 2004, http://www.laboreducator.org/darkpast4.htm

Ann Louise Bardach, *Without Fidel: A Death Foretold in Miami, Havana and Washington*; Scribner; Reprint edition, 19 April 2014.

"Operation 40," http://spartacus-educational.com/JFKoperation40.htm

Eva Golinger, "Venezuela Rejects CIA, But Opens Doors to FBI & DEA," 29 June 2005, https://venezuelanalysis.com/analysis/1220

Letter from FBI Director Clarence M. Kelley to Secretary of State Henry Kissinger, National Archives and Records Administration, 5 November 1976, declassified and released 9 May 2005.

"Interrogation of Orlando Bosch," U.S. embassy cables, 1977; National Archives and Records Administration, declassified and released, 22 May 2009.

Michael Carlson "Orlando Bosch: CIA-Backed Cuban Exile Implicated in Numerous Anti-Castro Terrorist Operations," *The Independent*, 28 April 2011.

Blake Fleetwood, "I Am Going to Declare War," *New Times*, 13 May 1977.

Ann Louise Bardach, "Twilight of the Assassins," *The Atlantic*, November 2006.

Peter Kornbluh, "Former CIA Asset Luis Posada Goes to Trial," *The Nation*, 11 January 2011.

"Posada Carriles Stars in Anti-Castro Rally in Miami," *Havana Times*, 21 December 2014.

"Anti-Cuban Terrorist Participates Freely at Miami Demonstration," *Telesur*, 21 December 2014, http://www.telesurtv.net/english/news/Anti-Cuban-Terrorist-Participates-Freely-at-Miami-Demonstration-20141221-0029.html

Bill Weaver, "On Why Luis Posada Carriles Will Not Be Extradited," *Narcosphere,* 1 September 2005, http://narcosphere.narconews.com/notebook/bill-weaver/2005/09/on-why-luis-posada-carriles-will-not-be-extradited

"Posada File: Part II," National Security Archive,

Notes

http://nsarchive.gwu.edu/NSAEBB/NSAEBB157/index.htm

Felix Rodriguez and John Weisman, *Shadow Warrior: The CIA Hero of a Hundred Unknown Battles*, New York: Simon & Schuster, 1989.

United States v. James Heller, 579 F.2d 990 (6th Cir. 1978), Court of Appeals for the Sixth Circuit; Argued Nov. 30, 1977, Decided June 30, 1978.

Memorandum from Bruce Berckmans Jr. to John K. Aurell, "Ricardo Morales Navarrete and the Niehous Kidnapping Case, 25 May 1978.

Rabbi Samuel Silver, "Paraguay Protects Mengele," *The Indiana Jewish Post*, 17 January 1969.

Hilda Inclan and Helga Silva, "Secret Agent Morales…A Man Without a Country?" *The Miami News*, 12 April 1978.

Letter from FBI Director Clarence M. Kelley to Secretary of State Henry Kissinger, 5 November 1976.

Letters from Bruce Berckmans Jr. to Ricardo Morales, 24 May 1978 and to Janet Reno, May 1978, Containers 2-3, David Atlee Phillips Papers, Library of Congress.

Bruce Berckmans Jr., "The Niehous Kidnapping in Venezuela - Summary of the Case and Request for White House Guidance and Assistance," 19 August 1978, David Atlee Phillips Papers.

Robert Parry, "Contra-Narco Terrorists," *Consortium News,* 15 October 1998, http://www.consortiumnews.com/1990s/consor30.html

John Rothchild, "The Informant: Meet the Biggest Dealer in Miami's Biggest Industry," *Harper's,* January 1982, p. 29-39.

Al Messerschmidt, "Macho Pride May Have Killed Morales," *Miami Herald,* 23 January 1983.

Edward Cody, "Black-Edged Legend Is Ended in a Vulgar Miami Bar Brawl," *The Washington Post*, 6 February 1983.

"Mercenary, Informant Morales Dies of Bullet Wound," *Sarasota Herald Tribune*, 23 December 1982.

Jim McGee, "Anti-Castro Terrorists Blamed in Bombing, *Miami Herald,* 10 April 1983.

Notes

"Possible Release of Amcit Kidnap Victim Niehous," Cable 1979STATE157667_e, from U.S. embassy to State Department, 19 June 1979, retrieved from Wikileaks.

Rafael Morales (a Venezuelan blogger), "The 40 Most Wealthy and Influential People, http://rafael-rafaelmorales.blogspot.com/p/los-40-personajes-mas-ricos-y-con-mayor.html

"Jorge Rodríguez padre no era un "angelito" (The father of Jorge Rodríguez is no "ángel."), 27 August 2016, http://www.opinionynoticias.com/opinionpolitica/27353-jorge-rodriguez-padre-no-era-un-angelito

Megan Rosenfeld, "Escape From the Jungle," *The Washington Post*, 4 July 1979.

Author interview with Donna Niehous, by telephone, 19 October 2015.

"U.S.A.: Businessman William Niehous Returns Home From Venezuela After One of History's Longest Kidnappings," *National Broadcasting Company*, ITN Source, 1979.

Paul Vitello, "William Niehous Survived Three Years in Captivity in Venezuela," *The Globe and Mail*, 22 October 2013.

William Niehous, "Hostage Survival - A Firsthand Look," American Society for Industrial Security, abstract, *Security Management* vol. 23 issue 10, November 1979: p. 6-8, 10, 50-52, 54.

"Casualidades o No disparan soy Niehous al fin quien secuestro a Niehous el de Owen Illinois," (Coincidence or not kidnapping of Niehous from the Owen Illinois finally ends)," comment by David Nieves, 27 October 2010.

"This Week in Venezuela," U.S. embassy cable, 3 February 1978, retrieved from Wikileaks.

David Robarge, "DCI John McCone and the Assassination of President John F. Kennedy," Central Intelligence Agency, approved for release, 29 September 2014, National Security Archive, http://nsarchive.gwu.edu/NSAEBB/NSAEBB493/docs/intell_ebb_026.PDF

Gaeton Fonzi, *The Last Investigation: What Insiders Know About the Assassination of JFK,* Skyhorse, 2013.

"AFIO Early Years," *PERISCOPE*, Newsletter of the AFIO, 2005, Double Issue, vol. XXVI, no 2; vol. XXVII, no. 1, 2005,

Notes

http://www.afio.com/publications/Periscope05.pdf

David Atlee Phillips, *The Niehous Ordeal: An American Family Survives a Terrorist Kidnapping*, undated, unpublished manuscript, Niehous, Container 3, David Atlee Phillips Papers, Library of Congress.

David Atlee Phillips, "The Man Nobody Bothered to Call," *Columbia Journalism Review*, January-February 1987.

Daniel F. Gilmore, "CIA Officer Wins Retraction of Allegations in Letelier Murder," *United Press International*, 14 February 1986.

"Ex-Agent Settles Libel Case," *Associated Press*, 14 February 1986.

"Resolution of David Atlee Phillips's Lawsuit against the *London Observer*," Jury List No. 85 1372 1984 - P - No. 3868, In the High Court of Justice Quwwn's Bench Division between David Atlee Phillips and *The Observer* Limited, Defendants, http://www.jfk-online.com/dapobserver.html

"David Atlee Phillips, Sergeant, United States Army, Central Intelligence Agency Operative," Arlington National Cemetery, http://www.arlingtoncemetery.net/dphillip.htm

Antonio Veciana and Carlos Harrison, *Trained to Kill: The Inside Story of CIA Plots against Castro, Kennedy, and Che*, Skyhorse Publishing, 18 April 2017.

Gerardo Reyes, "De secuestrador a zar de la educación" ("From abductor to education czar"), *El Nuevo Herald*, Caracas, 11 February 2001.

José de Córdoba, "To Fix Venezuela, Ex-Guerrillas Want To Make 'New Man'" *The Wall Street Journal*, 24 December 2004.

Articles by Carlos Lanz Rodríguez can be found at, http://www.aporrea.org/autores/lanz

Katiuska Hernández, "Rodriguez: There Will Be No Recall Referendum in Venezuela," 16 September 2016, http://www.caracas.gob.ve/alcaldiaDeCCS/submit-an-article/blog/noticias/rodriguez-no-habra-referendo-revocatorio-en-venezuela

Francisco Toro, "The Day Jorge Rodríguez Overreached," *Caracas Chronicles*, 22 September 2016.

Gisela Salomon, "Carlos Andres Pérez, Two-Time Venezuelan President, Dies at 88, *The Washington Post*, 27 December 27, 2010.

Notes

Simon Romero, "Carlos Andrés Pérez, Former President of Venezuela, Dies at 88," *The New York Times*, 26 December 2010.

"Chamorro Denies Venezuelan Charges," *United Press International*, 19 January 1995.

Fabiola Sanchez, "Body Carlos Andres Pérez, Former President, Returns to Venezuela," *Associated Press*, 5 October 2011.

"Body of Former Venezuela President Carlos Andrés Pérez Repatriated," *The Guardian*, 5 October 2011.

Tim Shorrock, "Labor's Cold War," *The Nation,* 1 May 2003, https://www.thenation.com/article/labors-cold-war

Nick Miroff, "Venezuela Declares a Two-Day Workweek Because of Dire Energy Shortages," *The Washington Post,* 27 April 2016.

Hannah Dreier, "Protests as Venezuela Embraces Two-Day Workweek to Save Power," The *Washington Post,* 27 April 2016.

Sofia Barbarani, "Venezuelan Women's Response to the Country's Economic Crisis: Get Sterilized," *The Washington Post*, 24 December 2016.

"Venezuela's Humanitarian Crisis: Severe Medical and Food Shortages, Inadequate and Repressive Government Response," *Human Rights Watch*, 24 October 2016.

Rachael Boothroyd-Rojas, "CEPAL: There Is 'Definitely No Humanitarian' Crisis in Venezuela," *VenezuelAnalysis.com*, 27 October 2016.

Javier Corrales, "Don't Blame it on the Oil," *ForeignPolicy.com,* 7 May 2015.

Simon Romero, "Venezuela's Cup Runs Over, and the Scotch Whiskey Flows," *The New York Times*, 20 August 2006.

"Venezuelan Asylum Claims in the U.S. Soar as Economic Crisis Deepens," *The Guardian,* 16 June 2016.

"Jonathan Watts, "Venezuela's Crisis Brings Economic Boom but Social Tensions to Brazil Border Town," *The Guardian,* 1 November 1976.

Nicholas Casey, "Hungry Venezuelans Flee in Boats to Escape Economic Collapse," *The New York Times*, 25 November 2016.

Jens Manuel Krogstad and Gustavo Lópe, "Venezuelan asylum applications to

U.S. soar in 2016," *FactTank: News in Numbers*, 4 August 2016.

Jim Wyss, "Dueling Data Blur Venezuelan Murder Rate," *Miami Herald*, 8 February 2016.

"Global Study on Homicide 2013," United Nations Office on Drugs and Crime, Vienna, March 2014.

"Germany Leads World in Penis Enlargement Operations, Venezuela is Second," The Star, Nairobi, 31 July 2014.

Roque Planas, "Venezuela Has World's Second-Highest Homicide Rate: NGO," *The Huffington Post,* 30 December 2014.

"Venezuela Battles Obesity Amid Dearth of Good Food, *Daily Mail,* 27 August 2014.

Rebecca Bintrim, "Cosmetic Surgery in the Americas," *Quarterly Americas*, Winter 2015.

Ernesto Londonov, "Venezuela's Tone-Deaf President," *The New York Times*," 3 November 2016.

Michael Barbaro and Megan Twohey, "Shamed and Angry: Alicia Machado, a Miss Universe Mocked by Donald Trump," *The New York Times*, 27 September 2016.

ACKNOWLEDGEMENTS

This book is based on a journal I kept in Venezuela, the hundreds of letters I sent to my seven siblings, friends and my parents as well as Peace Corps newsletters, handbooks and memos.

I would like to thank Mike Valentino and Kate5, from Editage, a division of Cactus Communications, for editing and talking things over, asking questions, offering comments, and making the book better.

Thanks to Bill Hawken and Fred Schram for the fun in remembering Venezuela and to Tim Rozwadowski for reading and commenting on early drafts. Bill also shot the cover photo while we were hiking in Guatopo National Park one weekend in October 1974.

Above all I want to thank my wife Barb who read and commented on early drafts and supported and encouraged me in spite of the time I spent on the book on the third floor.

ABOUT THE AUTHOR

Mike Kendellen was a Peace Corps Volunteer in Venezuela and Morocco in the 1970s. After Peace Corps and until he retired in 2014, he directed programs in various refugee and post-war settings in Asia, the former Soviet Union and the former Yugoslavia. From 1999, Mike supervised, monitored, researched and surveyed projects on three continents associated with the Anti-Personnel Mine Ban Convention, landmine survivors and surveys. He and his wife, Barb, live in Washington, D.C.

Made in the USA
Middletown, DE
03 October 2017